Antiques from the Victorian Home

ANTIQUES
from the Victorian Home

Bea Howe

CHARLES SCRIBNER'S SONS
New York

Contents

Acknowledgment
and Sources of Illustrations

It would be impossible to thank all those who have helped me over the years that I have been involved with Victoriana. But in regard to Editors, I am most grateful to the late Mr. Iolo Williams and Mr. James Bishop, till recently Features Editor of *The Times,* Mr. John Adams of *Country Life,* Lady Georgina Coleridge (Director, *Homes & Gardens* etc.), Miss Alison Brand (*Collector's Guide*) and Miss Whitford, late Editor of *The Lady,* for giving me encouragement and support by printing my articles at a time when Victoriana was not the fashionable subject it has now become.

Then there are those concerned with the world of antiques, always of importance to writers and collectors like myself. In the late Valentine Ackland who ran a small but unique business from her Dorset home, I had continual assistance in forming my own collection of Victoriana for years. Although she did not always see eye to eye with me or follow my taste, she invariably found (as she did for so many others) with patience and care the object one was after. Moreover she was a dealer of scrupulous honesty. Hilda Gardener (Mrs. Sebastian) of Bridge House, Coggeshall, Essex, invaluable book-finder and general informant on Victorian side-lines; Mrs. Marjorie Grinling of Coombe House, Lewes, Sussex; Mr. Thomas Higham and Mrs. Alison Wilson I would also like to thank for their help at various times.

On the matter of finding illustrations, unusual and suitable, (always a hazardous job) I found immediate co-operation and facilities for taking photographs of fresh subjects from Miss Helena Gibbon, recent Director of The Harris Art Gallery & Museum, Preston, Lancs, Miss Rachel M. R. Young, M.A., Assistant Director of the City of Norwich Museums and Miss Pamela Clabburn, Assistant Keeper of Social History of the same museum. To Mr. Maurice Littledale I am also very grateful for supplying me with many special photographs on request.

Lastly there is my husband, Mark Lubbock, always ready to advise and look out for yet another forgotten Victorian work of fiction besides my friends who have rallied round lending me some special particular possession to be photographed.

And this brings me to Mr. Michael Seymour of Maldon, Essex and the Broseley Studio, London who have coped so carefully with all my photographic work during the years I have been appearing in print.

Sources of Illustrations (publications, museums and private collections in alphabetical order)

The late Valentine Ackland (24); *Art Catalogue of the Industry of All Nations* (Great Exhibition), 1851 (27-8, 75–8, 89, 92, 189); Author's Collection (29, 31, 49–51, 55–7, 62–7, 70–2, 79–82, 86, 90, 93, 96–7, 108, 111–112, 117–22, 124–28, 130, 132, 141, 145, 147–50, 165, 170, 174–5, 179–80, 182–3, 187, 194–5, 197–8, 200, 214, 216, 220, 224, 226, 229, 231, 236–9, 241, 243–4, 246, 248–52, 254–6, 258, 259–61, 263–5, 267, 271–2, 279, 285–92, 294–301, 305, 309–12, 316–19, 322–7, 329–48, 350, 358–71, 376–9, 381–8); Mrs. Bachus (69); Lady Barker, *The Bedroom and Boudoir,* 1878 (142, 166, 188, 191–3, 218); Mrs Beeton's *Housewife's Treasury of Domestic Information* (18, 32–4, 45, 88, 98, 105–6, 156, 167, 191, 217, 293); Alan Bott & Irene Celephane, *Our Mothers,* 1932 (85, 186); Birmingham City Museum & Art Gallery (211); Cassell's *Household Guide,* 1875 (47–8); Castle Museum, Colchester (304); City of Norwich Museum (53–4, 59, 99, 163, 225, 227–8, 233–5, 262, 266); Lady Cunliffe (320–21); *Country Life* (245–6); Lucy Crane, *Art and the Foundations of Taste,* 1882 (159–60); Dorchester Museum (215); Charles Eastlake, *Hints on Household Taste,* 1878 (2, 155, 219); R. W. Edis, *Decoration and Furniture of Town Houses,* 1881 (1, 36, 39, 140, 161); Messrs Garrard, Crown Jewellers, London (83); Rupert Gentle (184); The Glandford Museum, Norfolk (269–70); Mrs Goodday (232); Mrs. Marjorie Grinling (58, 151–4); Mrs. Betty Harris (247); Harris Art Gallery and Museum, Preston (100–1, 129, 131, 196, 199, 201–5, 209, 212, 268, 273–4, 281–2, 354–7, 372); Mrs. Shirley Hibberd, *Rustic Adornment for Homes of Taste,* 1856 (134–5, 139); Mrs. Hodgshow (138); James Foundry Co. Catalogue, *c.* 1830 (3–9, 16, 17, 26, 173, 177–8, 181); E. & A. Landells, *The Girl's Own Toy-Maker,* 1860 (278); Maurice Littledale Esq., (10–15, 19–21, 30, 35, 94, 104, 137, 164, 373–5); London Museum (116, 208, 210); Jane Loudon, *The Ladies Companion,* 1849 (136) and *Encyclopaedia . . . ,* 1835 (22–5, 38, 40–4, 88, 167, 169, 190); Messrs James Macintyre & Co., Burslem, Stoke-on-Trent (84); Miss Malling, *Flowers and How to Arrange Them,* 1862, (46); D. Marks (171); The National Museum, Wales (74); The National Portrait Gallery (306); Mrs. Lionel Neame (172); *Oetzmann's Illustrated Catalogue* (87, 143, 157–8); the late Eric Ravilious (313–15); W. &. H. Rock (302); Royal Gardens Museum, Kew (253, 257–9); Mrs. Hilda Sebastian (60–1, 109–10); Thomas Stanford Museum, Preston Manor, Brighton (221–2); Lady Studholme (95); Sir Henry Studholm Bt. (230); Tunbridge Wells Art Gallery and Museum (185); Lady Upjohn (73, 257); Victoria and Albert Museum, London (102–3, 123, 144, 146, 271–2, 280, 303, 349, 353); Mrs. Wallis (68); Whitby Museum (380); N. M. Woodall (351–2).

In the jacket photograph, taken by Atlas Ltd., all the objects are from the Author's private collection.

Introduction

It was after some thought and much trepidation that I set out to write yet another book on Victoriana. And here, I must stress, that mine is purely a personal approach: one that I took up over 30 years ago, when as a recently married young girl with a strong, collecting urge inherited from an antique-loving and knowledgeable mother, I began to acquire some small pieces of furniture, ornamental china and decorative pictures for my home. It was at this moment of time that my mother stepped in and began to produce for me, one day, a small rosewood chiffonier with brass rail; another a Shell Valentine found in Sidmouth while visiting there; a third, a bouquet of multi-coloured wool flowers arranged in a lemon-yellow striped vase under a glass shade, which delighted me.

'If these things appeal to you as they do to me because I knew the world they once represented, collect them now for they are out of fashion and will cost you next to nothing', she said. Then she paused to add with a smile, 'but don't just take them for granted because you may find them odd or charming or – in some cases – rather touchingly ugly! Get to know something of their background. How they were made and why and for whom.'

And that is how my complete involvement with the world of Victoriana came about. In 1930, the word Victoriana which vaguely embraces today a strange hotch-potch of miscellaneous and uncorrelated objects assembled in antique shops and highly priced, was seldom if ever heard. Both lovers and collectors of Victoriana formed a minority group then though the *Victorian Exhibition* of 1931 whose Committee published a charming, informative little book on *Victorian Crafts* showed in what direction the wind of change had begun to blow in the world of collecting antiques.

Today we are all pressurised by articles in the press or by programmes on the air (including the fabulous, record-breaking one of Mr. Arthur Negus), into collecting some object or another because of its period value or rarity. In fact, we have been turned into a nation of wildly enthusiastic collectors and junk-hunters. Nothing, from old Victorian ships' figureheads costing anything between £100 to £500 to a small collection of ladies' button hooks with ivory or silver ornamented handles of varying designs dating from the 1880s to 1912, comes amiss to the up-to-date collector.

But what is most attractive and saleable to buyers of Victoriana comes not from the notable great houses of that day like Alfred Waterhouse's Eaton Hall (1867) Cheshire, or Pugin's Scarisbrick Hall, Lancashire (1837–67) for their appurtenances would be beyond the average collector's purse even if they did come into the sale room, but from the solid, comfortable homes

1

of the prosperous and secure middle class. For this reason, I have placed the things I undertook to write about in their proper social context and background, i.e. the Victorian home, room by room. I have tried to show too the enormous contribution made by women to the ornamentation of their homes through their intense absorption in the minor arts and crafts of their day which supplied the only outlet for their creative and artistic abilities, denied full expression by conventions ruling then.

In connection with Parlour Pastimes of the nineteenth century, a word continually met with, is 'Repository'. It crops up in contemporary letters or in novels, say by Charlotte Yonge or Miss Braddon; or in small books dealing with ornamental arts such as Mr. Gandee's *The Artist* (1835). Only the other day, my book completed, did I discover its correct meaning and why 'Repository' played such an important part in the production of the many objects now termed Victoriana! The explanation is given by Mrs. Gaskell in her short story 'My Lady Ludlow' first published in *Household Words*, 19 June 1858:

'It was the custom in those days of wealthy ladies of the county to set on foot a repository, as it was called, in the assize-town. The ostensible manager of this repository was generally a decayed gentlewoman, a clergyman's widow or so forth. She was, however, controlled by a committee of ladies, and paid by them in proportion to the amount of goods she sold; and those goods were the small manufactures of ladies of little or no fortune whose names, if they chose it, were only signified by initials.

'Poor water-colour drawings in indigo and Indian ink; screens ornamented with moss and dried leaves; paintings on velvet, and such faintly ornamental works were displayed on one side of the shop.'

In this way, then, that phenomenal output of Victorian ladies who pursued the minor arts at home, was brought about. Another door was opened to future collectors by Victorian travellers and holiday makers, irrespective of their class and social standing. For all Victorians were mad souvenir hunters whether they went to Mentone or Blackpool. Besides this they were sentimental possessors of Commemoration Ware that recorded either national events or some personal milestone in their lives, like family births, marriages and deaths.

Lastly, the common or garden things belonging to humble cottage folk such as their china, glass and furniture, besides rustic bygones from farm house or village pub are all being tracked down today and reassessed for the first time as antiques for collectors. So they, too, have a place in the overall pattern of my book.

Although my own involvement with the world of Victoriana has drawn to a close, something of what I learnt and enjoyed while exploring that world may be of interest, I hope, to those still blazing their own individual trails today.

1 The Hall or Vestibule

1 *Sketch for a hall in modern jacobean style by Robert Edis*

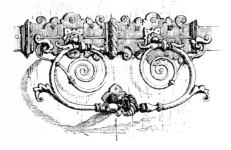

It was a fine old vaulted hall, a place to love and remember when far away. The walls were all of darkly-bright oak panelling, save where here and there a square of tapistry hung before a door or a painted window let in the light. At one end there was a great arched fireplace, the arch surmounted with Squire Tempest's armorial bearings, roughly cut in freestone. A mailed figure of the usual stumpy kind, in helm and hauberk, stood on each side of the hearth; a large three-cornered chair covered with stamped and gilded leather was drawn up to the fireside.

Miss Braddon, *Vixen*

The Hall or vestibule of a Victorian house whether found in a town or in the country, whether large or small, well-lit or gloomy, was always of some importance and its furnishing usually conformed to a traditional pattern. This pattern indicated the social status, more or less, of the owner coupled with the actual neighbourhood of his home.

Traditionally, an Elizabethan or Gothic-styled bench – a pair if space permitted – stood in the hall with some chairs of similar design; an ornate hat-and-umbrella stand; a torchère to support a bronze lamp, statuette or pot-plant; a circular brass gong on a mahogany stand; a console table or two on which a silver salver, papier mâché tray or beadwork basket was placed to hold visiting-cards and a brass-bound letter box, glass-fronted, following the introduction of the Penny Post in 1840. Finally, there might be a wire flowerstand in a corner or a terra-cotta plant pedestal or mignonette box to add a floral touch.

If the hall was an imposing one, the floor was paved in a black-and-white design and there would be a grandiose mantel-piece adorned by two handsome terra-cotta vases in the Etruscan style, while the grate would be of polished steel complete with fire-dogs.

When members of the New Rich society went too far, as they could in patronising ostentatious fashions, Mrs. Harriet Beecher Stowe (1811–1895) launched an attack on the housewife who put ornate furniture and ornaments before domestic hygiene, sanitation and kitchen cleanliness. She wrote:

'Of what use are brick houses whose fronts are plated with brown stone, whose entrance doors are exquisitely rimmed with carving, fine metal work and engraved glass panels when such showy houses lack even a bath-room and food is prepared in an unpainted gloomy kitchen?'

Of course, Mrs. Beecher Stowe was right.

Still, with the exception of a minority group of enlightened and kind mistresses who genuinely cared about the health and well-being of their servants it was a long time before conditions 'below stairs' as well as those far above in the attics where the maids slept were improved.

The natural start for my survey of small antiques from the Victorian home should, I think, begin at the front door.

4

DOOR KNOCKERS

The first thing that anyone calling at a house saw in Victorian times before electric bells came into general use was the front door knocker or 'Rapper' as it was once romantically called: a name which derived from Tudor times when it was customary for a gentleman or the servant accompanying him to lift the wooden stave in his hand and 'rap' on the door for entry.

Since those days, a door knocker or 'rapper' had been in constant use and seen many changes in design and workmanship which Miss Therle Hughes has dealt with more fully in her *More Small Decorative Antiques*. Here only those of Victorian origin are given. It was about 1839 that The Coalbrookdale Company in Shropshire established a new method for producing well-burnished and hand-chased knockers, profitably. Ten years later, electro-gilding was used on them. The Coalbrookdale Company are among makers that have registered their designs at the Patent Office to prevent piracy: so collectors are advised to look for the 'diamond' mark on a knocker which will then date it as being registered between 1842 and 1883.

By 1850, brass knockers were having their heyday. For there is nothing so rewarding to keep brightly polished as a handsome brass knocker

5–7   Three popular recurring designs for Victorian door knockers including the Dolphin still produced today

on the front door! There are many kinds to choose from: from a Medusa with her snaky locks, to the Egyptian Sphinx or a lion's mask cast in high relief. Classic motifs like a lyre or urn, a dolphin or spur, even an elegant, slim-fingered hand clasping a wreath or ball can be found as well. Possibly one of the most famous knockers to have survived long usage is the one on Number 10 Downing Street that features the mask of a lion holding a ring in his mouth.

As a result of the introduction of the Penny Post in 1840 a 'hatch' knocker was put on the market which combined a letter-flap with a scroll-type knocker. Then, as today, a brass knocker could be protected from the vagaries of the English weather by a process known as 'bronzing'.

Finally, an illuminating note on Victorian behaviour in regard to one door-knocker which I found in Miss Carola Oman's *The Gascoigne Heiress*. It relates to what happened when Frances Gascoigne, the future second Marchioness of Salisbury was lying ill at her father's home in Great Stanhope Street. A next door neighbour sent round a note enquiring whether 'he (Mr. Bamber Gascoigne) would wish my knocker taken off, lest it disturb. I hope he will let me know.'

To muffle a knocker in case of illness was often done in the same way that straw was put down in a street, but to take a knocker right off the door was surely the height of courtesy.

3–4   Pair of door knockers fanciful in design

DOOR PORTERS

Door stoppers or 'Porters' as they are more often called were widely used in the Victorian home and produced by the same firms who dealt in door

knockers. Chief among these firms was the Coalbrookdale Company who finished their 'porters' with the same care they gave to their knockers. One of their most popular and saleable examples was that of an armoured 'Knight' with spear and

8–9 *Pair of door porters in Berlin black or bronz'd: gothic knight under canopy; soldier with cocked hat*

10 *Cast iron door stop in the form of an early train, 1825. Early example of door stops reflecting current events*

shield under a Gothic canopy that went well with Gothic-styled furnishings in the hall. Made of cast-iron with a bronze finish, this knight is often to be found with an inscription on the back of his plinth: 'The Coalbrookdale Company, Registered (October 28th, 1841).' Modern reproductions of this same 'Knight' show him to be about one inch shorter in height than the original model from which he was copied.

Made in malleable cast-iron or brass, door porters came in as many designs as knockers. There is an attractive range, too, in glass while individual examples occur also in earthenware, terra-cotta, Derbyshire marble or wood, hand-carved. Roughly, they can be divided into two or three groups: those that are modelled in the form of different animals, like deer, swans, lions, cats, dogs and even some eagles; those which represent well-known celebrities of the day like the figures of the Iron Duke with his cocked hat, Lord Nelson and Jenny Lind, the vogue for them dating from about the 1820s; and those which reflect current happenings like the first appearance of George Stephenson's engine 'Locomotion' (1825).

When Richard Doyle's famous drawing of 'Punch' and his dog made their debut on the front cover of that magazine, a whole progeny of Mr. Punches and his Dog painted in iron, or brass, began their long years of service as door-porters. They had as their companion his wife 'Judy' or 'Judy with Baby'. In a comical genre, there was 'Ally Sloper', always popular. Another rare door-stop was the cast-iron model of David Lang, the

11–12 *Popular door porters: Mr. Punch, 1849; Judy with Baby*

13 *Miniature cast iron fire grate, c. 1860*

famous Gretna Green 'blacksmith priest' of 1827. This stands about 6 inches high, is painted cream colour and shows a capped and be-spectacled man with a book, presumably a marriage register, under one arm.

In the 1860s, the elephant Jumbo in cast-iron with painted rug and harness was much in demand. For Jumbo was as much a 'zoo celebrity' in her day as Chi-Chi the giant lady panda has been in ours. Jumbo is marked, incidentally, with the Patent Office's diamond registration mark of 1882.

Regimental 'Porters' date from about the 1830s and include those that incorporate the coats-of-arms of the family who ordered them. The latter date from about 1830 to the 1860s. Now and then a door porter may be come across made for a specific purpose, such as a 'Pestle-and-Mortar' that once stood outside a chemist's shop, or a 'Black Doll' for a marine store dealer. Glass door-stoppers known as 'Dumps' in the West Country are among the most attractive and were produced by Nailsea and Bristol from about 1828. Two years later, in 1830, Birmingham and Castleford were doing them. But theirs are in green bottle glass which tends to be harsher in colour than those of Nailsea. Dumps were also 'blown' and hawked about by travelling glass-blowers (Chapter XI: Cottage Glass).

Clear flint-glass porters are more expensive and have a smoky tinge which is the result from using lead oxide. They date from about 1840. Inside their

14 *Attractive old cast iron door stop in shape of a swan*
15 (right) *A handsome brass Regency lion's paw door porter Sheraton in style*

transparent domes, entrancing little bubbles of air rise and one may see a charming pot of flowers, or spray, enclosed. Another type of flint-glass porter shows coloured glass flowers inside them that so gleam and sparkle they seem larger than life. To my mind, they bear some affinity to those mid-Victorian glass paperweights which now fetch such high prices.

FOOT SCRAPERS

A cast-iron foot scraper has almost vanished from its traditional place by the front door because so

16–17 *Two now seldom seen cast iron door scrapers, 1868*

few people need to use them in these days of motor transport from door to door. But walk through Redcliffe Square, London, S.W.10: whose tall six-floored houses with their gloomy porticoes and serpentine pillars have remained intact since Victorian times, and one will often find a pair of heavy and ornate foot scrapers in cast-iron by each front door. Defiantly they have resisted the call for 'scrap iron' in two World Wars and have survived. Any 'old iron relics' like them together with door knobs, bell pulls, fire-dogs and fire backs, street lamps and individual old shop signs that can be found lurking in the corner of a down-at-heel 'junk' yard or adorning the scrap merchant's barrow are worth collecting; for their like will never be seen, again, and they can be put to good decorative use in a town garden or patio.

HALL BENCHES AND CHAIRS

18 *Good example of a Victorian gothic hall chair*

Most halls of adequate size possessed a simple rectangular hall sofa, or bench, in Gothic or Elizabethan style which was 'positioned', as they say today, against a wall. During the 1850s they were made in oak in both these styles but are comparatively rare to come by.

On the other hand, the so-called Elizabethan or 'hall' chair is still about. It is based largely on late seventeenth-century design, having a high back with barley-sugar, twist columns and can be found in oak, mahogany and, sometimes, rosewood. For the normal Stuart canework seat, upholstery was introduced or a Berlin wool-worked panel contributed by the lady of the house if she was a needlewoman. Another kind of hall chair that aped Elizabethan styles was richly carved and had pronounced 'cabriole' legs. Later examples of this chair in disagreeable shades of oak and yew wood are not nearly so attractive as their earlier prototypes. For they are apt to be meanly carved and display poor attempts at 'inlay' work.

The characteristic 'hooded' chair designed for, and occupied by, the Georgian hall-porter who attended to the needs of callers had, more or less, disappeared in Victorian times along with its occupant, for there were bells everywhere in the house to ring and policemen on duty outside. So the hall-porter (*i.e.* the watchful guardian of the house) had departed to hotels, clubs and City business houses. Instead of his 'hooded' chair in private houses one might see an 'Etruscan' styled iron chair, recommended for a hall by John Claudius Loudon (1783–1843). For Mr. Loudon very much favoured the use of metal furniture that was coming into fashion with the enormous advance made in ornamental cast-iron work based on new techniques established in England's flourishing foundries. In Loudon's giant tome, *An Encyclopaedia of Cottage, Farm and Villa Architecture* (1833) he wrote:

'The introduction of iron into the furniture of farm houses would be attended with considerable economy, at least in the article of dining-tables, side-boards, bedsteads and hall, lobby or porch.'

One Etruscan 'lobby chair' in cast iron was actually designed by Mr. Robert Mallet of Bath, who firmly supported the theory that carved ornamental work in furniture would be found cheaper done in cast iron than wood, even though a small number of the articles in question were needed.

In spite, though, of Mr. Mallet's firm belief in the efficacy of his metal chairs, they did not take on and only a few examples were on view at the Great Exhibition of 1851. On the other hand, The Coalbrookdale Company had better luck with their ornamental pedestal iron tables, marble-topped and richly ornamented. Among those seen at the Exhibition there were also:

'Cast-iron Chess-tables; Hall or Console tables in cast-iron painted white and gold with marble

19–20 (left) *Front and back view of original hall chair made from Irish elk horn*

21 *Oak chair, gothic-styled, made by W. Woolett from 20,000 small oak pieces*

22–3 *Examples of hall chairs having tab-lets, or panels on back, for heraldic shields or crests, generally painted, 1833*

24 *Hall bench with tablet (centre back) for heraldic insignia designed by Mr. Dalziel, 1833*

Mr. Mallet of Bath's well known cast iron lobby chair in Etruscan style

top; Large table with cast-iron legs, painted oak.'

To furnish sun rooms, verandahs and patios, this type of table is now in great demand and prices have rocketed. But even when found in poor condition, they are still well worth buying as they lend themselves admirably to recon-ditioning and are quite transformed by a fresh coat of paint.

HAT-AND-UMBRELLA STANDS

This often extraordinary, fantastically horned and over-decorated piece of furniture designed for hanging-up bowlers, caps, deer-stalkers and Homburgs or to put away tidily silver-topped canes and umbrellas was once the prop and mainstay of hall furnishing. Never will its like be seen again.

One hat stand described in a trade catalogue of the period had:

'Intricate iron casting, bronzed and marbled, arranged with pedestals for hats, coats and umbrellas, containing also a pillar for a lamp and looking-glass with boxes both for letters, brushes and an inkstand.'

This last-named item makes curious reading. For compulsive letter-writers though the Victorians were, surely it was not *comme il faut* to pursue that occupation in the hall? Or was it? One will never know. Another more conventional but also typical cast-iron umbrella stand (*c.* 1845) could be ordered from The James Foundry Company. It was listed in their catalogue as having four finishes: Japanned; French Bronzed; Fancy Bronzed; and Berlin Black. In mahogany, bentwood or cast-iron, the Victorian hat-and-umbrella stand still survives and is of period value to decorators and collectors

26 *Ornate mid-Victorian umbrella stand with bird decoration available in four finishes, Berlin black, japanned French bronze etc . . .*

9

alike. A nice point to remember is that a hat-stand was never used by a gentleman when calling. To hang his glossy top-hat up on it, would have been an act committed in the worst possible taste. For a top hat had to be taken in one hand into the drawing room always and put down beside the chair occupied. Yet another container for sticks and umbrellas was, for a time, tall crane-like birds in majolica ware which were also placed in conservatories.

TORCHÈRES

Quite a number of tall, pillar-like stands in carved or gilt mahogany as well as in cast-iron, coloured to look like bronze or brass and having a small platform top can still be picked up, singly, or in pairs in the sale-room or antique shops. Such stands were considered highly appropriate to place both in the hall or drawing-room either to carry a lamp or palm (when the latter had their day) or any other favourite pot-plant. Originally, they were copies of Sheraton and Chippendale candle-stands but copies certainly not to be despised in their day nor in ours. For there is no more useful support on which to stand a striking arrangement of flowers or an imposing lamp than a Victorian torchère. The most popular type that appeals to modern taste and much collected is the 'Black-amoor' light or plant bearer who descends from his more elegant Regency counterpart but is far less expensive.

The first carved 'Negro' lamp bearers seen in England were imported usually from Venice, where their prototypes had first landed, being brought into exile for domestic service by ships trading with the Orient. These figures differ of course in style and design from those who were later 'anglicised' in Regency times; and these differ, again, from their Victorian descendants when they took up their position from about the 1850s in the Victorian hall or drawing-room.

However, a 'Blackamoor' torchère was not to everyone's taste. In particular not to Mrs. Haweis (1848–1898), an arbiter of taste and general adviser on interior decoration to Victorian ladies. For she comments rather acidly in *The Art of Decoration* (1881) that:

'A candlestick, lamp or any other support ought to be a pretty and consistent object. Cleopatra's Needle a-light at one end and streaked with pink and blue is scarcely a work of art. Pheasants and monkeys adhering to portions of the room and upholding lamps are by many degrees removed from a correct feeling for either art or nature. Large Negro lads with glass eyes and arsenic-green draperies starred with gold are not so suitable in a great hall as a bronze Hercules or a really well-modelled elephant.'

But in spite of Mrs. Haweis's strictures, Negro lads with glass eyes continued to stand as plant and lamp bearers in Victorian halls and passage-ways till the end of the century. Today they are again in their ascendancy and much sought after.

HALL STATUARY

From the Queen down, to have some example of statuary whether in marble, alabaster, terra-cotta, bronze, plaster or cast-iron in their home gave enormous satisfaction to most Victorians. Was it not generally known that Her Majesty preferred the plastic arts to the graphic and had surrounded herself with small marble and bronze effigies of her children (attributed to Mrs. Thorneycroft) in symbolical attitudes and fancy costumes, besides those of her pet dogs? On the staircase at Osborne stood the life-size figure of her adored husband, the Prince Consort, which she had to pass by daily. In loyal devotion, her subjects followed the Queen's lead whenever they could in regard to domestic fashions and habits. So statues, and busts of every kind, sentimental or severely classical, embellished their homes, conservatories and gardens. In particular, was the hall honoured by those in marble or terra-cotta. These took the form of copies of the world's most famous pieces of sculpture or were the bust of contemporary figures.

However, from about the 1840s, the ornamental

cast-iron industry made such strides forward in technical production that a staggering amount of inexpensive metal sculpture ranging from figures to Landseer's historical stags and dogs, appeared on the market. An instantaneous success, metal sculpture was bought for halls. Then, between the years 1840 to 1870, 'French Art Bronzes' had their day, followed again by cheap versions of them in spelter. This form of metal ware was made possible through a clever invention by which a zinc-casting was given a thin coating of bronze, thus reducing production costs of copying the original French 'Art Bronzes' considerably. Spelter copies of 'The Marly Horses', which stands in the Champs Elysées, Paris, now took almost first place in popularity as a 'Hall' feature. Among a whole host, too, of pensive maidens, chivalrous knights and romantic cavaliers in spelter, the figure of Mercury standing upright, poised on a winged foot, was another favourite.

Nude figures, too, made in Parian ware (Chapter III: The Drawing-Room), classic-inspired, also graced passage-ways and halls. They were put out by George Jones at Stoke-on-Trent and usually stood on a majolica-ware pedestal.

27–8 *Suitable hall statuary. Copy of Mr. Thomas's 'Mother and Child' and 'Saher de Quincy, Earl of Winchester' (bronze) by J. S. Westmacott for the House of Lords*

CARD RACKS AND HOLDERS

To leave cards at a house was an essential social duty performed, at regular intervals, by Victorian ladies and gentlemen particularly after a dinner party or when the lady of the house was 'At Home' to her friends and acquaintances. There were also those sad occasions when a family went into mourning; then, deeply black-bordered cards were left as a sign of respectful condolence. On these occasions, cards were merely handed in at the door and no one was shown into the drawing-room.

Victorian visiting cards are small and narrow pieces of pasteboard with the name and address engraved (never printed) in fine copperplate. Some very early examples may be embossed; others used in less fastidious circles composed of the *nouveaux riches* were actually decorated with 'flourished' birds or even applied scraps of decalcomania (Chapter IX: Parlour Pastimes).

Birthday and greeting cards reached a high standard of lithographic art in the '70s and '80s and some charming examples survive which are well worth collecting. Such cards were left by young gentlemen when calling on a favoured young lady's birthday or at Christmas or on New Year's Day. To keep track of them, they were put into the card rack or bead-work basket placed on the hall table. card racks of bone, wire, or gilded paper were acquired from the Fancy stall at a charity bazaar or fête and were made by ladies. It is said that a 'harp' design was much favoured as cards could be slipped in neatly between the strings as it hung above a hall table. For a while, card racks came to be decorated even with dry fir-cones and moss during the Rustic Movement (Chapter IX: Parlour Pastimes).

In several Victorian ladies' journals I have come across instructions for the construction of a 'Visiting Card Pier-Basket'. This was made from fine Bristol board with fancy ornamentation. Towards the end of the century when big-game hunting became fashionable and much indulged in by gentlemen travellers in India, America and the Rockies, a large, stuffed grizzly bear came to

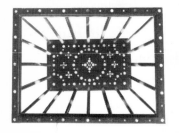

29   *Card Holder in porcupine quillwork showing resemblance on base to pique work. c.1860*

30   *Stuffed monkey stand for a card salver in the hall, mid-Victorian*

31   *Stuffed life-sized grizzly bear presenting card tray to visiting lady. From an album of Victorian advertisement prints, c. 1875-80*

stand in a Victorian hall holding out a card tray in his paw. At Clandeboye, Ireland, for instance, two small stuffed bears once stood (they may still today) on either side of the archway leading from the entrance lobby into the principal lofty hall. They are relics of the time when the then Lord Dufferin was Governor-General of Canada (1872–1878). If a stuffed bear was not forthcoming from the sporting head of the family, a large carved Swiss bear was pressed into service, instead. These popular hall figures were imported from Switzerland. When the postal service was established, a square wooden letter box with brass corners and slit was put in the hall to be cleared regularly by a manservant. Fitted with a brass lock and key, these boxes are now being collected.

PLANT STANDS AND PEDESTALS

Plant stands and pedestals in majolica or terra-cotta were much seen in the hall from the 1850s onwards.

At the Great Exhibition, Herbert Minton introduced his new 'Imitation Majolica ware' in which a variety of flower-pots and plant stands were made. Visitors to the Exhibition were intrigued and what was described as a 'new ceramic marvel' caught on quickly.

Minton commissioned Baron Marochetti, the sculptor, to model an enormous plant vase recommended for its design, colours and great size. Majolica tiles modelled in bold relief with tulips and other flowers done in natural colours to decorate flower-boxes soon followed. Potters entering into competition in this field of work with Minton substituted their word 'English' for his 'Imitation' majolica.

Among producers of English majolica ware for the hall and conservatory are Daniel Sutherland and Sons of Longton whose goods are impressed *s & s* and George Jones of Stoke-upon-Trent who was awarded several gold medals at the following exhibitions: Paris, 1867; London, 1871; and Vienna, 1873. His wares are marked *G. J. Jones*.

Terra-cotta was equally favoured as a medium for the production of ornamental vases, flower-stands and boxes for the hall. Minton contributed some outstanding terra-cotta examples after the designs of well-known industrial artists. William Baddeley, son of William Baddeley of Hanley, founded his own terra-cotta works at Longton in the late 1860s. He used a similar mark to his father's (impressed W. BADDELEY) and among his principal wares were different vessels for the conservatory with characteristic ornament that featured well-modelled trees and plants in high relief.

Flower-holders in a hard, dense terra-cotta evolved by William Kirkham, impressed W. KIRKHAM came on to the market about 1860 and were among the best of their kind.

Another specialist firm was the Wilnecote Works established near Tamworth in 1862 by George Skey, whose name is virtually unknown to collectors according to Mr. Bernard Hughes. His authoritative and interesting chapter on Terra-Cotta in *Victorian Pottery & Porcelain* should be read by collectors. The Wilnecote Works produced many large conservatory ornaments in terra-cotta. They were glazed in brown tinged with green and catalogued under the name Rustic Ware. The impressed mark in an oval is 'GEORGE SKEY/ WILNECOTE WORKS/NR TAMWORTH'.

Outstanding terra-cotta 'Wicker Baskets' came from John Matthews at Weston-super-Mare which were massed with garden flowers imitating the style of flower-encrusted Coalport baskets in bone china. Their mark: the Royal coat-of-arms shown above the inscription: John Matthews/Late Phillips/

Royal Pottery/WESTON-SUPER-MARE. For Charles Phillips the former owner of these pottery works held a royal warrant as terra-cotta maker to Queen Victoria from 1845 until his death in 1870. He specialised in conservatory terra-cotta.

In close competition with majolica plant vases and terra-cotta jardinières and baskets were elegant 'wire stands' in which to hold exotic foliage plants and flowers. These stands were strongly recommended by Shirley Hibberd, then a leading garden journalist as 'noble window ornaments' to be filled with blooms. He advised ladies to study 'lightness and elegance of outline' when choosing them. Furthermore they had to be kept 'bright, clean and gay with not a trace of the rustic!'

Today these stands when they survive are in great demand and expensive. Incidentally, at the Great Exhibition of 1851, John Reynolds of New Compton Street, London, showed 'an ornamental flower-table' which was made entirely of wire. In the form of three serpents, posed uprights on their tails they look more like sea horses than snakes. On their heads rest a circular top with wire gallery. How this curvaceous hall stand would have delighted Mr. Hibberd! Furthermore what an entrancing 'find' for collectors of hall embellishments today.

32–34   *Trio of flower stands for the hall. Gothic-style low plant container;* (centre) *grecian urn on carved legs;* (right) *jardinière in Louis XV style*

13

MIGNONETTE BOXES

Both Jane Loudon and Henry Phillips have recorded at different times how 'whole London
streets were quite oppressive with the odour of
mignonette' in early Victorian times. The enormous
popularity of this modest little plant with its
greenish-red flower that has such a sweet and
penetrating scent was largely due, it is said, to the
Empress Josephine, who first grew it at Malmaison
from seed sent to her from Egypt by the Emperor,
who well knew her love of flowers.

Not long after mignonette had established itself
for ladies as their favourite indoor plant, Herbert
Minton began to produce some attractive and
individual boxes in the warm red tones of terra-
cotta for its cultivation. On the panels of some of

his boxes were bas-reliefs in white parian copied
from Thorwaldsen's 'Four Seasons'.

Later, about 1847, the Denby Pottery used
Bourne's patent three-chambered kiln to produce
some lightweight mignonette boxes and flower
vases in terra-cotta. These are all impressed with
the name BOURNE & SON.

Charles Canning of Tamworth, who had made
his name in architectural terra-cotta, also produced jardinières, flower vases and mignonette
boxes that were enamelled in a combination of
bright and dull colours. In his wares, the con-
volvulus is often featured as it was a fashionable
flower at the time. Canning's ware, though
impressed DELLA ROBBIA, bears little resemblance
to Minton's similarly named goods which appeared
about 1850 to cater for those with less expensive
tastes.

In conclusion to this chapter on the Victorian
hall and vestibule, there were many, of course,
which reflected the individual taste of their owners
and were not so conventionally furnished. By and
large, though, a Victorian hall was regarded simply
as an entrance to the house through which the
family, visitors and servants passed but never
sat in.

However, towards the end of the century, this
view changed and with it the old-style hall. A
keen observer always of the domestic scene, Mrs.
Talbot Coke described the new-look Victorian hall

35 *Handsome brass
hall lantern, portable,
with 'horn' windows,
c. 1860*

in *The Gentlewoman at Home* published during the
'90s:

'Amongst my own earliest mind-pictures, stands
out the square inner hall of an old west country
manor-house with large, receding latticed windows, the top panes filled with coats of arms
blazoned on coloured glass, the curtains faded old
red Genoa velvet. Dark oak-panelled walls were
lighted up here and there by groups of gleaming
armour and beaten brass scones, curious old
Venetian lamps swung from the dark rafters, the
walls above the panelling showed tawny, large-
patterned brocade, the huge open fire-place was
lined with blue and white Delft tiles from Biblical
subjects, with a brass dog, sentry-like, on either
side of the hearth.

'A tall carved oak settle with orange velvet,
fringed pillows and hospitable-looking armchairs
clustered round; the floor of dark oak showed old
Persian rugs with, here and there, the skins of
tiger and leopard; a large dark table in the centre
held a great Nankin bowl, never filled as was the
fashion some thirty years ago ('60s and '70s) with a
hideous mosaic of every flower in the garden but
with one decided note of colour – a bough of
fragrant lilac, sturdy red peonies, fiery orange or
snowy-white lilies. . . .

Nor were books and papers forgotten, for the
hall was a favourite *rendez-vous* between tea and
dinner.'

And as such the Hall has remained, more or less,
ever since.

2 The Dining Room

36 *Interior of dining-room showing artistic treatment and suitable fittings for fireplace, walls and decorated door. Designer: R. W. Edis*

The dining-room should be characterised by the massive appearance of its furniture and the richness of its hangings. The curtains may be of maroon-coloured cloth or moreen, trimmed with gold. The carpet should be Turkey or Axminster, and should not quite cover the room but leave a part to be rubbed bright or painted. You should have a large handsome chimney-piece and a large grate, so contrived with a plate at the bottom, as to contain wood as well as coal.

The Lady's Country Companion, 1845

So wrote Jane Loudon of the early-Victorian dining-room, repeating the same views, of course, held by her husband, John Claudius Loudon in regard to how it should be designed and furnished in the homes of the well-to-do.

As one knows, the Victorian dining-room was the focal point of family entertaining and changed little during the century. Meals were long and courses many, so chairs had to be of solid make to support masculine weight. Equally solid and imposing was the massive, mahogany side-board which dominated the whole room by its size and elaborate ornamentation.

Traditionally, the walls of a dining-room were covered in dark crimson paper and hung with dull and pompous family portraits by mediocre painters in heavy, gilt frames. Sometimes, a pair of chiffoniers with matching book case were placed against one wall while dead-centre stood the large mahogany dinner table, with square or rounded ends, which could be extended to twice or more its length by adding leaves. Few people need such tables today unless buying for a school or public building.

Since 1914, no greater revolution has taken place than in the world of domestic entertaining coupled with the change in our feeding habits. Apart from royalty, millionaires and the dwindling number of owners with 'stately homes' who can still command some form of restricted domestic service, we sit down to meals taken in the most unexpected places. It may be in the re-conditioned basement of a town house because it is adjacent to the kitchen and so handy for a cook-hostess; the small dining-area screened off in a open-plan living-room; or even in the kitchen itself, complete with every mechanical cooking and washing-up device, skilfully camouflaged. But rarely is it in a conventionally appointed dining-room used only at meal time.

Should one ask the modern housewife to explain the meaning of a 'drugget' or 'crumb cloth', would she be able to supply the correct answer? I doubt it. But there was a time when no self-respecting mistress (in particular if she owned an expensive Brussels or Turkey dining-room carpet) would have foregone the commonplace ritual of laying a large square of linen cloth or drugget under the dinner table to catch what crumbs fell or what food was spilt. Even Queen Victoria used a drugget at Balmoral to preserve the pristine glory of her specially woven plaid dining-room carpet. This 'drugget' was solemnly lifted, and shaken, after each meal by a flunkey.

Today not only has the drugget vanished but so, too, have doyleys, napkin rings, menu cards and holders, besides unwieldy cruets and condiment sets. The once grandiose epergne is rarely seen on a dinner table unless it has been transformed into modern dress; nor does a Self-acting Table Fountain ravish the eye and charm the ear of important guests as once it did. What of the tantalus, now a museum piece, or those rows of heavy cut-crystal decanters which to keep replenished with wine and spirits would cost a small fortune? They have gone by the board. What, too, of those hand-painted and lavishly gilt decorated dinner and dessert services of 72 and more pieces marked with the name of Spode, Minton, Copeland and Wedgwood. Who can afford to use them today? Instead, they go for vast sums in the sale-room to help finance their owners. Precious Waterford table glass and heavy Victorian silver has gone the same way. Our dinner tables are small and bare of fancy extras.

So much, then, for what the Victorian dining-room with its conventional furnishing and snobby, class-conscious awareness of how to entertain correctly once stood for. What remains of interest in it for the collector? Plenty, I think, by way of a glittering crystal epergne or rosewood chairs, table glass and china, besides small attractive items like mustard pots and salt cellars, hand-painted doyleys, menu holders and little silver table bells. For all these objects had their own appointed place in the Victorian dining-room which could be, as it certainly was in the old vicarage home of Mrs. Dulcimer at Little Yafford in Yorkshire, a room full of period charm.

'It was a long low room with three square casements on the southern side, and a wide old fireplace, bordered with blue and white Dutch tiles. On each side of the fireplace was the deep recess filled with old oak shelves on which were ranged the odds and ends of porcelain and delft which had dropped from the family tree into Clement Dulcimer's lap. Aunt Tabitha's Swansea tea-set with its sprawling red roses on a cream background; Uncle Timothy's quaint Lowestoft jugs; Cousin Simon's Bow punch bowl; Grandmamma's Oriental dessert plates; a Chelsea shepherdess minus an arm; a Chelsea shepherd piping to a headless sheep.

'A bowl of chrysanthemums, a ham, a game pie, a sirloin and a salad made a glow of colour ...

'At the end of the room facing the fireplace stood the fine old sideboard of Chippendale period, familiarly known as Uncle Joseph.'

Miss Braddon, An Open Verdict

It is with the sideboard, not Chippendale but pompous Victorian that I will begin my survey of the dining-room.

THE SIDE-BOARD, TABLE AND CHAIRS

Apart from film designers wishing to set up, in replica, a dining-room of the 1850s and '60s, the typical Victorian side-board with its capacious small cupboards and shelves, its large back-mirror and heavy rich carving is in little demand today. So no one need anticipate trouble in locating one for quite a moderate sum. Once considered almost *the* most important buy for the home, there were in Victorian days, three to four principal styles of side-board to choose from. These were the so-

38 *A neat plain sideboard in so-called cabinet-maker's gothic*

39 *A richly dressed sideboard for a wall-papered and mores fitting-room type of dining-room, presented by Messrs Jackson and Graham*

called Elizabethan style and the Greek; the French and the Gothic. One splendid example of the Elizabethan-styled sideboard with panels showing carved pictorial scenes was designed by Hughes Protat and made by William Cookes of Warwick in 1853.

The Paris Exhibition of 1855 inspired some sideboards to be made after the French style of Louis XVI which were quite successful. In his excellent little paperback *Victoriana* (Hamlyn) Mr. Juri Gabriel appears to be drawn to their rich curves and crestings. For he writes: 'They have a vulgar, bosomy appeal and can look marvellous in a modern interior if they are not treated with undue reverence'. Be that as it may. Their heyday lasted till about 1860.

40 (left) *A three-shelved sideboard with little carved decoration*
41 *Nice example of a Chiffionier type of dining-room pier table, early Victorian*

Other designers of sideboards were William Kendall of Warwick, a skilled craftsman who followed, more or less, current taste, and Bruce Tarbet, viewed in his day as the leading exponent of the Early English style in sideboards which were much admired.

But it was Sir Charles Eastlake (1793–1865) president of the Royal Academy and the author of *Hints on Household Taste* (1867), read by thousands of would-be artistic and house-proud Victorians, who has left behind him one of the best descriptions of the 1850 sideboard:

'It was bowed in front and "shaped" at the back; the cupboard doors were bent inwards; the draw fronts were bent outwards, the angles were rounded off: tasteless mouldings were glued on; the whole surface glistened with varnish.'

On the whole this was just criticism and one that Eastlake supported rigidly when creating his own upright examples of sideboards on which he placed the minimum amount of unnecessary mouldings and ornament with the exception of a few flourishes where forged-iron work appeared by way of hinges.

Some mid-Victorian pedestal sideboards with mirror decoration have been adapted to modern use quite successfully. Two excellent examples of this type of sideboard are illustrated in John Claudius Loudon's *Encyclopedia of Cottage, Farm and Villa Architecture* (1833). This style is termed somewhat loosely as 'Cabinet-maker's Gothic'. Well-proportioned with well-placed ornament,

42–4 . *Three different types of small early Victorian dining-room tables, table on carved pillar with revolving top based on a card table;* (centre) *Round 'loo' table in rosewood;* (right) *Dining-room table known as a 'cottage' or Pembroke table*

Loudon makes no comment on their design himself, other than that they were 'neat and plain' to his mind and had 'no claim to merit in point of style'.

A charming little chiffonier pier table also appears in Loudon's *Encyclopedia* and it is these small pieces, once used for the storing of laces and chiffons (hence their name), that are in demand to act as sideboards in the small dining-rooms of today.

The regulation large and imposing Victorian dinner table of gleaming mahogany with its far too thick and solid legs is like its stable-companion – the sideboard – more or less a drug on the antique market unless needed for a specific purpose. Far more suitable in every way for our restricted entertaining is a good quality early Victorian rosewood 'loo' table or traditional rectangular 'drop-leaf' which can seat eight comfortably when extended.

However, when it comes to buying Victorian dining-room chairs, there is no problem, as so many are still about. If one thinks of how many chairs must have been wanted by those horrific large families gathered together at meal-times, this is not surprising. The only stipulation put forward as to their use a century ago was made by Robert Kerr in *The Gentleman's House* (1864) when he advised his readers never to place them in an unbroken line against the dining-room wall as they would then give that pompous room the air of a tavern! And how right he was.

The most commonplace type of Victorian dining-room chair, indeed, of most chairs of this period was the *balloon-back* which made its first appearance during the 1830s and stayed in fashion till the late 1860s. At first, this chair had a basically rectangular back with a horizontal rail splat and a

45 (top) *buttoned dining chair;* (middle pair) *dining chair with stuffed morocco back and seat, mahogany, with morocco seat;* (bottom three) *gothic oak; mahogany and morocco, stuffed damask seat with painted back*

horizontal yoke-rail. Within ten years, though, this yoke-rail lost its overhang look and gained rounded corners. Instead of there being a solid vertical block of the uprights, a curved link came between them, giving that 'corseted' look with which we are all so familiar. This look was soon rounded off into the true 'balloon-back' of the 1850s when cabriole legs finally replaced the old, straight, turned ones in front. Such chairs are found in mahogany, walnut or rosewood and are usually upholstered with plump buttoned seats. Horsehair was used too. Well-made, strong and comfortable to sit on, such chairs are extremely good buys.

THE EPERGNE

46 *Miss Maling's own trumpet-shaped dinner table vase*

About 1850, a curious domestic revolution took place in the Victorian dining-room which led not only to a completely new way of serving meals but also to 'dressing' the table for the first time with fruit and flowers. For centuries, the English had set all dishes of fish, meat, poultry and game directly on the table spread with a fair white cloth which was removed, or as the expression went, 'drawn' after the cheese course. Then, and only then, did the dessert appear. But this custom had its drawbacks. For instance, it was difficult for a large family seated at table with guests to cope with the distasteful accumulation of dirty dishes and plates collected before them till the cloth was 'drawn'. While that ceremony was in progress under the butler's supervision, the conversation naturally halted and had to be re-established by a hostess already on tenterhooks lest a forgetful servant did not put the dessert plates in their correct position or supply finger bowls.

When about 1850, *le diner à la Russe* was introduced to England from the Continent it soon established itself as the best medium for entertaining elegantly, although it changed considerably the traditional set up of the English dinner table. To begin with, every course from soup to sweet was handed round by Russian servants instead of being put down in front of those at table as in England. The cloth was never 'drawn' either but remained firmly in place. This necessitated the use of a large sideboard where a large dish containing a saddle of mutton or haunch of venison was carved instead of being put before the host to perform that ceremony. With the table-cloth never removed, it was possible for flowers and fruit to be arranged tastefully in a new range of glass and china vases. Although ornate silver or silver-gilt Georgian epergnes (*see* G. Bernard Hughes, *Country Life*, 19 May 1955) had been a striking feature of the eighteenth-century dinner table, they were only used to present highly

47–8 *Pair of charming dressing glass stands (or epergnes) made by Messrs Boucher, Guy & Co., Glassmen to Her Majesty, 128 Leadenhall Street*

flavoured sauces, pickles and relishes enjoyed by gourmets. However in 1851 when the first models of newly-styled glass and china table-centres, or epergnes, made their debut at the Great Exhibition in Hyde Park, the massive silver epergne of Georgian times was quickly superseded by what *Cassell's Household Guide* described as 'Pyramids of exquisitely chased crystal – light, airy, sparkling and fragrant with blossom.' These new table ornaments fascinated the female eye and became rapidly fashionable. Moreover they were christened by individual names and those feminine. There was the 'Josephine' after the lovely French Empress and the 'Excelsior'; the 'Rosa' and the

'Exhibition'. These last two epergnes inspired the production of a whole host of others which were put out by Messrs. Boucher, Guy and Co., Glassmen to Her Majesty at 128, Leadenhall Street, London.

At the Council House, Mary Stevens Park, Stourbridge, Worcestershire, a fascinating collection of Victorian glass epergnes and table-centres are housed. But in view of the interest American collectors have taken in them for some time past, their fashionable come-back has naturally caused prices to rise. First favourites are those in ruby glass, or in ruby-threaded crystal, with snake-like hooks fixed to the stand from which dangle small baskets to hold nuts and fruit. A great number of china table-centres were produced by Minton, Copeland, Spode and other firms to match accompanying dessert services. Another floral fashion conceived for the Victorian dinner-table was a range of little glass, or china, baskets which were placed at regular intervals down the table, usually one before each guest. They were filled with tiny posies of multi-coloured florets; or, again, with fresh strawberries. Such baskets went by the name of 'Denmark' or 'Alexandra' baskets in honour of the lovely Princess of Wales who used them on her table when entertaining at Marlborough House. Other favourite table ornaments besides baskets, were tazzas or china cherubs holding a shell in which sweetmeats could be served.

One of the first books on flower-arranging appeared in 1862. Called *Flowers and How to Arrange them* it was by a Miss Maling, who stressed the importance of 'the arrangement of what Florists call "Cut-Flowers" owing to the universal

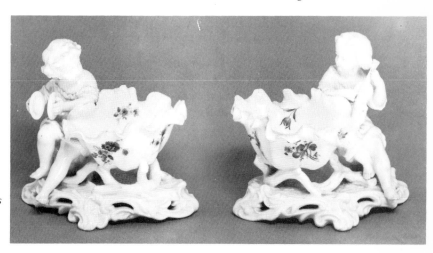

49 *Pair of glazed white china cherubs with musical instruments (cymbals and fiddle). Sweetmeat containers for the dinner table. Marked, Moore Bros.* c. *1862*

adoption of the *diner russe* which requires so many flowers.'

Miss Maling designed her own table vase in frosted glass: a design she pointed out, to assist 'the ease and convenience of separating the flowers and fruit while still obtaining the full "Embellishment" that each gives to the table, the faculty for cleaning and the useful attribute of holding much or little fruit to lie on its own leaves.'

Miss Maling preferred fruit like peaches, grapes, plums, etc., to rest on their own foliage at the base of the trumpet-shaped vase she had designed while above them flowers and ferns 'made a graceful waving shade above without interrupting the view across the table which is such a great discomfort'.

She recommended, too, that small, pretty, white china groups or figures in Parian ware should also hold a decorative place on the table. Such figures repeated the theme of little cherubs, or boys, and are sought by collectors today. At the Great Exhibition and others that followed 'Sets of dessert ornaments of eight pieces in white parian statuary enriched with gilding' were always on view. From Messrs. W. H. Kerr and Co., Royal Porcelain Works, Worcester, there came in 1863, the celebrated Shakespeare dessert service of 24 pieces in in a combination of Parian statuary ware and lead-glazed bone china enriched with gilding. The free-standing statuary showed different characters from 'Midsummer Night's Dream'.

Following Miss Maling's lead in suggesting new ideas for 'dressing' the dinner table *à la russe* came a Miss Hassard of Norwood and Mr. Cypher of Cheltenham. They worked as floral artists during the 1870s and were present at many an exhibition where Miss Hassard's style was described in the press as 'exquisitely airy and refined' and Mr. Cypher's as 'being more dashing, precise and hard as befitted a man!'

It was Mr. Cypher who won first prize in the gaslight competition staged by the R.H.S. in 1873 at Birmingham. He is recorded as having used three brilliantly shining glass epergnes, the central one, three-tiered, on whose base of silvered glass was arranged a circle of multi-coloured flowers. A set of small matching table vases carried scarlet geraniums, white eucharis and red roses relieved with sprays of astilbe, stipa, milium and maidenhair. The central epergne had pink heaths and white and pink roses with grasses and ferns to soften the outlines while the two side epergnes displayed modified arrangements of this floral theme.

Unfortunately, the gracefully designed epergnes of glittering glass whose hanging baskets were characteristic of the late 1850s, '60s and '70s gave way eventually to more clumsily modelled and cheaper versions (some even electro-plated) till at last the epergne came in for heavy censure from that noted arbiter of domestic taste and floral arrangement, Mrs. Talbot Coke. She wrote in *The Gentlewoman at Home*:

'Those of us who can recall dinner-parties of some twenty-five years ago will not need to be reminded of the amount of ugliness to the square inch an epergne was capable of holding. I can see the tasteless, lumpy mass of silver with tortuous branches holding up the cut-glass bowl into which the gardener stuck, at his own sweet will, a specimen of every flower in the garden, with a cheerful edge of box and yew and asparagus fronds waving above; and on this we had to feast our eyes all through dinner which was the long-drawn affair it is not today.'

Before the epergne died a natural death it was demoted to a very inferior position in middle-class homes. This was on the sideboard where, if money permitted, it was filled with nuts and fresh fruit; if not, with wax imitations made by the daughter of the house which gave rise to the catch-phrase – 'There's always fruit on the sideboard!'

TABLE CLOTHS, NAPKIN RINGS AND DOYLEYS

There appears to have been two schools of thought on the question of what kind of table cloth should be used in the 1850s. Should it be the best British table-damask, satin-like in texture and relying only on the gloss obtained from the weaving of warp and woof or those recently arrived from Dresden with striking new designs showing the famous Zwiebelauster or onion pattern in coloured borders? Colour in table linen! It was a novel idea that caught on immediately. By 1872, scarlet and blue threads came to be worked into embroidered initials and monograms on damask cloths. In *Woman's Handiwork in Modern Homes* (1881) a table cover with matching napkins and a sideboard cloth was starred for its design of scattered field poppies worked in washing scarlet thread interwoven with German text!

But like the epergne, coloured table linen soon came to be vulgarised, especially when the mistress of the house, proud of her needle-skill, decided to add her own decoration to it.

'Terrible cloths and centre-pieces were perpetrated in crewel work and crazy work', recorded Mrs. Talbot Coke, honest as ever. 'It became sometimes quite a question whether the most despised epergne would not have been preferable to such badly designed dinner table work. For horror's crown of horrors which my own eyes saw once in a grand house was a strip of vivid rose-coloured satin with edges of sham ivy sewn round it.'

Whatever, though, the dinner table might be covered with, either by an ice-smooth white damask linen cloth or one embroidered in violent colours, a napkin had to be folded in one of an amazing variety of shapes for each guest. No Victorian parlour maid or footman worth their salt could dare confess to ignorance as to how to fold them correctly.

Napkins have been in use in Britain since Roman times, for they were part and parcel of eating habits at banquets. From about the early sixteenth century till 1800 they were beautified by a wide range of subjects, hunting-scenes, etc. being woven in the damask. In Victorian times, napkins reached their apogee of splendour when a dozen, and more, complicated ways of 'folding' them was devised. The more elaborate the better. *Cassell's Household Guide* (1875) supplies a long list of these ways and their names. For instance, there was the Shell and The Basket; The Slipper and The Mitre; The Victoria Regia (after the famous water-lily) and the Cornucopia. The proper place to fold napkins was in the pantry or housekeeper's room, then they were carried into the dining-room on a tray. The following morning, all napkins were re-damped, ironed and then slipped through a napkin ring to be used by members of the family till they were exchanged for fresh ones. On account of this habit, napkin rings became necessary. In silver they were considered a suitable christening present for a child, particularly when 'boxed'

50 *Two pairs of Victorian napkin rings. One, silver, engraved with the signs of the zodiac and initialled; one made of pearl shell, shell-shaped*

together with a matching silver mug or porringer. Victorian napkin rings can be very pretty. They were made in gold and silver, mother of pearl, ivory or carved wood. Some were plain, some highly ornamental, being engraved with the recipient's name, initials or the family crest. There are napkin rings, too, made of beadwork, embroidered in gaudy Berlin wools or bought, like those in Tunbridge ware, as happy holiday souvenirs.

Though napkins are still with us, the rings to hold them appear to be unfashionable except as collector's items.

In one way, this can be said also of doyleys. Once upon a time, no finger-bowl appeared for desert at table minus the decorative little mat on which it stood. The doyley has quite a history and its curious name derives from a Queen Anne warehouseman called Thomas Doyley who carried on his business at Number 386 the Strand. But his house, which once stood beside Hodsoll, the banker, has long been demolished. Determined to make his doyleys of material which 'might be both cheap and genteel' Thomas Doyley did so and made his fortune besides preserving his name.

During the eighteenth century, doyleys were in constant use as miniature wine glass napkins in the dining-room; then, about 1850, they changed their character and came to be placed under a glass finger-bowl where they have since remained.

Circular in shape, doyleys were cut to fit inside a dessert plate and were made usually of white

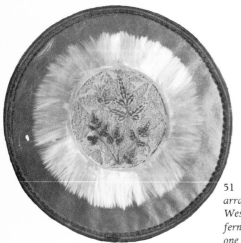

51   *Doyley featuring arrangement of West Indian dried ferns and grasses, one of a dozen, c. 1890*

doyleys with original drawings by Beatrix Potter taken from her *Tale of Jemima Puddleduck* fetched £700 in the sale-room.

About the '90s, the fashion for using doyleys appears to have been on the wane and a small manual *Manners and Tone of Good Society* by a 'Member of the Aristocracy' gave this advice: 'Plates and d'oyleys are not used in good society at "Afternoon Tea"; to use them, then, would be considered bad style'.

During the opening years of King Edward VII's reign, table mats as opposed to doyleys appeared for the first time on a 'bare' dinner table which had been denuded altogether of its white damask cloth. This fashion was introduced from America by Lady Randolph Churchill. Other smart hostesses followed, suit so that the full beauty of polished wood reflecting, like a mirror, the sparkle of glass and silver was seen for the first time in the English dining-room. The following description of a late Victorian dinner party table will give an idea not only of its loaded but also quite magnificent appearance, even when the hostess seems to have been carried away by her love for a 'pink-and-white scheme' in its entirety:

'All the ornaments on the table were plain white Sèvres, lovely in shape and finish. Even the candelabra were white Sèvres figures. The flowers used were pink and white roses, heaths and carnations charmingly arranged in baskets of different designs. There was no fruit on the table only pink and white bonbons and small cakes in silver shell-dishes; all the set china pieces stood on rose-

satin jean whose matt surface lent itself to decoration. Doyleys with pen-and-ink drawings for which were commissioned the work of famous illustrators, are well worth collecting. Favourite subjects include genre and landscape; Japanese scenes, so much *en vogue* during the '70s and '80s; comic situations derived from *Punch*; and the hunting-field. The collector can come across sets which are faithful copies of Sir John Tenniel's (1820–1914) famous illustrations to *Alice in Wonderland* or Florence and Bertha K. Upton's entrancing *Golliwog* books. Kate Greenaway, Walter Crane and Beatrix Potter all tried their hand at decorating doyleys in their early days. In December, 1968, a set of circular silk-fringed

52–4   *Lace-trimmed, circular doyley showing pen-and-ink drawing of Tweedledum and Tweedledee taken from Sir John Tenniel's* Alice . . . *illustrations, 1860;* (centre) *Pressed fern-frond on net, lace-edged, 1870 and* (right) *'Prince Frederick Charles' one of a series of six portrait doyleys*

coloured velvet stands about an inch and a half high; the candles had small pink silk shades; and even the wine-glasses that were not clear crystal were of lovely pink and white Venetian glass with twisted stems. All the china used throughout dinner was of white and gold Sèvres with rose-coloured dessert plates. The dinner cards were to match.'

MENU AND DINNER CARDS

Nothing brings home more the great changes that have taken place in national eating habits than reading the lengthy menus supplied by the arbiter of culinary taste, Mrs. Isabella Beeton (1836–1865). To begin with, the quite ordinary menus she suggests for a Victorian middle-class household run from four to five, and more, courses at every meal. This made menu cards obligatory which led, in turn, to the production of many delightful and different kinds of china menu holders.

In her memoirs, *Under Five Reigns* (1912) Lady Dorothy Nevill who was a leading social figure and a great hostess in Victorian and Edwardian days, records how 'Illuminating verses of poetry, texts and menu cards' were a popular pastime for ladies during the 1870s and '80s. Furthermore, she collected them. Among the many examples Lady Dorothy possessed, one, most prized, was a large menu card commissioned by the Corporation of the City of London when that august body entertained the old Shah of Persia at a Banquet in the Guildhall in 1873. She describes this card as being decorated in an over-all Persian design that encircled a portrait of the Shah and showed both his arms and that of his hosts plus a majestic view of Mount Demavend capped with eternal snow.

When not made of fine cardboard, hand-painted

55   Front and back of flower-decorated white china menu holder having a small socket for candle, c. 1879

56–8   Example of simple white china 'tablet' menu card holder, 1870; (centre) Menu holder in biscuit china, yellow-brown, made in the shape of two walnuts on stem-base, c. 1880; (right) Amusing menu card holder featuring two mice performing on musical instruments, Lambeth Doulton, attributed to George Tinworth, 1886

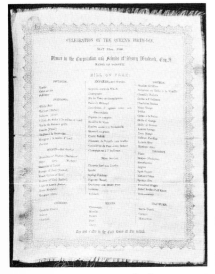

59–61 Fringed silk menu card in celebration of The Queen's birthday, 24 May 1850 held in Norwich; (centre) menu card designed for a dinner given by The Sette of Odd Volumes at the Willis Rooms, 7 May 1886; (right) Menu card designed and signed by Harry Furniss for dinner given at The Freemason's Tavern, 2 April 1886

and engraved, menu cards were made of silk or satin with fringed ends. Both doyleys and dinner cards were made to match. These last-named objects were small gilt-edged and hand-decorated slips of pasteboard inscribed with a guest's name. They were made with great care and artistic skill by the lady of the house. Different writing techniques were studied in the school room such as the Italian, or Gothic hand, for use on menus.

62 Tablet form white china menu card holder with painted figure and painted floral border, c. 1890

In fact, many boring hours were spent in pursuing this absurd accomplishment and the writing-out of a menu card was often vetted by dear Mama. Such a well-bred Mama as Mrs. Tempest who on watching her daughter, Violet, at this task, declared:

'If you would only slope more, Violet, and make your upstroke finer and not cross your Ts so undeviatingly. A lady's T. ought to be less pronounced. There is something too assertive in your consonant, my dear.'

Miss Braddon, *Vixen*

Designs on menu and dinner cards were usually repeated on doyleys. For instance, at a celebration Christmas dinner both menu and dinner cards are recorded as cut from cardboard with tiny pictures of a turkeycock, game and plum pudding done in watercolours with doyleys to match.

To facilitate the traditional custom of a gentleman offering his arm to the lady that he has to conduct downstairs to the dining-room, he was handed on arriving at the house a small envelope by the butler. This contained his partner's name. One example I have seen showed a floral stamp on the right-hand corner of the envelope with an imitation postmark indicating the name of the flower and the date of its blossoming (i.e. Arbutus, April 15th). A corresponding one was held by the partner.

In a recently published book, *Life with Queen Victoria*, Marie Malet writes to her husband of a menu card used at a Royal Household luncheon when she was 'in waiting' on Queen Victoria. It carried a small painting of a gay young woman dancing the can-can! 'What do you think of our menus?' she wrote. 'I hope you don't think we have a conversation to match!'

Here is the menu for that luncheon:

HOUSEHOLD LUNCHEON
Rissoto à la Milanaise
Grilled Mutton Chops
Poulet aux nouilles
Asperges à la sauce
Tapioca Pudding
Meringues aux fraises

In less august households than those belonging to a Queen of England or the aristocracy, menu cards were far simpler in design, of course, but still obligatory.

'"It seems hardly worthwhile writing the names of so small a party", said Mrs. Mulholland, ambling round the dinner table with little strips of paper in her hand. "But I always think it safer, do not you, dear Nan?"'

Rhoda Broughton, *Mrs. Bligh*

But if they wished, fashionable hostesses could always commission an artist to design her own individual menu and dinner cards. Walter Crane, Kate Greenaway and Beatrix Potter all experimented at one time in this fascinating field of Victorian paper ephemera that waits to be more fully explored by the collector.

TABLE CHINA

In contrast to the limited number of dinner and dessert services used today, limited on account of storage space and the lack of domestic help, a Victorian home possessed at least three to four vast China table services to cope with the garganuan meals served both in the dining-room and servants' hall.

One standard service, for instance, made not of fine china but ordinary blue-printed earthenware for everyday use, which was issued by Spode a few years before Queen Victoria came to the throne, numbered 134 separate pieces. These included fan-shaped dishes and covers, four square dishes and covers, one octagonal dish, liner and cover, two sauce tureens and stands for ladles, two oval egg stands each with 12 cups, six octagonal meat dishes, four oval dishes, a salad bowl and 24 each of soup, dinner and dessert plates. Apart from these, a Victorian hostess might decide to present her fish course in a separate service by Minton with a painting by W. Mussill of a different fish on each plate.

The Victorian hostess tried to muster as much fine table china and glass as she could in her dining-room to show off to her guests. If she hadn't got it, she borrowed, as little Mrs. Haweis did from her mother, Mrs. Joy, wife of a fashionable Victorian portrait painter:

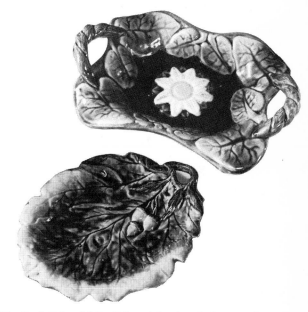

63   (top) *Colourful English majolica bread platter with ivy-leaf pattern and raised marguerite centre;* (below) *One oval shallow dish in highly glazed majolica-ware ivy-leaf-shaped and decorated with acorns, 1860*

Number 16 Welbeck Street,
July 17th, 1869

My dear Ma,

We are coming to you for pickings. We want your china bowl for claret cup – the tazza-spoons and forks innumerable – all the rarities you possess

65–7   *Teapot stand composed of a shell-patterned Minton tile mounted in pewter;* (centre) *Lattice-edged fruit plate (marked Pirchenhammer) nineteenth century, Austrian;* (right) *White china bread platter with painted spray featuring a pansy always a popular Victorian flower motif, c. 1860*

we shall take home in a cab this week. And why? We are going to have the Archbishop and Mrs. Tait to lunch – likewise the Cowpers William on Sunday !!! We want some splendid things about. So look out. . . .

Yours affectionately,
M.E.H

From about the 1840s, many imitation Sèvres table services were put out by different leading china firms. This fashionable trend was followed by another, that of using a different make of china for each course. Thus dinner might begin with the soup served in Sèvres; then fish in Minton; and game or poultry in Rockingham or Copeland. Finally, for dessert, a set of imitation Dresden fruit plates that matched frail little china baskets with forget-me-not decoration, candelabra and a pretty china Cupid, astride a swan with blue forget-me-not reins already placed on the table.

When not in use, the traditional place to keep candelabra was on the dining-room sideboard or mantel-piece – never anywhere else.

A complete table service (i.e.: 24 covers) by a well-known china firm in mint condition will command a high price in an antique shop or sale-room today. On the other hand, because they were of such a monumental size and because so many of the old homes from which they came have disappeared, it is quite possible to pick up a 'harlequin' service or even a small set of perfect Minton table dishes and plates for a modest sum after careful search. Individual items of a service such as fruit and sweetmeat dishes; sauce boats and pickle jars; honey-pots and jam jars; a monster soup tureen or handsome meat charger – all lend themselves to being collected, one by one, so as to form an interesting assembly of representative Victorian table ware in china.

68   (left) *Small round blue-and-white transfer printed Worcester menu card holder, 1860s*

69   (right) *Oval china dish from a service showing Esher Place in parkland with a folly, c. 1840*

FASHIONS IN FISH PLATES

During the Middle Ages, monks were greatly addicted to eating fish as they had to observe many meatless days according to Church regulations. In most monasteries, a stew-pond was established in which carp, eels, perch and other edible fish were kept.

Stew-ponds or 'Fishing-warrens', as they came to be called in the eighteenth century, were also maintained by noblemen and big landowners in their country seats.

In an interesting article entitled 'The Mazarin for Elegance' (*Country Life*, 14 March 1968) Mr. G. Bernard Hughes tells how the mazarine, a large pierced oval silver dish, fitted over a shallow bowl or under-dish holding hot water to keep, first a fricassee or ragout, then fish, was introduced by its inventor Charles Marguetel de Saint Denis de Saint Evremond (1613–1703) to the Court of St. James's. In turn, this same dish inspired potters to produce a similar type in creamware from about 1730, listed in Georgian trade catalogues as 'Fish Drainers for Dishes'. Made in eight standard sizes ranging from 10¾″ to 28″, the numerous circular perforations on them were arranged in attractive patterns. Still later, they were produced in Staffordshire blue pearl ware with transfer-printed decoration that usually feature a picturesque view of some historic contemporary scene. They are well worth collecting.

Incidentally, the name 'mazarine' given by Saint-Evremond to his long-surviving platter was in honour of Hortense Mancini, Duchesse de Mazarin, a noted Chelsea hostess and friend of King Charles II. She used one always for serving asparagus, a vegetable she much enjoyed. Sometimes, in an old inventory of household china found in country-houses, a 'mazarine' is referred to as 'a hortensia'!

As much as fish like boiled turbot with caper sauce, or salmon and whitebait was relished by Victorians, so, too, was shellfish. First in favour were oysters which in the nineteenth century had not priced themselves out of existence as they have with us today. For oysters were eaten by rich and poor alike. Second in popularity came whelks, mussels, shrimps, cockles and winkles.

In the varied world of dinner plates, large or small, that were put out by china makers for a specific purpose, oyster plates are very decorative.

70 *Fish plate from a service with fluted gilt trim showing hand-painted fish swimming in underwater foliage, c. 1880*

71 *Bevelled gilt and pale green border with perch as principal motif, fish plate from a service, c. 1890*

72 *Brown earthen-ware scallop-patterned dish from a Yarmouth shellfish stall, c. 1890*

73 *A scallop-edged gilt-and-white oyster plate showing delicate seaweed patterns, recessed, c. 1880*

74 *Three Victorian cockle plates. Left and right are products of the South Wales Pottery; middle example, marked Dillwyn & Co., Swansea*

Generally they feature richly gilded scallop-edges with shallow compartments for serving the best Whitstable or Colchester natives and carry designs of floating gilt seaweeds. A whelk plate in my possession has shell-shaped recesses in which to serve them. Henry Mayhew has recorded that at one time as many 4,950,000 whelks were sold annually in London alone and at Billingsgate, the big fish market, three different varieties were listed under the names of White, Red and Almond Whelks.

Equally in demand were cockles: cockles from Leigh-on-Sea and Southend. The cry of the cockle-seller patrolling the dingy streets and alley-ways of the East End was as well-known and loved as the cry of the Muffin Man heard in Belgravia and Brompton.

Not only has Charles Dickens written about cockles taken with a dash of vinegar and eaten with bread-and-butter but many another Victorian author. So it is not surprising to find some very pretty, little china cockle plates with characteristic designs, chief among them being marine emblems like shells, fishes and anchors. Others, again, have mottoes or are engraved with the arms, and crests of companies such as the Oddfellows and Buffaloes used when they staged their celebrated Cockle Feasts in the City.

A fascinating collection of cockle plates can be seen at the National Museum of Wales, Cardiff.

TABLE GLASS

As much as the Victorians enjoyed using a vast number of table dishes and plates, so did they enjoy an equal number of wine glasses, goblets and decanters.

Beside each place setting it was customary to see four to five wine glasses in position. For both red and white wines (i.e. clarets and burgundies, champagne, hock, sherry and port) and later in the century liquers, were offered at a dinner party. Tumblers, however, were always kept on the sideboard and produced only on request. Wine was offered from decanters that stood, again, on

the sideboard, with the exception of the port decanter which was put down before the host and then sent round the table clock-wise. Hence the enormously wide range of wine glasses with their different shaped bowls and stems that were used in Victorian times.

Since the Excise of 1745–6 the English glass industry has been in a parlous condition and unable to expand, although in the field of clear lead crystal with cut decoration it was unrivalled, leading the world. But when this exorbitant tax was repealed in 1845, important glass centres like Stourbridge and Gateshead set themselves out to catch up, even out-class, some of their Continental rivals; in particular they wished to rival Bohemian and East German glass men who, by concentrating their skills solely on producing coloured glass wares, had become the top-producers of it in Europe.

Almost immediately, at the Manchester Exhibition of 1845, Benjamin Richardson of Stourbridge staged a display of coloured, opal, cased and painted glass. Following his lead George Bacchus and Sons, Rice Harris and Son as well as Benjamin Richardson showed exciting use of colour in one glass form or another at Birmingham in 1849.

An important and novel feature in George Bacchus's wine-glasses was the use of multi-coloured threads in their stems; stems which were often convoluted. With their distinctly Venetian touch they were much admired by Ruskin. Such glasses swiftly caught the eye of buyers and released a perfect flow, with others in green, ruby, topaz, and other shades (one known as Vaseline) from the Midlands into London shops. Goblets with engraved or cased bowls were now seen on the dinner table with slender-stemmed tall hock glasses aping the Bohemian style. Although Waterford glass still held its place for unsurpassed brilliance and design, other makes of cut-crystal were phased out and not seen again until the 1880s.

What mattered the dull and heavy surroundings of the dining-room, with its massive sideboard and gloomy family portraits, if, at night, by soft illuminating candle-light, a hostess could achieve such a magical effect of colour as this?

'The centre-piece was a glowing mass of scarlet poinsettia and white japonicas, the latter cut with long stems and having dark glossy dark-green foliage. Side-dishes at dessert, finger-bowls and

75 *Two intricately cut flint-glass decanters and one table goblet shown by The Brooklyn Flint Glass Co., Washington, at the Great Exhibition, 1851*

76 *Trio of cut-crystal table decanters, designs being cut in very bold relief. By Mr. Summerfield of London*

77 *Three very ornamental glass table goblets, work of Mr. Conne of London, exhibited at the Great Exhibition of 1851*

78 (below) *Five examples of different types of wine glasses featuring grape and vine-leaf patterns*

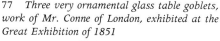

81 *Attractive examples of a tall water tumbler, sherry and port wine glasses in star-patterns of the 1880s*

ice-cream plates were ruby Bohemian glass. The doyleys were etched with red silk in tiny ruby glass, and the red wax candles had each a little jaunty cap, or shade, of scarlet silk. The sparkle of fire-light and candle-light over all, recalled the impression produced upon Jane Eyre by the drawing-room of Thornfield, '"a general blending of snow and fire".'

A bobeche, by the way, was the small circular glass or porcelain cup used to catch the drippings of candle-wax. It was often decorated and could be had in blue china; Venetian glass beaded and lipped with colour; in crystal starred with gold; and in Bohemian ruby, rose and blue glass.

At one time, decorated candles for dinner had a certain vogue, but they were superseded by plain white, crimson or rose candles that remained traditional colours for the dining-room. When a wedge-bottom to fit into the socket of a candle-stick was invented, and patented, it became an easy matter to have tall or short, slender or thick candles as preferred. Coloured paper shades painted with floral motifs were made to match candles. This work was looked on not only as an agreeable occupation for genteel ladies but as a reliable source of income for those living in reduced circumstances.

Generally speaking, Victorian table glass can be divided into three main groups, or types, which are easily identifiable. First there are the glasses and decanters made of clear flint glass, finely cut and featuring the 'diamond' and 'strawberry' pattern which date from the 1830s and were in use till the Great Exhibition of 1851. Next comes the 'thumb-print' design on the bowl of the glass which had a 'cut' stem. Finger bowls and decanters were produced to match. A complete set of such wine glasses would include those with a shallow and more open bowl for serving champagne in with a larger, more goblet-like glass for burgundies and clarets. Claret was first put in, and poured from, a tall, slender ewer, or flagon type of jug modelled on classic lines and often fitted with a lid. By 1846, or so, complete sets of coloured table glass in amber, apple-green and amethyst (this colour is scarce) shades had appeared and soon were in use everywhere.

Mid-Victorian wine glasses and decanters made their debut, at the International Exhibition of 1862. In deep green, rose-red, ruby and topaz colours, many had clear-glass stems and feet, while decanters showed a Renaissance influence in their design, having lost their rings and with stoppers of a mushroom shape. As hock and Moselle were now popular table wines and much drunk, glasses whose bowls were engraved with grapes and vine leaves after Bohemian styles were seen and still remain in production.

Then, in 1865, through his invention of a geometrical 'etching' machine, John Norwood introduced his 'famous key' pattern which had an instantaneous success. Established as a favourite design for table glass it has never been ousted.

Late Victorian table glass has a thin, fine, clear look and was decorated either by that well-known and pretty 'star' pattern or by fern-engraving, ferns being a highly popular motif on everything at this time owing to their cult by Victorians. By now, decanters were long and slender of neck and there was, too, a vogue for coloured wine glasses which stood on ribbed, opaque stems in rose-white, and dark-green and white shades.

Sometimes, the collector of period table glass may be confronted with the term 'Cabaret Sets'. The name alludes to a claret jug, or decanter, sold with two matching goblets that were often given away, together, as a wedding present.

PRESSED GLASS

One of the most distinctive kinds of late Victorian table glass, long ignored but being very much collected now is 'pressed' glass, which was first produced in America about 1825 by means of mechanical pressing. The process for making 'pressed' glass was simple and cheap, molten glass being dropped into a patterned mould followed up by a tightly fitting plunger forcing it into every part. Pressed glass is surprisingly heavy and part of its charm to those attracted by it are the occasional flaws found! Because it could never be re-heated and lacked the brilliance of 'blown' glass, its familiar 'lacy' or 'stippled' look was devised to produce the necessary sparkle. Originally intended to serve as 'poor man's cut glass' it rapidly developed so much character that it established itself as a popular glass ware in its own right.

Inspired by the success that pressed glass was having in America, the method of producing it

82 *Pretty pressed glass plate showing sunburst; (centre) A small cream jug commemorating the Silver Wedding of the Prince of Wales to Princess Alexandra (1888); (right) attractive leaf-shaped pressed glass dish with handle*

between a mould and a plunger was introduced to England by some Midland glass manufacturers in the 1830s. Among these firms were Thomas Hawkes, Bacchus & Green and Rice Harris. Though early English 'pressed' glass copied America's 'lacy' styles and patterns like the 'daisy and button,' the 'hobnail'; the 'heart' and the 'star' on finely stippled grounds, in England cut-crystal designs were repeated on this cheaply-produced glass, as was only natural in the country to which cut-crystal decoration was native.

In the 1870s and '80s, England's thriving 'pressed' glass industry concentrated on producing an enormous quantity of small table items such as custard and jelly cups, bread platters, butter dishes, milk and cream jugs, cup-plates (Chapter XI: Cottage Glass) for homes all over the country. These items are all highly collectable.

Yet another field open to the collector who is drawn to pressed glass is that of 'Commemoration' pieces still available and very decorative. Nearly every royal occasion that took place in Queen Victoria's reign was faithfully recorded in pressed glass for her loyal subjects to buy and treasure. Jubilee plates, candlesticks and jugs celebrating the wedding of the Prince of Wales to the lovely, Sea King's daughter, Alexandra, Royal Christening mugs and even a sad death were all commemorated in plain and pressed glass, lovingly inscribed and dated. The choice is wide still and prices not prohibitive.

SALT CELLARS AND CONDIMENT SETS

From earliest times, the economic importance of salt has played a leading role in those countries where it was discovered. Equally, it has had many social and religious implications. A 'covenant' of salt is recorded in the Bible, while the shipment of salt to the coast led to the building of one of the oldest roads in Italy. To this day, the Persians speak of a man as being 'untrue to salt', meaning by this, disloyal. In England, a 'standing salt' occupied the most important place on the medieval table. Placed before the head of the household, or lord, those seated 'above the salt' were of higher social rank than those seated 'below'. Containers for salt have answered to many names. They include the first early 'standing' salts or trencher salt; salt dip and salt cup; salt cellars and shakers. But this last name is more common, I think, to America, where 'salts' in every size and shape have long been collected.

One of the most magnificent salt dishes ever made was by the famous Renaissance goldsmith and sculptor, Benvenuto Cellini. The humblest were those put out by travelling glass-blowers (Chapter XI: Cottage Glass) in the nineteenth century. Made in crude bottle-green glass, they were sold for a penny or so to cottage folk.

Victorian salt cellars can be found in many mediums, beginning with gold and silver and then descending in the social scale from fine porcelain to glass, wood and pewter. In pressed glass, the shape and pattern of salt cellars is endless, for they were produced in vast quantities from the 1870s onwards. Novelty glass 'salts' may come in the form of a duck or a tulip, a pedestal or a broken column! Then there are those typical little Victorian 'salts' which are made of Britannia metal dip-lined with ruby-red or cobalt-blue glass linings because of their pierced sides. Pewter and pressed glass pepper pots appear to date from about the 1830s, but pairs of salt and pepper shakers do not seem to have been common much before 1875. When painting on china was taken up as a 'parlour' hobby by young ladies in the '70s and '80s, many hand-decorated salt and pepper pots came into being to be given away as presents. Favourite flowers painted on them were the rose, the violet, pansy and arbutus. They were also much ornamented with gold.

An amusing line of salt and pepper sprinklers with screw top cover or stopper together with Mustard Pots were known as *Hygenic Cruets*. They were put out by Messrs. James Macintyre & Co. Ltd. of the Washington China Works, Burslem towards the end of the nineteenth century. They were modelled and coloured to imitate birds' eggs (Chapter VI: The Best Bedroom); another range were decorated with flower-and-leaf designs. Matching Coquetiers (i.e. egg cups) and Muffineers were also available from the same firm. It must be remembered as a nice note on Victorian etiquette,

83 *Victorian silver 'monkey' condiment set*

84 *Example of a smooth brown 'hen's egg' pepper pot, c. 1880*

that cruets were *never* seen on the dinner table in the homes of gentle folk but kept firmly in their traditional place – on the sideboard!

Mustard pots which can form a fascinating collection in themselves date from the seventeenth century or even earlier. In Georgian silver, they are both rare and expensive, but there is a wide range of glass and china pots used in Victorian times which are modestly priced and appealing. Such pots were produced by most well-known china firms like Doulton, Copeland, Spode and others; in pressed glass they were 'hawked' by the glass-blower. An interesting side-line on how mustard was once sold is contained in the old-fashioned name of 'Tewkesbury Balls' or 'Fire Balls'. These were small balls of dried mustard, the process to make them involving the grinding of mustard seed in a small hand-mill called a 'mustard querne', then mixing the ground seed with damp pea flour into the shape required. This way of selling mustard was taken over in the eighteenth century by one of 'milling' mustard seed to produce mustard flour; a process which originated in Durham. Mustard pots, first known as 'mustard cans' or 'mustard tankards', have an equally old and interesting history as 'salts' and 'pepper shakers'. Messrs. Colman of Norwich, the famous mustard producers, own a fascinating collection of their own characteristic pots and others commissioned by them from firms like Minton, Royal Doulton, etc. to mark national events.

There are many commemorative mustard pots in pressed glass, for instance, or in china still to be picked up in the 'Sentimental Souvenir' and 'Royal Occasions' class. In conclusion, salt and mustard spoons must not be overlooked. Until about 1850, the former were made in silver and pewter and measure about 3 to $3\frac{1}{2}''$ in length with bowls which are about $\frac{3}{4}''$ in diameter. By the 1880s, they measured even less as they were produced for use with very small salt cellars indeed. Little salt spoons come in bone, horn, ivory and china, as do mustard ones.

3 The Drawing Room

85   *Queen Victoria's sitting-room at Osborne House, Isle of Wight, 1880*

A visit with her husband to a fashionable warehouse resulted in a carpet that resembled moss bunched all over with full-blown roses, and two hearthrugs to match. A rose-wood suite was also selected, consisting of six elegant chairs, a sofa and a settee, upholstered in green damask. A large looking-glass was chosen to fill the space over the mantelpiece, and a marble-topped chiffionier surmounted by a mirror added to the general effect by reflection.

The room was well proportioned though not large, and Mrs. Danvers did not consider it complete without a circular table of walnut wood and a grand piano. Damask curtains with tasselled testers framed the high windows and a polished steel fender and fire-irons adorned the hearth.

A Book with Seven Seals (c. 1845–50) (Anon)

Not even Mrs. Loudon writing at very much the same time on how to furnish a drawing-room could have faulted Agnes Danvers on her elegant choice of a Wilton carpet, rosewood suite, circular walnut table and soft green damask curtains. She might have even congratulated her warmly when on hearing a voice, the high-pitched voice of a street-seller, outside her home, crying: 'Ornaments for your Fire-stove', Mrs. Danvers hurried out and bought a *Cataract Screen*. This was 'a gorgeous cascade of white horse-hair and gold paper shavings to suspend from a hook concealed in the chimney to hide the ugly aperture when a fire was not leaping in the grate.'

Jane Loudon's description of an Early Victorian drawing-room suitable for the young wife of a rich country squire differs little from Mrs. Danvers's Chelsea one.

'The walls may be filled in with fluted silk with a gilt moulding round them; or the walls may be covered with flock or satin paper with a gilt moulding under the cornice . . . against the walls there should be a few choice cabinet pictures which should be characterised by delicacy and beauty rather than force. A Claude or two, some of Guido's exquisite female heads, and one of Raphael's Madonnas would be very suitable. There should be large mirrors in panels or in richly gilt frames and a very handsome white marble chimney-piece, with a very rich-looking steel grate, made low to show an ornamented back . . . The three windows opening on the terrace are quite sufficient to give light to the room and that at the south end I should like to see opening into a conservatory . . .

'The curtains should be silk or silk damask and made with a piped valance or very deep gold fringe; the inner muslin should be trimmed with silk fringe of the same colour as the outer curtains. Chairs should correspond and have a great deal of gilding about them. . . . There should be several sofas and ottomans and ornamental stools; an excellent piano and a harp; ornamental screens; consoles with richly gilt frames and looking-glass slab brackets for ornamental china; candelabra for lights; an elegant ormolu clock; in short a variety of articles that will suggest themselves. Only take care not to crowd the room lest it have the air of an upholstered warehouse rather than drawing-room.'

By and large, women are natural hoarders, buying things often for pure sentiment and keeping them too for the same reason. It did not take much time, then, before a whole bevy of unrelated objects made their appearance – as Jane Loudon feared they might – in Victorian drawing-rooms. And once there, there they remained till the death of their owners.

Those two little words 'snug' and 'cosy' so frequently used by Queen Victoria are synonymous with the 'cluttered' look which prevailed always in her rooms at Windsor, Balmoral and Osborne, and those of her loyal subjects. No longer were mantel-pieces kept almost bare except for a pair of classic urns in Blue John set one on each side of a magnificent ormolu clock. Though the mantel-piece itself maintained a Regency air, its style coarsened while the marble it was made from was either glaring white Carrara or displayed the mottled, dark-red and green hues of Cornish serpentine. Short stout columns supported a deep shelf which afforded ample space to show off a motley crew of ornaments that ranged from fancy French gilt clocks, bronze statuettes, the Leaning Tower of Pisa in alabaster to lustres dangling their crystal drops, Parian hands, Bohemian glass ware and bouquets of artificial wax, feather or shell flowers incased in monstrous domes of glass.

Everywhere small occasional tables had their place and these tables came to be draped to the ground in a rich velvet or plush cloth, while sofas and sociables, footstools and chairs were so luxuriously padded, buttoned and fringed till they bore little resemblance to their original shapes. Such chairs were anathema to Mrs Haweis (1848–1898) an arbiter of domestic taste who declared them to be 'dropsical velvet and satin monstrosities which the upholsterer turns out by the thousand and are hideous; a good spring-seat covered with a *little* wool or handsome silk or tapestry, uninsulated by buttons requires less material and is far more comfortable'.

The only kind of furniture that was relatively free of embellishment by way of button and fringe, silken tassel and guimpe, was papier mâché which has been considerably written up. But even papier mâché chairs, cabinets and tables (the best coming from the Birmingham firm of Messrs. Jennens and Betteridge) lost their first dramatic impact and colourful appeal when used too lavishly. When a whole drawing-room came to be done in papier mâché the effect was ponderous and vulgar.

Another menace in regard to ladies' uncontrolled taste and poor powers of selection was the fashion to bring home whatever had taken their fancy while travelling abroad. No drawing-room was, perhaps, so representative of this mania than Lady Cheriton's:

'The drawing-room was as frivolously pretty as the library was soberly grand. It was Lady Cheriton's taste which had ruled here, and the room was a kind of record of her ladyship's travels. She had bought pretty things or curious things wherever they took her fancy, and had brought them home to her Cheriton drawing-room. Thus the walls were hung with Algerian embroideries on damask or satin, and decorated with Rhodian pottery. The furniture was a mixture of old French and old Italian. The Dresden services and the ivory statuettes, the *Capo di monte* vases and Copenhagen figures, had been picked up all over the Continent without any regard to their combined effect; but there were so many things that the ultimate result was quite delightful, the room being spacious enough to hold everything without an appearance of over-crowding.

'The piano stood in a central position and was draped with a Japanese robe of State – a mass of rainbow-hued embroidery on a ground of violet satin almost covered with gold thread. It made the piano a spot of parti-coloured light amid the more subdued colouring of the room – the silvery silken curtains, the delicate Indian muslin draperies and the dull tawny plush coverings of sofa and chairs.

'The room was lighted only by clusters of wax candles and a reading-lamp on a small table near one of the windows.'

Miss Braddon, *The Day Will Come*

How far removed from the delicate charm of rosewood furniture, green damask curtains and a carpet showing bunched roses of Mrs. Danvers' Chelsea drawing-room is Lady Cheriton's in Dorset. How different, again, is Charlotte Brontë's famous drawing-room at Thornfield with its white carpet brilliantly garlanded with flowers, its crimson ottomans and couches, its sparkling Bohemian ruby glass and 'general blending of snow and fire' that fascinated her heroine Jane Eyre when she first looked on it.

That striking colour scheme of crimson and gold (like the best Opera Houses) of cut-crystal and ruby glass, lamp-lit, was typical of the upper-class, Victorian drawing-room. But, unfortunately, it was only a nostalgic memory by the 1860s. A memory, however, very dear to Mrs. Talbot Coke who never forgot one drawing-room of her childhood whose:

'Walls were covered with what had once been red brocade faded into a softly fitting background for old paintings and family portraits. The carpet was a dull red Aubusson with a broad creamy border; the curtains of red Utrecht velvet. A tall Vernis Martin screen stood near one polished rosewood door and a stately gilt harp near the other.

'The gilt furniture seen on 'dinner-party' nights to be upholstered with cream brocade with Watteau-like scenes in varied colours was covered with chintz of large red peonies and green leaves at other times. At the end of the room was a high arch through which came the scent and verdant vista of an orangery, the plash of a fountain and the song of birds from an embowered aviary.'

It is in such a drawing-room with its Brontesque 'blending of snow and fire' that the collector of Victoriana would best like to find himself today, and not, with all due respect, in Lady Cheriton's.

THE WHATNOT

There is no word more evocative of the Victorian domestic scene than *Whatnot*. For it conjures up immediately the picture of a drawing-room having at least several of these three-to-four tiered square or rectangular stands made of rosewood or burrwood whose shelves supported by well-turned spiral bobbin or barley-sugar columns were loaded always with an extraordinary assembly of diverse objects. Objects that ranged from the gleaming irridescent beauty of a Nautilus shell, a small glass swan filled with Alum Bay coloured sands or a lump of South Sea coral to a pair of pottery baskets or china shoes, a plate marked simply 'A Present from Brighton' and a small bust in Copeland parian of Her Majesty the Queen.

There are some people who still confuse a *whatnot* with an *étagère*; others who hold that a whatnot *is* an *étagère* which it certainly is not! The best kind of Early Victorian *whatnot* dates from the 1830s and there is one example, three-cornered in design which, if come across, is most useful for placing in the corner of a room or passage. Unfortunately, about 1850, the whatnot came to be vulgarised through the addition of fretwork, while its shelves tended to be mirror-backed or lined with plush. An *étagère* is made in a four-square Louis VI style with a brass gallery and is adorned with ormolu. Its two to three, graduated tiers (oval in shape) are supported by ormolu pillars or ornamental brackets. *Étagères* stand usually on cabriole legs and come in tulipwood, kingwood or inlaid satinwood. Ladies gave quite large sums for them as they were much prized.

Some smaller types of *étagères* were oval in

shape and bow-ended. The favourite motif for their flying brackets support of the tiers was a rococo spray of roses and ribbons.

Yet another kind of *whatnot* in buhl and ormolu were produced in pairs and stand about 18 inches high.

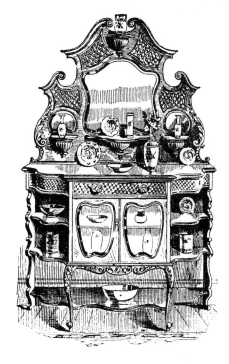

87　*Carved dark mahogany drawing-room cabinet with lower part enclosed for china; upper half has bevelled edge silver plates and brackets for more china, 1880*

SOFAS, SETTEES AND SOCIABLES

The best examples of Early Victorian sofas imitate the Grecian style and with their double-scroll ends and graceful lines have a simple elegance that appeals to modern taste. By the 1850s, though, their lines had thickened; so much so that sofas came to bear little resemblance to their old shape. Finally, the Grecian style for sofas was abandoned and Louis XV rococo took its place.

With every curve exaggerated now and fretwork seen more often as ornamentation than restrained and delicate wood-carving, Victorian sofas even of this period are worth buying. Good workman-ship has gone into their making and their solid frames continue to survive Time's battering. In spite of their profusely buttoned and over-padded look, a mid-Victorian sofa is always worth consideration so long as the chesterfields of our day command such prohibitive prices.

Settees, the twin companions of sofas, perform a useful function. They have a country counter-part (equally in demand) in the 'Windsor settee' which features a 'combined' or 'bow' back. A high-backed 'oak settle', is another familiar piece of furniture usually seen in a country farmhouse or pub. It will always attract buyers.

An average-sized settee can accommodate from

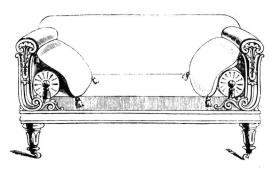

88　*Typical buttoned and padded couch with rounded ends, 1870. (right) Earlier grecian style of sofa with carved ends, detachable cushions and tassled bolsters*

89   *The ever favoured 'Sociable' or 'causeuse' in patterned rich damask, carved top, sides and front, c. 1850*

two to four people and there is one kind of Hepplewhite 'Window settee' with tapered legs and scroll ends that fits most happily into a window embrasure, hence its name. Three to four,

even five-backed settees are also procurable. The 'love-seat' whose charming name implies that it was designed for the use of a couple, only, is usually painted white-and-gold and has cabriole legs. One of this family, popular since the reign of Queen Anne, can fit into a corner and is generally found with button upholstery in a light chintz.

Almost as typical of the Early Victorian drawing-room as the *whatnot*, is the 'Sociable' (or *Causeuse*) which had its heyday in the 1850s. A 'Sociable' was formed of two chairs linked together, side by side, or placed the one opposite the other, so as to allow their occupants every facility to carry on an intimate conversation or flirtation even, uninterrupted. Sociables were usually made of walnut or mahogany with cabriole legs, button upholstery and much fretwork ornamentation.

ORNAMENTAL TABLES

With their inordinate love for displaying family treasures either for snob reasons or to create what we call today 'a talking-point' in dull company, Victorian ladies scattered a number of decorative little tables all round the drawing-room. On these little tables, so easily moved about, they placed their precious bits of china and glass, silver knick-knacks, photograph frames and boxes. But they also liked to have another type of table, peculiar to this time, that was a drawing-room decoration

in itself and remained bare except for a book to be taken up and read, some time.

These little round tables on a slender pedestal can be found either with a beadworked, slate, inlaid marble or mosaic top and are essentially Victorian. So are others in papier mâché, Tunbridge Ware or Victorian pine with ebony inlay. The choice for this type of table is wide and the search fascinating.

The round pedestal table of rosewood or dark mahogany with its coloured marble or slate top derives from an earlier Regency example. This

90   (left) *Finely made Tunbridge-ware occasional table with front panel showing Windsor Castle, c. 1840*

91   (centre) *Scallop-edged papier mâché table with gilt decoration. 1865*

92   (below) *Over-ornate, carved and painted table on tripod base, c. 1850*

was a console or heavy gilt tripod table whose separate scagliola top, imported from Italy, was fashionable. Whereas the multi-coloured often precious types of marbles used on the tops of Regency tables show geometric patterns, those on Victorian tables are more likely to feature naturalistic motifs like a cloud of butterflies or trails of ivy. Cornish serpentine, Derbyshire spar, porphyry and slab agate were often used to decorate these tables in preference to more expensive Italian lapis lazuli and malachite used later.

In papier mâché, a table of the 'Tilt-up' variety, when not in use, could be removed in its 'resting' position to a corner where it still remained decorative! One papier mâché 'Tilt-up' table commissioned by Queen Victoria had its circular top painted with a group of the Royal Children plus their dogs and ponies and a view of Windsor Castle in the distance. Such famous views as Melrose Abbey under the artificial light of a 'mother of pearl' moon were depicted too on fragile little drawing-room papier mâché tables. Incidentally, the name 'papier mâché' which means *mashed paper* is misleading as this ware originated, not in France, but in eighteenth century England; the best factories for its production centred round Birmingham.

During the 1860s and '70s when the Victorian cult for growing ferns was at its height some pretty parquetry fern tables with ormolu mounts and brass galleries were introduced to display them. In this same category, other small flower-and-plant tables can be found.

Few English ladies have given their names to pieces of furniture which became so celebrated as Madame Récamier's sofa. But there is one small Victorian table with wide flap leaves and pull-out leg supports which, successor to the popular Georgian sofa table, was called a 'Sutherland' table after Harriet, Duchess of Sutherland who was its originator. Made of ebonised walnut, rosewood, satinwood or mahogany, afternoon tea was usually served on it.

ORNAMENTAL CHAIRS

Although a drawing-room suite composed of a centre table, a sofa (sometimes a pair) and two arm chairs was often favoured, a number of purely ornamental chairs were also essential. These are still easy to come by as they were produced in quantities; they are easy to identify, too, for each type carries an individual name such as the Bergère chair, the Cameo Back, the prie-Dieu, the Abbotsford or Baronial chair. The ever popular and much reproduced bent-wood rocking chair invented by Herr Thonet of Vienna, which made its debut in England at the Great Exhibition of 1851 with staggering commercial success must not be forgotten either.

The Abbotsford or Baronial style chair derives its name from the romantic influence of Sir Walter Scott's Waverley novels and dates from about 1835. It is a florid version, really, of a seventeenth-century Stuart or Jacobean chair of state. Made of dark oak or walnut, its back is formed of a narrow T-shaped upholstered panel with a carved crest that is flanked on either side by barley-sugar uprights. Materials used for the upholstery were a rich, figured velvet or tapestry.

The Cameo Back chair with its open, oval back, cabriole legs and brocade-covered seat much seen from the 1840s came in rosewood, walnut or mahogany. It was often sold with matching arm chairs that bore lightly carved flower decoration along their back and knees. Few chairs had arms at this time so that they could accommodate a lady and her huge crinoline more easily. After crinolines went out of fashion, arm rests returned and the sloping back of most chairs returned to their normal vertical position.

Between 1850 and 1880, the Bergère chair from Georgian days was revived and became popular as ladies could display their fine needlework on them. Some Bergère chairs have gilding on them or an ebonised and gilt finish; others with cane panels and seats are gilded all over or carved in Louis XV style when they are painted white. Yet another kind are large with square seats and high, crested backs. Boldly scrolled with padded arms, they command a high price.

In contrast to the Bergère chair, ladies assembled fragile sets of papier mâché chairs with cane seats in the drawing-room and bedroom besides some made in satinwood or maple with oval, cane-panelled backs. This latter type once known as 'Rout' or 'Soirée chairs can fulfil a useful (and inexpensive) role as occasional chairs today. But

93–4 *Similar pair of broad, low-seated chairs with single padded top rest and walnut frame. One covered in velvet (buttoned), the other with floral beadwork in delicate colours*

95 *Very decorative low-seated lady's 'sewing' chair covered in richly coloured Berlin worked poppies, c. 1850*

the most comfortable, strong and still graceful chairs capable of bearing masculine weight are those nineteenth-century chairs belonging to the best Louis XV period. Often carved and gilded with upholstered backs and seats and having nice elbow rests, they can be recovered in *petit point* or crewel embroidery by enterprising needlewomen today. The result – a very handsome appearance.

With its low seat and long straight back terminating in a short, horizontal bar on which a lady could rest her arms while praying in a kneeling position on it, a prie-Dieu chair was considered

more suitable for the bedroom than drawing-room where it now stands as a prize specimen of Victoriana. But the general design of the prie-Dieu chair can be found, incorporated in a sister-type of parlour or boudoir chair covered with Berlin woolwork. And finally, the Bentwood rocking chair, that favourite of today, which is being reproduced everywhere in beechwood by up-to-date furniture shops and workrooms. Collectors must beware when seeking original examples.

The idea of an elegant parlour, bedroom or drawing-room chair in bent-wood to be evolved on

96 (left) *Small ebony-black Bentwood chair with embroidered seat*
97 (centre) *Cane-seated, balloon-back, occasional chair with a scatter of mother of pearl decoration on back*
98 (right) *Prie-dieu type of mid-Victorian chair with long sloping back, richly upholstered*

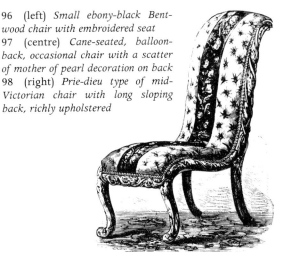

the lines of long-established wooden 'rockers' known to cottage folk of many countries was first developed by Michael Thonet (1796–1871) in Vienna where it became the rage. Seen in England at the Great Exhibition of 1851, it repeated its continental success.

The wood used for a rocking chair of Thonet's design was birch, as this was found to be more pliable for the various 'steaming' and 'bending' processes it had to undergo to achieve the graceful curves and lines of the final product. The whole chair was then stained a fashionable glossy black.

At one time, a bent-wood rocking chair and those made later in wicker and bamboo were subjected to ornate treatment during the 1870s and '80s. This was a period when ladies could not resist decorating them with a plush cover or a piece of 'crazy work' besides tying them up with perky bows of ribbon. In America, rocking-chairs in particular those known as the 'Shaker' produced by the Shaker brethren of Lebanon were made of hardwood, stained and varnished a rich mahogany brown, have always been popular.

On her first visit to America in 1885, Mrs. Haweis was so much attracted at the sight of countrywomen sitting all day long on their 'rockers' in their porches, knitting, that she brought one home and installed it in her well-known home, Queen's House, Cheyne Walk, where it was much talked about.

FOOTSTOOLS

When ladies, fragile and feminine, took more and more to remaining in their drawing-rooms, reclining either on a sofa or easy chair patiently awaiting the arrival of the next 'little one', a footstool to support their tiny, slippered feet came into prominence. Victorian footstools are still to be found in large numbers in most reputable antique shops besides turning up often at country sales and elsewhere. For the moment, moderately priced, they are highly collectable on account of their general prettiness, especially when decorated in beadwork or in *gros point* and *petit point* with multi-coloured wools. Flowers, birds, and fruit designs may all be found decorating the top of a pretty little Victorian footstool.

At least one pair, if not more, was considered essential in a drawing-room or boudoir. Often one stood in front of each armchair. The first Victorian footstools were oval or rectangular in shape with low, cabriole legs. They are mostly made in walnut and often match the oval-backed chairs they were bought with. Then they are usually covered in velvet and nicely padded: others that followed were smaller, lower and rounder with little china, or wooden, knobs for feet. Their frames might be ebonised or gilded and the wood they were made of, walnut, rosewood and mahogany. An oblong or square type of footstool that stands on 'turned' wood or 'fluted gold' legs often served a dual purpose. For their hinged tops could be lifted open to disclose a workbox or a metal container to hold hot water when they performed the duty of foot-warmers!

There are special gout-stools, too, oblong in shape with short legs or comforting 'rockers'. On them a gentleman could lay his swollen and painful foot and rock it gently. In this category comes a very large gout-stool which opens rather like the lid of a grand piano and which can be adjusted on wooden rachets to the angle or height required. Long and narrow fender-stools, about 4 ft. in length, should not be overlooked. For they are usually covered in the most charming embroidery that follows a traditional pattern, i.e. lilies on a black, turquoise or scarlet ground. Miss Broughton knew all about such fender-stools, describing on that turned up at a village fete:

'Oh! Sir Thomas, please let me put you down in the raffle for a fender-stool; so handsome! White arums of a red ground; do let me, so handsome!'

Rhoda Broughton, *Red as a Rose is She*

DRAWING-ROOM BUSTS AND FIGURINES

Attention must be drawn here to the numerous charming and small statues, busts and figurines of young girls or children that were considered suitable ornaments for the drawing-room and boudoir. Singly or in pairs and groups, they were modelled in marble, alabaster, Parian ware, terra-cotta or even in plaster. For collectors attracted to small pieces of minor statuary that was so adored and collected *en masse* by Victorians, these figures and busts can still be found for fairly modest sums.

To begin with marble. This medium is, of course,

99 *Charmingly sentimental and suitable marble 'Child with Dog' for a lady's drawing-room, c. 1850*
100 *Parian ware: The Veiled Bride; jug decorated with classic figures in relief; Peasant girl with pitcher*

the most costly, particularly for good copies of figures done by notable period sculptors like John Gibson famed for his *Tinted Venus* or Hiram Powers, an American, whose original statue *The Greek Slave* caused an international sensation at the Great Exhibition and when copied by Copeland 'sold by the thousand'.

Victorians, especially the female sex, were deeply enamoured with the pure snow-whiteness of marble and alabaster which they likened to that floral darling of theirs, the madonna lily. Fortunately, with the arrival of steam-driven machinery, marble came to be more easily worked and thus made cheaper. A single marble bust, or figure, lent considerable cachet to a middle-class home if certain rules as to where it stood were observed. For instance, in *The Gentleman's Home* (1864) Robert Kerr advised the ignorant householder how to avoid a social solecism by not placing the wrong type of alabaster group or Parian-ware figure in the drawing-room, when it should grace the hall or library. Today we can place our finds anywhere.

The gradual evolution of Parian statuary which is only of recent popularity extended over several years. It began, actually, in 1837, the year Queen Victoria was crowned; a queen who was to be a great buyer of Parian ware in all its manifestations. In 1837, Herbert Minton issued a near-Parian bust of William Wilberforce, the celebrated slave-trade reformer. Five years later, on 3 August 1842, under the direction of W. T. Copeland the first example of his firm's pure Parian statuary was released to china sellers. This example was a copy of *Apollo as the Shepherd Boy of Admetus*, after the original sculpture by R. J. Wyatt, R.A. owned by the Duke of Sutherland. Minton instantly retaliated by producing several more models and achieved several successes recorded in 1844. Owing to its marked resemblance to the ivory-tinted marble quarried in the Greek island of Paros, Minton's gave the name 'Parian' to their statuary.

In 1851, at the Great Exhibition, Minton displayed 46 different subjects catalogued as 'Parian Figures'. Among them was *Una and the Lion* and *Dorothea* (a character from Don Quixote) both after John Bell, R.A. The vogue for Parian statuary had begun and quickly gathered momentum in the years to come.

In his interesting article on 'Parian Statuary for Victorian Homes' (*Country Life*; 2 January 1964)

Mr. Bernard Hughes tells us from a catalogue published in 1854 by Minton that the trade price for their figure of 'Dorothea' was only £1.17.4. One of the most appealing 'little-girl', drawing-room figures at this time was Copeland's *Go to Sleep* (1862) after John Durham's original.

Parian ware busts of Queen Victoria are many showing her at different stages in her long reign, from the happy young matron of Balmoral to the mourning Widow of Osborne. Other popular reproductions were those of *Venus* (Copeland issued at least seven different examples of this goddess) after the sculptors Canova, Thorwaldsen, John Gibson, R.A. and others.

Josiah Wedgwood and Sons also joined the ranks of Parian producers, evolving their own whiter but less transparent brand of Parian which they named Carrara Porcelain on account of its resemblance – not to the marble from Paros – but to one quarried in Tuscan mines. Wedgwood's Carrara porcelain statues include *Triton, Cupid* and *Psyche* and later, about 1851, The *Infant Hercules, Morpheus* and *Venus and Mercury*.

By the 1860s, at least 50 Staffordshire pottery firms had become Parian-minded and were busy on its manufacture. Their figures took over in popularity from the one time traditional and colourful 'image toys' which had been sold by itinerant pedlars and the Image Man (Chapter XI; Cottage China). So, for the first time, miniature copies of fine, contemporary sculpture came within reach of the lower classes. The artistic education of the masses had begun.

Besides Minton, Copeland and other firms of their standing which remained supreme in producing top-grade Parian ware, there were two Midland potters who impressed their names, or initials, on their own Parian goods. One was Charles Meigh and Sons of Hanley: the other Robinson & Leadbetter at Stoke-on-Trent.

TERRA-COTTA VASES AND FIGURES

Next in popularity to Parian statuary were small figurines made of terra-cotta and delightful they are in their warm, red tones. But they were considered more suitable to decorate the hall, library and conservatory than the drawing-room.

The name 'terra-cotta' is apt to be a misleading one as examples in this medium can be found not always in the attractive red colour familiar to most of us but others silvery-grey in hues or the flushed pink tone of a dawn or sunset sky. Terra-cotta means, literally, *baked clay* and was, originally, no more than purified clay, hand-shaped and hardened merely by baking in the sun of Mediterranean countries. Two thousand years ago, clay was first fired in primitive kilns, the end-product resulting in such lovely objects as the terra-cotta Greek and Etruscan vases which can be studied in the British Museum.

The manufacture of English terra-cotta in Victorian times was a highly skilled branch of the potter's craft. A sharpness of detail distinguished it, then, from earlier and softer qualities while colours ranged from the brilliance of a lobster's boiled shell to the smooth, more matt appearance of brick-dust. All these colours, of course, were obtained only after firing.

It was not long before terra-cotta became a fashionable medium for the production of handsome hall and library vases and tazzas; to full-scale figures for passage-ways and the conservatory; besides delicate small figurines and little busts for the drawing-room. In the dining-room, terra-cotta was seen by way of an immense, dome-lidded cheese dish or a ewer. As for the conservatory, it became full of decorative hanging baskets and pots of every shape and size in terra-cotta.

Although that great potter, Josiah Wedgwood had discovered how to produce a type of terra-cotta, harder in substance than any before in the 1760s and one to which he applied, most successfully, a shiny black pigment to decorate it, no other potter appears to have been interested in this clay till a Sir Frederick Fowke, Bart., founded a small terra-cotta works on his estate at Lowesby in Leicestershire. Using deposits of a local red-burning clay, he produced antique-styled vases and bowls decorated with black designs after the Etruscan fashion. Other plain vases, he had sent to London to be enriched with coloured enamels and burnished gilding by his agent, a Mr. William Purden whose show rooms were in King William Street. However, Sir Frederick's venture was doomed to failure, and no terra-cotta was made at Lowesby after 1840. Now and then, though, some charming and rare 'pieces' of his turn up such as one vase I have seen, globular at its base and tapering into a slender neck, besides a cup and saucer. Both vase and cup and saucer were covered with delightful shiny pink flowers and pale-blue butterflies and marked by a fleur-de-lys (this flower being incorporated in the Fowke family coat-of-arms) besides the name LOWESBY, impressed.

A highly vitreous terra-cotta which was ideally suited for classical scenes in brilliant polychrome enamels was put out by F. and R. Pratt of Fenton from the 1840s. This firm is known to have made in 1848 the largest pair of drawing-room vases ever seen. They were bought by Prince Albert. Clock-cases painted all over in mosaic patterns in vivid colours, to stand on a drawing-room mantel-shelf, was another of their specialities.

Less well known than F. and R. Pratt but of interest to collectors is the Torquay Terra Cotta Company, established in 1875 at Hall Cross, near the east corner of Torquay cemetery, Devon. About two miles away at Watcombe, another terra-cotta Clay Company, established earlier in 1869, had Charles Brock of Hanley as technical director.

Watcombe's delightful range of little figures included some larger for the garden, while Torquay kept mainly to small statuary, plaques and domestic objects. For instance, reproductions of John

Gibson, C. B. Birch and other sculptors' work was done in terra-cotta at Torquay besides casts from original models of birds and other figures done on the spot. Torquay terra-cotta wares differ from Watcombe's by being more decorated, with emphasis laid on circuit lines and details in gold. Less use was made of turquoise-blue enamel which is characteristic of the older pottery's wares. Fine and smooth as is the Torquay body, it is very brittle; far more so than that of Watcombe which may be why so little of it has survived in good condition today.

For collectors, Torquay marks from 1875 to 1890 consist of the words Torquay Terra Cotta Co. either in an oval girdle surrounding the word LIMITED or together with LIMITED surrounded by a mere oval line. Two other marks used at any time in the life of the pottery (from 1875 to 1909) consist either of the word Torquay alone impressed or the monogram TTC designed vertically and impressed or printed in black.

Watcombe products are all marked WATCOMBE POTTERY or WATCOMBE impressed or printed in black. From 1876, the printed mark was a woodpecker perched on a branch against a distant landscape and a ship at sea, encircled by a garter inscribed WATCOMBE POTTERY.

---

101 (left) *Lady's black papier mâché hand-screen painted in full colours and gilded scroll patterns, c. 1830*

102 (right) *Stand-up screen with cheval frame of carved maple-wood, enclosing a panel of coloured wool embroidery, 1890*

SCREENS

At a time when 'screen-dividers' are being used in rooms and 'screening' is an operative word in the language of modern decor, it is not surprising that Victorian screens, hand-painted or embroidered, in scrap-work or papier mâché, japanned or decorated with pressed flowers and even fans, have staged a fashionable come-back and are much in demand.

Though screens trace their early beginning in Oriental countries, a rude kind of screen made from animal skins hung over a wooden frame or one, rush-woven, once stood in the great halls of medieval England as a kind of primitive draught-protector. Since that time the screen has undergone many forms. Possibly its most artistic and charming expression is found in the shield-shaped, walnut and satinwood pole screens designed by Chippendale and Sheraton for Georgian homes in the eighteenth century. For under their glass-fronted shields, exquisite floral embroidery in pale silks on a satin ground or in ribbon work is preserved. But by 1840, Georgian pole screens had given way to others of a sturdier build. This is when a cheval frame of maple wood or mahogany, handsomely carved, enclosed a panel of gaudy Berlin work featuring parrots, macaws and flamboyant flowers like the dahlia or cabbage rose.

Later, during the 1860s and '70s, the folding screen came into its own when there were many kinds to choose from including those with three to four folding panels. Like footstools, the Victorian drawing-room had many screens; from painted gilded leather ones to papier mâché. Some in rococo frames had a panel of glass in their upper half; in their lower, a piece of rich brocade.

103   A fine two-wing Victorian 'scrap' screen composed of six brilliantly coloured prints with floral motifs placed in between

104   Characteristic three-wing screen with embroidered Pre-Raphaelite figures designed by William Morris, 1860

Though a scrapwork screen was a hot favourite for children in the nursery (Chapter VI: The Nursery) many lovely and individual scrap screens were produced for the drawing-room by ladies. For instance, at the Carlyle Museum in Cheyne Row, Chelsea, Jane Welsh Carlyle's scrap screen can be seen. It was much admired by Mr. Thackeray and others of her circle and is composed of four large panels on which cut-out pictures from contemporary illustrated papers are stuck. There are views of Stonehenge and the Coliseum at Rome side by side with Landseer's famous Stag at Bay and Lord Byron's handsome head!

Another literary lady who tried her hand at making a scrap screen was Mrs. Oliphant (1828–1897) a prolific novelist. Hers, though, must have been a delightful creation as she used only tiny and delicate sepia and grey, French prints. Endowed with fine taste, her drawing-room was the last word in elegance as she debarred the furniture of her day and used only genuine Queen Anne pieces.

During the craze for Japonnerie and the Oriental way of furnishing, folding-screens with paintings on thin silk were fashionable. They could be made in many different materials such as silk, satin or velvet; the new 'Morris' art fabric; besides such common stuffs as crash or Bolton sheeting. Screens of all these different types have a period value today.

One use for a screen in the Victorian home was to

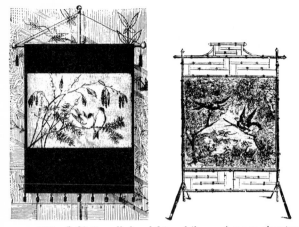

105 (left) *Tasselled and fringed 'banner' screen showing Japanese influence in needlework design, 1881;* (right) *bamboo screen with ferns and birds decoration, c. 1870*

106 *Three-panelled folding screen in gilt frame with over-all feather patterns, c. 1870*

107 *Tea screen designed by Miss Doris Wheeler depicting Morning and Evening, 1881*

mask the entrance downstairs to the kitchen in the basement which was genteely known as 'the descent to Avernus'. Another use, equally snobbish, was to place it in front of the door which led out of the dining-room so as to hide the coming and going of the butler and his minions with their plates and dishes.

A lady's journal of the day went so far as to give this expert advice:

'With a certain exercise of tact, a screen can easily transform a long uninteresting parlour into a series of small boudoirs, full of charm. Scatter in them easy chairs, foot-stools, lounges strewn with cushions, work-stands and jardinieres and you will have a sort of *Bazaar* society where delicious mysteries may be confidentially discussed.'

So much, then, for the folding screen in its many guises. There were others of even a more individual character such as the floral screen which showed, under a glass panel, delicate designs of pressed flowers when a lady was botanically-minded! There was the Tile Screen featuring hand-painted tiles set in a mahogany or ebonised frame. There were small, triple-fold screens framed, again, in ebonised wood with a design of real peacock feathers appliquéd on to a background of old-gold silk. There were screens with panels of gilded canvas, framed in variegated bamboo, on which were painted in oils bunches of chrysanthemums besides a great number of small banner screens. Finally, of course, there was Mrs. Danvers' *Cataract Screen* made of long, frayed strips of tarlatan which could cascade down, like a miniature Niagara Falls, when pinned on to the mantelpiece to hide the grate below during the summer when it was such an eyesore.

Towards the 1880s, the tea screen, with a small protruding shelf on which cups and saucers could be placed as ladies partook of afternoon tea in the drawing-room, became very fashionable. A striking tea screen was shown at one exhibition of the Royal School of Art Needlework, South Kensington, during the '80s with embroidered panels after the design of Walter Crane. These panels illustrated the four senses, Seeing, Hearing, Smelling and Tasting, represented by four females worked on grey linen in greenish-brown silks. One clasped a basket of daffodils; another held a shell up to her ear; a third smelt a rose; and the fourth drank from a shell.

In her *Beautiful Houses* (1882) Mrs Haweis has

described a magnificent set of drawing-rooms, leading out from one another, in Mr. Reuben Sassoon's Belgrave Square home whose *leit motif* was adornment by screens. Screens:

'Covered, painted, and embroidered in gold with tropical birds or white storks and peacocks pluming themselves on every side. One screen, the quietest one in colour, was of a faint sea-water tint with birds and clouds and scrolls embroidered on it by the exhaustless Japanese fancy. Every stool, ottoman, and table glimmers with raised gold work on the new 'high art' plushes and velvets; but the finest specimens form the portieres which are large, heavy and gorgeous, doubled at every door and magnificent in colour. . . . Over the doors rise panels containing pictures of the Watteau School.'

So much for Mr. Sassoon's screens. Screens that would be far beyond the reach of the average collector's purse today and which will never be seen again in a Belgravian drawing-room unless it is one belonging to the Embassy of some oriental country.

DRAWING-ROOM TEA SETS

Afternoon tea once recognised as a popular form of polite entertaining very much enjoyed by Victorian ladies, has almost disappeared: killed by the rush of modern life. The words, indeed, 'Afternoon Tea', survive only in France, in that well-known and happy catch-phrase '*Le Five o'clock*!'

As for those gorgeous Minton and Spode china tea sets composed of dozens of matching cups and plates arranged on a handsome silver tray together with a large, imposing silver tea-pot, milk jug and sugar and slop bowl, besides a hissing tea kettle, where have they vanished to? The answer, of course, is to the sale-room like dinner services. For they are far too valuable now for everyday use.

During the 1840s, the fashion was to use Sèvres china only in the drawing room as well as in the dining room. Sèvres (genuine and imitation) was followed by much gilded and ornate Worcester, Coalport, Spode and Minton tea sets. Then, for a while, a slightly bizarre Worcester tea set known as 'Harlequin' was seen which aimed to stimulate conversation as each cup and saucer, different in colour and pattern, was examined. The Queen was said to own such a tea-set.

In the middle and lower income groups of Victorian England, only one china ware was in common use and that was blue Willow pattern earthenware. And so it might have continued, for people were conservative in their taste, if Prince Albert had not persuaded makers of ceramic ware to try their hand at bringing out some new colours and patterns for household china in the lower-priced markets. Rather reluctantly, they agreed. Success was immediate and Willow ware for such a long time a universal favourite gave way to a rapid and most profitable invasion of naturalistic designs on china such as insects and birds, butterflies and flowers, delicately drawn grasses and ferns. The moss-rose, the pansy, the violet and lily-of-the-valley were all seen on ladies' drawing-room and boudoir tea-sets. Queen Victoria dearly loved a moss-rose tea set she used. Indeed, such was the popularity of flower-decorated china that many ladies were inspired to take up 'flower-painting' on china with admirable results.

An interesting note on social behaviour at this time concerns the use of plates and doyleys banned from afternoon tea in the drawing-room. If they appeared it was considered extremely bad style. The only food offered was some very thin slices of cake and bread-and-butter. Pastry and jams only appeared at large teas when formal invitations were sent out. These at least are the injunctions given in a manual on *Manners and Tone of Good Society* published at this time. It was also considered bad taste to press visitors to a second cup or even to ask them 'If it was to their taste?' Such a question was reserved only for the housekeeper's room where tea was treated as a meal.

If a lady did live out in the suburbs, in a cottage near the Walworth Road, Dulwich, like pretty, refined Mrs. Sandford in 1850, the conventions for drawing-room tea were strictly observed.

'Sandwiches were triangular and cut very thin with minute sprigs of parsley on lace-bordered paper, the lemon sponge, in a cut-glass dish, the tablecloth finest damask bequeathed by a rich maiden aunt. Mrs. Sandford had this same aunt's Swansea china and diamond-cut glass and a little old silver.'

Miss Braddon, *A Lost Eden*

108–10 Three coal boxes: a black japanned coal box with brass handle, hinges and painted sprig of narcissi, 1870;
(centre) *Fine brass 'helmet' coal bucket, 1880;* (right) *Elegant copper 'scoop' coal scuttle, 1850s*

THE VANISHED COAL SCUTTLE

The age for the coal scuttle when one if not two scuttles at least were kept in every room of the house filled with shining lumps of the best sea-coal from Durham was between the years 1830 to 1860. At this time much care was given to their design and production by craftsmen. The first coal boxes fitted with lids were vase-like objects standing on a small base. They were known by the pompous name of Purdonium. Birmingham, Bilston and Wolverhampton – all centres for the japanned-iron trade – produced coal scuttles of japanned tinned steel with gilt decorations or a painted glass panel set in the lid. They were successfully exported abroad; a brisk trade in coal scuttles being set up between England and North and South America. In the 1850s some very handsome, glossy-black,

japanned coal boxes were designed on whose lids flowers were painted. Their hinges, handle and paw-feet were made of brass. An interesting reference to the wide range of coal scuttles available to the Victorian housewife comes in *The Pillars of the House* by Charlotte Yonge (1873). Standing in the department of a large store whose counters displayed dozens of coal scuttles, one of which alone must be chosen, Geraldine Underwood turned to her sister beside her and said:

'Is it not a curious study to see invention expended on making an intrinsically hideous thing beautiful by force of japanning, gilding and painting? You see the original design provided for a scuttle is the *nautilus* shell and unluckily that is grotesquely inappropriate! Just look at this row of ungainly things craning out their chins like overdressed dwarfs. I am decidedly for the simplest and least disguised though Robina is for the snail and Angel, I believe, for that highly suitable Watteau scene.'

By far more useful when brass-ware was cheap (which it is not today) were coal-scuttles in brass and copper though these were seen more in bedrooms and nurseries than in the drawing-room. Two traditional shapes were the Helmet and the Scoop. The Scoop became the favourite scuttle for the drawing-room as it was comparatively light in weight and easy to handle. Other shapes modelled on these two designs followed with slight variants. No better coal scuttles have been produced since nor will be again, now that central-heating by

111 A London fireman's painted red leather water bucket turned coal scuttle painted with the royal arms, c. 1890

electricity, gas or oil has taken the place of the old-fashioned coal fire.

There is one place, though, where the coal scuttle survives still and this is on the colourful, painted barges and 'long boats' of the canal folk. (Chapter X: Cottage). In metal, crudely painted with flowers and other symbolical signs, they are still being produced in midland river villages like Braunston on the Grand Union Canal near Rugby, to match the rest of the domestic ware used by the canal people, many fine examples of which are on view at the Waterways Museum, Stoke Bruerne. (Chapter XIII: Souvenirs of Travel).

Though coal scuttles have all but vanished from our modern homes, they still remain interesting and attractive objects worth the collector's attention and their value will continue to rise.

Recently, too, some collectors have begun to take an interest in Opercula. This word derives from the Latin, *operculum*, which signifies a lid or covering, and is the collective name for all coal manhole covers in London and other big cities.

It was in 1929 that a Doctor Shepherd Taylor first drew attention to the many intricate and often good designs he had found on coal manhole covers during the 1860s when a medical student living in London. He published his findings in a booklet called *Opercula* which has six illustrations to every page.

THE SHADE

There were few Victorian drawing-rooms or for that matter the parlour in a tradesman's or farmer's home that did not boast having a bouquet of fragile shell, wax or feather flowers preserved for posterity under an imposing glass dome. These objects were given their trade name of 'Shade' (i.e. 'Shade of Artificial Flowers' or 'Shade of Fruit', etc.).

A pair of shades might stand one on each side of a marble mantelpiece; on the top of a whatnot; or be sandwiched between the family album and other keepsakes on a circular rosewood table in the middle of the room. Today, there are few more Victorian objects to collect than 'a shade'.

In his *Tales of Mean Streets* (1894) which became a bestseller, Arthur Morrison included one called *Behind the Shade*. In this story, he describes a house set in a London slum whose genteel occupant – a lady – gave piano lessons.

'In the lower window in front stood a 'shade of fruit' – a cone of waxen grapes, apples, and hothouse peaches under a glass dome. Although the house was smaller than the others, it was always a house of some consideration. In a street like this mere independence of pattern gives distinction; and here the seal of respectability was

112–15 Group of Victorian shades: a trophy of wax fruits in wire stand; exotic stuffed birds in dried ferns grasses; basket of artificial gauze roses and ferns; bouquet of Berlin wool flowers in lemon-and-white striped vase.

116 (left) *Exquisitely frail bouquet of shell flowers in basket, c. 1850*

117 (right) *The milk-maid executed in paper cement, 1860s*
118 (far right) *Pair of hand-coloured wax figures: peasant girl with basket and Little Boy Blue, 1860–70*

set by the *shade of fruit* – a sign accepted in these parts.'

The fascination of collecting Victorian shades lies in their amazing variety. But they are becoming increasingly difficult to find in good condition and must be handled carefully. For if their domes which are made of a very thin and brittle type of glass . sustain damage in any way, they are practically impossible to replace.

One of the best collections of 'shades' I ever saw belonged to the late Thomas Lowinsky, a painter with a taste for Victoriana. During the late 1920s he picked up cheaply many glorious examples. I remember one, a Hair Tree, which I found later listed in a nineteenth-century ladies' magazine with instructions on how to make it. Fine strands of hair were collected by the executant from the heads of different members of the family concerned; they differed from Grandpapa's silvery

locks to the newest baby's golden fluff. From these strands a tree was made to stand about 8 to 9 inches high, complete with silvery-brown, chestnut red, tawny, raven-black or blonde foliage. At the tip of each branch, a tiny label was attached on which was printed the name and age of each donor of hair. Here, indeed, was a true Family Tree preserved for descendants to peer at sentimentally and try to decipher the fading names and dates.

Small wax figures such as an enchanting little girl with her dog, or a group of ladies having tea outside their Gothic villa can be come across under a shade. So, too, can some religious figures featuring the Holy Virgin and Child. These little figures were supposed to have been made commercially for Roman Catholic households where they adorned the shrine in a private chapel or were put in a wall-niche below which stood a lady's prie-Dieu in her bedroom.

ELEGANT HANDS

As a symbol of romantic sentiment an elegant china hand with wrist cuffed in a frill and long slim fingers either holding up a harebell, cornucopia or corncob or laid, delicately, outstretched on a narrow plinth as an ornament or paper-weight was as typical an object in a Victorian drawing-room as the 'shade' which so often stood beside it. In marble, in alabaster, in china and glass, in Parian ware or brass, hands are met with over and over

again. To make a collection of them would be most rewarding. For they possess not only great charm but feature an interesting variety of media and design.

It has been recorded that Queen Victoria might well have started the fashion for them. For she surrounded herself with reproductions of her beloved children's baby hands done in marble and alabaster. Her own pretty hand placed on a regal cushion, richly tasselled, came to be reproduced by leading china firms all over England and sold,

119–21   Elegant hands: china ring stand featuring a spread-out hand with painted Lilies-of-the-Valley at base and a hand clasping a bluebell; (centre) Parian-ware hand holding cornucopia-vase for flowers, turquoise and gilt bracelet round wrist; (right) Chubby hand with shell in blue-and-white and gilt decoration

by the hundred, to her devoted subjects in every walk of life.

A brass 'hand' was often used as a 'tie-back' for drawing-room curtains as well as for a door-knocker. But in Victorian times, a brass 'hand' let alone a china one was beyond the means of humble people and so cast-iron ones were made instead. These were much seen in Scotland, being produced by the Carron Ironworks in Stirlingshire.

Another popular medium for 'hands' was wood,

which was treated with an 'ebony' finish when it looked like jet. Both coral and jet 'hands' in the form of delectable little brooches can be found as at one time they were given as presents. In this context, the 'hand' is usually extended in a symbolical gesture of 'love' or 'friendship' and often holds a tiny envelope or a flower like the moss-rose. If two 'hands' are incorporated in the design they are nearly always lovingly clasped.

122   (left) *Ornamental urn-vase in dark purple glass with raised gilt decoration in greek style*

123   (right) *Minton vase (marked) in fine porcelain with applied decoration of white ferns and butterflies on celadon green ground, 1862*

FASHIONS IN FLOWER VASES

A striking feature of the Victorian drawing-room was the number of small flower vases to be seen. They stood everywhere; on little papier mâché tables, on the *étagère* and whatnot as well as on the top of a Davenport or the draped lid of a grand piano. With the conservatory usually leading out of the drawing-room, flowers were close to hand and in good supply. But until about 1840, it was the gardener (not his mistress) who selected the flowers of his choice for his lady to arrange in 'dumpy, tight-packed bouquets of mixed blooms and no foliage' for the drawing-room. If she disdained the job, he did them himself, crowding them even more closely together in a cut-glass bowl with a hideous stiff edging all round of yew or asparagus fronds.

However after Mrs. Jane Loudon had exhorted ladies to do their own flowers, carefully, and after the publication, too, of Miss Maling's book in

1862 (Chapter II: The Dining-Room) a school of lady flower arrangers began to emerge led by Mrs Haweis whose floral views were expressed in *Rus in Urbe* (1885). Others were Mrs. Orrinsmith, Mrs. Talbot Coke, Miss Rose Kingsley and, finally, the great Miss Gertrude Jekyll.

At first, Victorian ladies arranged their flowers in vases put out by leading china firms like Minton, Wedgwood, Copeland and Spode. These vases were richly ornamented and modelled on classic lines reproducing flagon, urn or slender ewer shapes. They were so over-decorated by hand-painted flowers, enamelling, or by high-relief figures that they killed, stone-dead, the delicate charm and colouring of the flowers arranged in them.

On the other hand, there was a small but far more suitable range of little flower-vases produced to hold posies of mixed flowers like primroses, violets, pansies and their like. These little vases which became very dear to the female heart were made in every kind of fancy shape such as rustic baskets or shoes, top-hats or even a coal-scuttle or watering-can. But never in the old, traditional shape of a classic urn or tazza.

To begin with shoes. Shoes in china, glass and slagware are very much collectors items. Much of their appeal derives from the age-old superstition that shoes are good-luck emblems and will continue to be so. Some of the prettiest china shoes are painted all over with clusters of tiny multi-coloured flowers. They are high-heeled with long tongues and have a rosette or buckle, imitating the style of a Chelsea china shepherdess's foot-wear. Others might have belonged to Cinderella for they are blown in clear, transparent glass; others, again, in glass of every hue, amber, blue, turquoise, rose-pink and *vaseline*, opaque or clear. Boots appear as well, either of marble glass or slagware in mottled purple, apple-green or tortoiseshell shades, and in china too. With their high, arched instep and row of buttons from top to bottom, they are essentially of the period but belonged more to cottage parlours than refined drawing-rooms.

Besides slippers for every taste, small models of hats in china and glass were utilised as flower-containers. Again, the choice was wide, from low-crowned derbies to bowlers, top-hats or a jockey's cap. (Chapter XII: Cottage Glass).

China and glass baskets had an enormous vogue

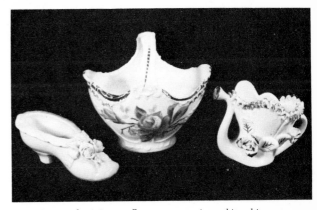

124 *Group of miniature flower vases: tiny white china shoe with floral buckle; (centre) Hand-painted floral spray on white china basket, 1899; (right) Pink and white china watering can with applied floral decoration*

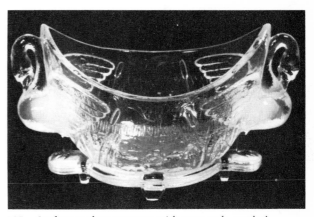

125 *Opalescent glass ornament with swan-ends, marked Sowerby Newcastle, 1870–80*

126 *Vaseline glass basket with raised scallop-shell decoration, 1860*

127–8 Two hand-painted 'milk' glass vases,
one showing a moss-rose; the other cluster of
purple pansies, c. 1860

129 Three flower vases in opague glass, popular shapes and
hand-painted with different flowers, c. 1860

for holding flowers and were thought pretty
knicknacks for the drawing-room. They even
appeared in the school-room:

'It looked more like a drawing-room. There
were so many pretty things about. A couch and
delightful easy chairs and flowers on the table;
a great bowl and a *white china basket* full of
daffodils.'

Rosa Nouchette Carey, *Only the Governess*

China baskets can be large or small, with plaited,
twisted or quite plain arched handles. Some are
painted with flowers or carry applied flowers.
Others are inscribed with a name, date or initial
and can record by transfer-printing some event
of national interest like the sinking of a well-known
ship or the opening of a bridge. The most collectable baskets to my mind are those produced by
Sowerby & Co., Newcastle (later Sowerby's
Ellison Glass Works) who used the peacock's-head
crest to mark products, 1870–1880.

They made these baskets in *Vitro-porcelain*, a
thick, white or sometimes black, opaque glass
locally called 'poor man's marble'.

To paint flowers on their china and glass vases
was a happy ploy for ladies with artistic talent
from the 1860s. Hence the large amount of them to
be found. For some ladies took this craft up professionally to augment a small income or to make
extra pin money. (Chapter IX: Parlour Pastimes).

Plain white china or coloured glass vases in
every known shape and size could be bought,

cheaply, from a china store by would-be paintresses
to do their best on or worst. These vases can be
roughly dated through the kinds of flowers
painted on them. For the earliest examples show
moss-roses and auriculas followed by pansies and
lilies-of-the-valley. Then came large cabbage roses,
dahlias and peonies such as were being worked on
canvas by ladies for cushions etc.

Much later in the 1870s and '80s, at the height
of the Japanese cult, floral decoration changed on
vases. Straggly branches of peach-blossom or
hawthorn, sunflowers, ferns and waving rushes
took the place of those old-fashioned flowers once
raised in cottage gardens. At one time during the
1930s, the shelves of small junk shops besides the

130 Bohemian amber glass vase,
one of a mantelpiece pair

131 *Amphora-shaped opaque white glass vase, painted. Stourbridge, c. 1855*

132 *Large white china jug with painted pansy motif*

133 *Mary Gregory type of cranberry-pink glass jug with painted white, raised figures*

stalls of the old Caledonian Market were loaded with every kind of flower-painted china vase or those in variegated glass. For a few shillings one could pick up delectable specimens of what is, today, known as Victorian Art Glass which has been so carefully catalogued by *the* expert on this subject Miss Ruth Webb Lee in her two valuable books *Victorian Glass* and *Nineteenth-Century Art Glass*. Collectors can explore the entrancing field of Victorian glass, striped, spangled or spattered, Satin or Peachblow, Opaline or Queen's Burmese with Miss Webb Lee as their best guide.

However towards 1880, ladies began to have second thoughts on using the highly-coloured and over-decorated drawing-room vases and tazzas adored by their mothers. The final blow came when Miss Rose Kingsley, (daughter of Charles Kingsley) who was known to be an excellent gardener and flower-arranger lashed out against:

'The variety-show posies in glass vases of evil crinkled shapes and yet more evil colours – crude blues, greens, yellows and pinks and ornamented

(save the mark!) by lumps of contrasting pinks applied to the surface like half-melted poisonous lollipops.'

She advised, instead, the use of Mr. Powell's glass from the Whitefriars Works.

'How perfect it is for our purpose; clear white, opal, straw-opal and bottle-green. The soft tints harmonise delightfully with any flowers while graceful and practical in form the vases give room for a plentiful supply of water for the stalks.'

Rose Kingsley, *Eversley Gardens and Others*

Gertrude Jekyll held much the same view as Rose Kingsley though she preferred, above all, vases of cream-coloured and smooth Leeds ware. An expensive taste today! She aired her views in *Flower Decoration in the House* and has these last words to say on the late Victorian drawing-room.

'There comes a point when a room becomes overloaded with flowers, greenery and knick-knacks. During these last years (1890–1900) I have seen a drawing-room where it appeared to be less a room than a thicket.'

ORNAMENTAL BIRD-CAGES

'There is no reason for keeping such interesting, lively and beautiful creatures as birds in ugly

cages that have so long been used; let their homes be beautiful to match themselves.'

Shirley Hibberd,
Rustic Adornments for Homes of Taste

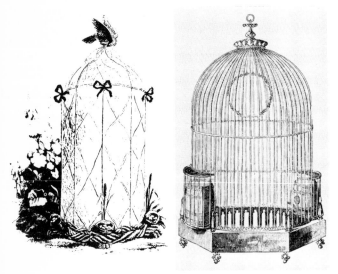

134–5 Two ornamental bird-cages by William Kidd of Hammersmith

So wrote Mr. Shirley Hibberd, a leading garden-journalist of the day, in 1856. And so did Victorian householders also think when they flocked to see Mr. William Kidd's ornamental bird-cages at Hammersmith.

It was kind and amiable Mr. Kidd who first imported German and Zollverein bird-cages to house the many pet canaries, bullfinches and goldfinches being sold as decorative embellishments for the Victorian drawing-room.

From importing fancy bird-cages, Mr. Kidd turned his attention to making them himself. His cages are recorded as being entirely made of metal, stamped and perforated in many lovely designs, the patterns of which were picked out in bright colours such as orange, scarlet, green, blue and crimson 'so that as Window and Conservatory Ornaments they are very showy and effective' went one advertisement. But it was Mr. Kidd's 'Fairy Bird-Cage' with its bars of transparent glass, its perches of ruby Bohemian glass and swing-perch made of crystal and malachite that achieved lasting fame for its fantastical air of beauty that delighted not only a buyer but its sweetly trilling occupant inside.

To prevent draughts when placed on a table, Mr. Kidd's 'Fairy Cage' was sold with a movable screen made of strong, tinted cardboard mounted on hinges. 'His screen', wrote Mr. Hibberd portentously, 'if painted would be a neat ornament', adding in his most characteristic vein, 'the happiness and whimsical conceit of birds living in 'fairy cages' particularly in the case of love birds, Australian paroquets, canaries, bullfinches and goldfinches can be but faintly conceived. They *feel* their importance and they *know* they are objects of admiration. It is, perhaps, difficult to say which is happier – the bird or his mistress.'

In the Victoria and Albert *Commemorative Album of The Great Exhibition* (1851) there is a fascinating illustration (Figure 196) of an Ornamental Japanned Bird Cage and Flower Stand which may have been a source of inspiration to Mr. Kidd. Actually, it was displayed by Messrs. Rau & Co. of Wurtemberg, Germany, in which country the expert breeding of canaries has always been maintained and ornamental cages made to house them.

Another kind of bird-cage known to a splendid writer of tales for children and adults is described in the following passage which includes the perfect picture of a small drawing-room of the period.

'Lucilla received him in a drawing-room scented with last year's rose leaves, and fresh with chintz that had been washed a dozen times . . . she leaned one hand on a chiffonier of carved rosewood on whose marble top stood, under a glass case, a Chinese pagoda, carved in ivory, and two Bohemian glass vases with medallions representing young women nursing pigeons. There were white curtains of darned net; in the fire-place white ravelled muslin spread a cascade brightened with threads of tinsel. A canary sang in a green cage, wainscotted with yellow tarlatan, and two, red rosebuds stood in lank specimen glasses on the mantelpiece.'

E. Nesbit, *Fear*

Besides Victorian ornamental bird-cages that attract collectors there are those in wicker, traditional, rustic, which cottagers hung outside their porch to house a pet linnet or jackdaw. These cages are shaped either like a hanging lantern or a casket with a flat bottom. Others are dome-shaped. The old name for a wicker cage was 'Pear-tree' forever associated in our minds with that enchanting carol 'The Twelve Days of Christmas'.

The first day of Christmas, my true love sent to me
A partridge in a pear-tree.

CONSERVATORY FURNITURE

'Your improvements would have been destruction. A conservatory opening out of that window would suggest a city man's drawing-room at Tulse Hill. I have seen such when Mother used to visit old people on the Surrey side of the river.'

Miss Braddon, *The Day Will Come*

So declared Sir Godfrey Carmichael's young bride on being shown over his home, the old grey Priory embowered in roses and passion-flowers, which lay between Wareham and Wimborne, Dorset. Already, in the 1870s, the one time fashionable possession of a conservatory opening out of a ground-floor room like a library or drawing-room had become vulgarised. Today, the wheel of fashion has come round full circle and not only is a small, up-to-date conservatory or patio craved by most householders but all the gear too (if it can be found) of its Victorian counterpart such as florid, Minton and Wedgwood majolica plant containers, rustic-styled terra-cotta urns and vases, wirework hanging baskets and cast-iron seats and benches, china and glass mosaic ornaments, and ornamental ceramic chairs.

One fantastic garden chair, illustrated in *The Gardener's Magazine* of 1833, was the forerunner of many to come. Painted green and priced only at 16/-, it had a wooden seat and its cast-iron back support and legs were modelled in the shape of 'acanthus, thistle or artichoke' leaves. Its designer, Matthias Saul of Sulyard Street, Lancaster, submitted this chair for the approval of Mr. Loudon, editor of *The Gardener's Magazine*. Needless to say, Mr. Loudon's re-action was unkind to say the least. For he wrote that garden chairs should be painted any other colour but green nor should they be supported by such an improbable and unpractical design as Mr. Saul's *leaves*. When Mr. Saul submitted a revised version of his chair, substituting intertwined vine-branches for leaves with applied decoration by way of detachable, fat bunches of grapes that could be painted – according to the season – green, black or red – Mr. Loudon's sole comment was: 'We like this design still less than the other.' However, in a way, Mr. Saul had anticipated the coming of the 'rustic' style in garden and conservatory furniture which was to sweep all before it from the 1840s to '70s and which is now being restored to high favour in modern examples produced in glass-fibre, perspex

136 *Iron conservatory built by Handyside & Co, Walbrook, London*

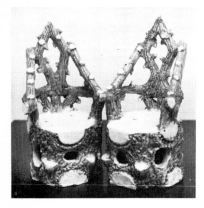

137 (left) *Pair of rustic armchairs*
138 (centre) *Rustic ceramic conservatory chair, c. 1865*

139 *Fern vase*

and new synthetic materials less costly than cast-iron work.

The 'Rustic' style is generally based on designs suitable for reproduction in cast-iron or ceramic ware like terra-cotta. They stress, for instance, the attractive 'knobby' appeal of bark combined with the close intertwining of twigs and branches (to give back support to chairs and benches) plus applied decoration of ivy, fern-fronds and other similar foliage. Actually fern-fronds tied up with the great craze for fern culture that took place in the Victorian home during the '60s and '70s. Ladies were led into making their own elegant pot-containers or other rustic ornaments for the Fernery, Conservatory or Flower-Garden utilising both moss-work and canework (Chapter IX: Parlour Pastimes) for their creations.

In her *Gardening for Ladies* (1841) Mrs. Loudon supported the 'Rustic' style for the production of plant containers which she said could be contrived from old wine barrels or casks, with moss-decoration declaring that alternatively Chinese tea-chests could be utilised such as Lady Grenville displayed at Dropmore. Wisely, Mrs. Loudon added:

'But in all cases where the materials employed are of little value, the flowers grown in them should be in the highest state of cultivation, so as to show that the rudeness of material had been the result of intention and not of carelessness or poverty.'

Mrs. Loudon knew her public.

Besides home-made, artistic barrel-containers, there were others similar in shape but commercially produced in vari-coloured earthenware showing applied ivy and vine garlands. Ornamental chairs made in terra-cotta or fireclay were also available

and their colours ranged from a rich red to a pale buff tint. Messrs. William Baddeley of Hanley, Staffordshire is one recorded manufactuer of 'Terra-cotta Conservatory Furniture', his characteristic tree-trunk sections being modelled in high relief. Collectors of ceramic garden chairs may find an impressed name or initials, often small and hidden, on them. But it is not always possible to attribute the name of the potter except under close and authoritive scrutiny of the ceramic itself.

Owing to the enormous interest being shown today in genuine Victorian-styled conservatory furniture prices have soared. On the other hand, many old patterns and styles are being reproduced in modern materials, which is just as well. For the one time large and often too magnificent Victorian conservatory has come under fire and is in the process of being given a new look. A conservatory described here such as Mrs. Alexander Fraser, a leading hostess and novelist of the 1880s, possessed at Carylls, near Faygate, Sussex, (now a home for old ladies) is completely out-of-date and would be impossible to maintain!

'Heated to a pleasant temperature, full of bright and rare blooms the gentle breath of sweet-scented gardenias and tuberoses pervades the atmosphere. Cages of many-coloured foreign birds, a gleam of Moorish lamps against the greenery overhead, comfortable lounges, wickerwork tables, Turkish rugs strewn on the tesselated floor – all combine to make a delightful place in which to while away Time with books or work'.

Yes, there it all is, the vanished splendour and domestic comforts of the Victorian conservatory which led off the drawing-room or library when time and money was of no object and gardeners and their boys to be had by the score.

4 The Boudoir

140　*Interior corner of an octagon boudoir in Adam style, c. 1880*

I write in a nook that I call my boudoir.

William Cowper, 25 June 1786.

So wrote the poet, Cowper, from his garden in Bedfordshire. And so might many a lady, but hers would have been from the boudoir proper and not some leafy nook out of doors. The word *boudoir* comes from France, that land of civilised living, and it derives from the verb *bouder* to sulk or pout. But how many women followed this practice in the small elegantly-appointed room to which they retired either to be alone or to receive, *sub rosa*, an intimate friend or lover, is a matter of conjecture. However, according to Charles Kingsley there was one sultry beauty, the heroine of his novel, *Yeast* (1851) called Argemone who was 'often found in her boudoir, too often a *true* boudoir to her'.

In the Victorian home, the boudoir lay near the drawing-room, or it might be found, upstairs, next to the best bedroom. Its furniture consisted usually of a *chaise longe* or *tabouret* on which a lady could recline at her ease in private; some elegant but rather fragile chairs; a pretty *escritoire* or *bonheur du jour* complete with writing paraphernalia; besides numerous china ornaments like miniature china watering-cans in Rockingham or Worcester, flower-encrusted vases or a pair of Belleek Boudoir Flower shells. Many small silver objects and photograph frames in silver-gilt or Italian mosaic work containing tinted portraits of beloved ones and pets would be scattered about together with trinket and cachou boxes and other costly trifles presented as gifts. In fact, everything in a fashionable Victorian boudoir imparted an air of expensive luxury to the visitor on entering it.

Surrounded thus by their sentimental keepsakes, ladies passed hours of agreeable leisure attending to their correspondence, embroidering or reading the latest novel from Mudie's. Their boudoir could be both a room for seclusion and rest; a hive of activity for pursuing some fashionable hobby of the moment; or a secret rendez-vous for lovers.

'It is a sweet hour', said Glorvina, sighing. 'It is a *boudoirising* hour', I replied. (*Harper's Magazine*, 1883)

But to what occupation these words refer, one can leave only to Glorvina and her companion.

More often than not, a young lady's den became her boudoir after marriage as in the case of the Honourable Juanita Cheriton:

'Lady Cheriton went straight to her daughter's boudoir, a room with an oriel window looking across the wide expanse of the park where the deer were wont to congregate. . . . The room was full of Juanita's girlish treasures – evidencies of fancies that had passed like summer clouds – accomplishments begun and abandoned – a zither in one corner – a guitar against the wall – an easel in front of one window – a gigantic rush work-basket lined with amber satin and crammed with all manner of silks, wools, scraps and unfinished undertakings.'

Miss Braddon, *The Day Will Come* (1890)

Generally speaking, then, the boudoir, like a lady's bedroom, expressed her own individual taste and personality more than a traditional pattern of colour décor and furnishings laid down

64

by those considered authorities on the subject. Such a boudoir was the Honourable Mrs. Fausset's in Upper Parchment Street which was bounded on the west by Park Lane and on the east by Grosvenor Square, London.

'For furniture and decoration there was everything pretty, novel, eccentric and expensive that Maud Fausset had ever been able to think of. She had only stopped her caprices and her purchases when the room could not hold another thing of beauty. There was a confusion of form and colour but the general effect was charming: and Mrs. Fausset, in a loose white muslin gown suited the room, as the room Mrs. Fausset.

'She was sitting in the bow-window, in a semi-circle of flowers and with heterogeneous styles of art – here Louis Seize, there Japanese; Italian on one side, Indian on the other, waiting her husband. The scarlet Japanese tea-table stood untouched, the water bubbling in the quaint little bronze kettle, swinging between a pair of rampant dragons.'

Miss Braddon, *The Fatal Three*

It is Mrs. Fausset's scarlet Japanese tea table that points to the arrival of eastern fashions which now found their best setting in the mid-Victorian boudoir.

BAMBOO AND WICKER FURNITURE

From about 1865, the Oriental Bazaar which had its natural habitat in Mr. Thomas Liberty's Regent Street Emporium drew crowds of admiring ladies to feast their eyes on an enthralling assembly of new, decorative objects. These included glossy-black lacqueur boxes; miniature pagodas carved in ivory; exquisite fans; brass gongs, and tall, embroidered screens across whose silken panels flew long-legged storks and cranes. With such wares, came bamboo and wicker chairs and tables, small work-tables, cakestands, wastepaper baskets

and their like. Whether painted, gilded or left *au naturel*, bamboo and wicker furniture became the rage.

On the whole Chinese bamboo chairs had a pleasing air of light elegance when sparingly used in the boudoir. There were also several kinds to choose from. One, in black wicker, was called a 'Market Harborough' chair and is described in one stores catalogue as 'a luxurious retreat for an idle moment'. It appears to have been cushioned in sage-green, stamped plush and decorated with bows of sage-green and pale-pink ribbon to stress its femininity. Another type was known as 'The

142 *Chinese sofa in bamboo with stuffed cushions (back) and bolster sides, 1878*

143 *Bamboo table floor lamp on Japanese afternoon tea table ornately fitted, c. 1880–5*

Oxford'. In natural-coloured rattan, ebonised in black and gold, it was upholstered, again, in blue plush. Plush was the operative word in the language of boudoir materials and seen everywhere for portières and piano draperies; for ottoman cushions and chair covers; even for wall-roundels in which hand-painted tiles, plaques or crayon portraits were framed to show them off. When Mrs. Baddeley undertook the decorations of her newly married sister's London flat off the Victoria Road, Kensington, she immediately got an introduction to a City oriental warehouse as the Japanese style was her passion. Very soon by purchasing gold-embroidered screens and bamboo blinds, by enamelled vases and curiously carved ebony cabinets, Helen Belfield's dull and modest little flat was transformed into a veritable Japanese bower where:

'Josses nodded in every corner and beaded bamboo blinds rustled at every door and where parti-coloured rush matting covered the floor except where lay a few costly Indian rugs.'

Miss Braddon, *Like and Unlike*

But even after all this work, Leo Baddeley was not content until she had filled every vase with poppies and nasturiums – those flowers of the moment – and every fireplace and lobby with palm leaves and bulrushes. Imagine her pain, then, and consternation when on the arrival of the honeymoon couple from the Continent, Valentine Belfield roared out to his wife Helen, and her sister – as he gazed in astonishment round him: 'Do you expect me to live in a place that looks like a stall at a Charity Bazaar?'

And with that, he departed in high dudgeon to his Club. His feelings, no doubt, were reciprocated by many other young husbands living at this time.

There has been a recent revival in bamboo and wicker furniture similar to the one that took place in the 1860s. Among the small, graceful and genuine 'pieces' in Victorian bamboo that have survived, bamboo music and newspaper stands, plant tables, cake baskets and umbrella stands are well worth the money that is being asked for them. For what was once tatty and of no lasting account has long succumbed to the rough and tumble wear of boarding-house life where it ended up.

THE TURKISH COSY CORNER

It was the arrival of the ottoman and divan in the Victorian drawing-room and boudoir which led to one rather horrific fashion that has yet, if ever, to be revived! Using the ottoman and divan as an inspirational basis for further experiments in Oriental decor, ladies enamoured of the Far East evolved for themselves 'The Turkish Cosy Corner' which swept all before it. No one was better equipped, either, to write about it than Mrs. Talbot Coke, a great enthusiast for everything Turkish, Moorish or Indian. In *The Gentlewoman at Home* she describes one boudoir blest with a 'cosy corner' that she deemed a real *tour de force*. It lay in:

'A room, quaintly shaped, with deep-set square bay window, the top panes shaded with leaded glass in white and yellow. A quaint turret-shaped recess, with three little lancet windows in the angle of the outside wall, showed the charm of a window in an unusual position. The walls were papered with a plain dull greeny-blue oil paper with very high dado of the now familiar Manilla grass cloth, tightly stretched, the vertical stripes being in dim yellow, dull red and greeny blue. The dado rail was a narrow shelf edged with bamboo, and here and there – above the writing-table – widened out into a large bracket for pottery, etc. On the narrow shelf stood all kinds of quaint things – a Jeypore shield, in red-brown horn, decorated with gold tracery; a pierced copper plate from Kashmir engraved brass ones from Cairo, lovely bits of colour in Mooltan ware, and lacquer from Japan.

'The floor was covered with Indian red matting and old Oriental rugs, russet plush curtains hung in the large window, a unique couch covered with leopard skins and with a fierce stuffed head snarling over the back stood across a corner with a spreading palm in a huge brass pot overshadowing it, and a tall group of tawny fringed grass behind it. Other large couches and cosy arm-chairs were covered with bold 'Liberty' fabrics and the large window held a divan strewn with cushions. Overmantel there was none, but merely irregular Mushrabeyah shelves with all kinds of queer pottery and Eastern curios in a sort of shrine, formed by a large bracket placed high and draped with a phoolkari, the mantel-board having a deep frill of the same glittering stuff.

'One corner of the room was cut off by a large mirror with curious Indian drapery which stood on the floor and reflected the turret window – the gem of the whole room. This was so arranged that one mounted to it by a step covered with a Persian rug. The circular wall was covered with a bold-patterned, red-and-gold leather paper, the ceiling with ivory and gold. The little windows had tiny frilled curtains of soft yellow Liberty silk. A low seat followed the outline of the wall and was covered, with frill to the ground with rich-looking, gold-figured velveteen. Two brass lamps, pierced and jewelled, hung between the windows, and gave a hint of what this charming little nook was capable of when night came.'

FASHIONS IN FANS

In 1876, the Fan Exhibition at South Kensington renewed the interest once taken in collecting fans both in England and America. This interest was further stimulated when Whistler began to use them for wall or mantel-piece decoration.

So, instead of re-discovering their true place which had been between the fingers of an eighteenth-century lady's delicate white hand, fans in every shape, size and colour came to hang on panelled walls or be wedged, in pairs or groups, behind picture frames. Some were even laced together by ribbon to form a wall-pocket in which loose odds-and-ends were kept. Indeed, there was no limit set to what absurd forms of extravaganza they could be put.

In one issue of *The Lady* (1885), a table lamp can be seen with its shade made of over-lapping fans whose fringed handles have been cut short and then tied tightly with ribbon to hold them together. Both open, flat or folded fans were tacked on walls to make a frieze, or they were placed, trophy fashion, over a draped doorway.

From India sweltering under the British Raj, came pierced and ribbon-threaded fans of sandalwood by the boxload to shed their distinct, sweet faint scent from whatnot or mantelpiece. From Japan, others were imported with characteristic motifs of iris and lotus flowers or hawthorn, instead of one time Watteau-like scenes. Tiny silk or gauze fans found an extraordinary use by being sewn along the border of a Japanese blue boudoir table-cloth with the tiniest of stitches.

But the most 'collectable' fan of this period, 1865 to 1870 must surely be the one designed for a ballroom, which had a tiny mirror inset in the guard. When held up to a lady's face, she could see who was approaching her and regulate her behaviour accordingly.

ARTISTS' PALETTES

The setting up of an easel as a purely decorative feature in the boudoir evoked one strange fashion.

'There is a rage today', recorded a writer in an issue of *The Parisian*, for palettes to be illustrated and signed. In every window where pictures or curiosities are sold, palettes are seen. The fashion, it seems, comes from America.'

On the contrary, the original idea was Paris-born. This came about when a dealer, paying a visit to the studio of a famous painter, offered to buy his palette if he left his colours on it. Amused by the idea, the painter ran the colours into a sort of surrealist landscape and putting his initials in a corner sold his palette for 100 francs. Repeating this scene in 50 other studios, the dealer, it was said, went to New York, where he sold his signed palettes for large sums. On returning to Paris, he became the proprietor of a successful Montmartre brasserie. . . .

In this way, an artist's ordinary brown wooden palette suddenly became a fashionable boudoir item, the more so when painted by sprays of flowers or a tiny landscape in oils by a professional hand. Palettes were generally hung on the wall against a square of maroon velvet-covered pasteboard. To make them even more glorious, peacock feathers were thrust through the aperture for the thumb. If such feathers were not available, bunches of gilded, dry oats or ferns or grasses were put instead. Some of these palettes are reappearing needless to say along with the Art Nouveau Movement which has taken place.

Decorated wooden palettes may appeal to some *avant garde* collectors, but what of a Victorian child's 'Wooden Spade', seen recently with a horrid little landscape painted on its blade while from its gilt handle dangled the ribbon by which it was once hung up?

144–8 *Group of boudoir shell ornaments:* (top) *irridescent shell on shell-decorated base (Belleck & Co. Fermanagh);* (centre) *small translucent pink-white Chamberlain's Worcester shell (marked),* c. 1825; (bottom row) *William Cookworthy's (1705–80) Plymouth china shell on shell-decorated base with painted lining; two representative late-Victorian shells, coloured and highly glazed*

BOUDOIR FLOWER SHELLS

These shells are among the prettiest of china objects once found on a boudoir chiffonier or what-not and they were made by two well-known china firms during the 1870s. One was Belleek at Fermanagh, Ireland; the other, W. H. Goss, the Falcon Pottery, Stoke-upon-Trent, Staffordshire, established in 1858.

As we have noted earlier, Belleek was a china ware much favoured by Queen Victoria, who had several table services made in this lovely translucent china. The chief modeller for Belleek was Gallimore, who, it is said, was responsible for the creation of Boudoir Flower Shells. These take the form of two dolphins placed, back to back, on a narrow plinth with their tightly curled-up tails supporting two small conch shells placed tip to tip and with their bodies tapering outwards.

When Gallimore left Ireland for England, he worked for Goss at his pottery works and produced more of his boudoir flower shells. But these differ from the Belleek Shell-and-Dolphin Group. Composed of two shells of a pale biscuit or pinky-beige colour that look more like baskets with applied small white flowers and pale-blue leaves, these shells are placed, side by side, on a low, coral-spiked base. Three small cherubs play among the coral sprigs that adorn the top, a pretty but far fussier object than its Belleek counterpart.

IMITATION DRESDEN CHINA

In this genre of ornamental china that was much loved by mid-Victorian ladies comes a wide range of flower-encrusted little objects modelled in the shape of high-heeled boots and shoes; arch-handled baskets; candlesticks; tea-pots, swans and watering-cans, covered with green moss china and little flowers like forget-me-nots, each piece features always the signature of a small white rose. Marks on this kind of china are seldom found but I have recorded on one or two examples a tiny blue swan, two fine red lines, and once the word GERMANY. Prices are still modest for this type of flower-encrusted china which is rapidly coming into favour among collectors.

149 *Miniature Dresden china cluster of daffodils, c. 1890*

150 *Ornamental shoe and small teapot in imitation Dresden china, applied green moss and flower decoration, c. 1890*

LITTLE CHINA WATERING-CANS

China flowers in any form or shape have always appealed to feminine taste; in particular, to one fine and lovely lady. Her name was Jeanne Poisson, created Madame de Pompadour by King Louis XV, of France whose beloved mistress she was. Incidentally, Jeanne de Pompadour is among the great collectors of all time and it is fascinating to read how she gathered together for her pleasure and to display in her many magnificent homes exquisite bibelots, pictures, engraved stones and gems, rare books and china.

In her famous Winter Garden of Porcelain Flowers, flowers that never withered or faded but bloomed in perpetual perfection, Madame de Pompadour received King Louis and taught him how to appreciate them as she did.

Another high-ranking lady who was a noted flower-lover, but of real flowers more than those exquisitely contrived from china, was Valentina, Duchesse d'Orléans who took a long, slender-necked and bulbous perfuming watering-pot to be her personal device in the fifteenth century.
Owing to the indoor cultivation of all kinds of ferns and foliage plants in the nineteenth century, Victorian ladies had a great use for, and love of, ornamental watering-cans. The prettier they were, the more there was a demand for them.

Watering-cans have a long history dating far

151–3 *An assembly of 14 different types of miniature to small-sized nineteenth century watering cans which include some in hand-painted china, one in silver filigree (third in first line top picture); and one in terra cotta (third in line in bottom picture)*

back to very primitive times. They are fascinating objects in themselves, whether made in fine china, painted tinware, gleaming brass and copper or plain terra-cotta. For watering-cans other than those Victorian, information can be obtained by the interested collector from Miss Therle Hughes' *More Small Decorative Antiques*.

During Queen Victoria's reign, a lady could use a pretty little china watering-can either as a scent sprinkler to sweeten the stuffy air of her bedroom or boudoir or to water pot-plants like musk or mignonette that she had surrounded herself with. Small or large, in every kind of medium, from delicate silver filagree to homely stone ware, an assembly of watering-cans can afford the collector endless interest and fun in tracking them down. In fine china, Josiah Spode, Bloor of Derby, and Chamberlain of Worcester all produced their own type of watering-can. The latter favoured 'japan' patterns from about 1806, which were followed by some showing flowers and leaves in high relief done in natural colours. Coloured grounds of watering-cans date from the 1830s, onwards. Some cans may be marked in red script *Chamberlain Worcester* but the majority remain unmarked.

With its attractive and characteristic apple-green colour and much lavish gilding on their rustic-styled handles, a Rockingham watering-can has great appeal. Some, like those of Worcester, come in 'japan' designs, with reds ranging from rose-pink to rich maroon; others with glittering gold leaves and coloured flower-sprays in high relief can be found bearing the familiar puce griffin mark of this factory. Coalport cans feature a long, six-inch spout which tends to lose its gilt rose in use. The tricky problem of a projecting spout, so easily damaged, was tackled, and perfected, by John Davenport of Longport. His cylindrical little cans may be identified by the small animals and other similar motifs found supporting the finials of their domed lids. Even more conspicuous for collectors are their spout design, which feature about six small tubes protruding from the rose to regulate the flow of water and make certain that it fell exactly on the required spot. Davenport left white spaces on his cans for his enamellers to paint in with little coloured posies, and from about 1830 such cans are marked with the words *Davenport's Stone China* in a circle with a full anchor.

For use in a drawing-room conservatory or for

154 *Two very handsome large watering cans with rich applied flower decoration of Continental origin, c. 1890*

watering the mignonette boxes and fern-stands elsewhere, large cans were put out by William Baddeley of Normancott Road, Longton in rustic terra-cotta from 1862. His 'rustic' style that represented sections of bark-covered tree trunk plus twig and branch is best found in his ceramic conservatory chairs.

Watering-cans in miniature, which delighted Victorian ladies and which they liked to put on their whatnot shelves or tables, feature usually the straight, wide-rose spout, the arching handle and half-hood plus cylindrical form of the genuine japanned iron conservatory watering-pot. But Spode produced some charmers with rose sprays after the style of William Billinsley of rose-fame at Swansea. Some Swansea marks can be tracked down on little flower-painted cans issued in the '40s by Henry Morris, late decorator to Swansea, now closed. From 1862, Stevenson & Hancock of Derby marked theirs with the Derby crossed swords over a script D flanked by S & H while Sampson Hancock continued making little watering-cans right up to 1900 at the 'Old Crown Derby China Works'.

PLATES AND PLAQUES

In his *Hints on Household Taste*, Charles Eastlake gives an illustration of some pieces of artistic pottery suitable for display on 'Overmantel-shelving'. This form of decoration led, in time, to the appearance of 'the plate-rail', a grooved wooden moulding which acted as a protective small barrier between the body of the wall and the frieze of a room and which cost next to nothing to instal. Hence its popularity. The presence of the plate-rail, then, in the home called forth all the collecting-instinct of Victorian householders, in particular that of china-lovers who were soon bent on acquiring a wonderful assortment of decorative china plates and plaques.

71

To begin with plates: Victorian plates of every size, shape and make. In the pursuit of them, in tracking down both the rare and commonplace plate, the collector would not only feel the exciting lure of the chase but is quite likely to come across some exceptional example impressed with the name of its maker, a left-over from a large table-service by Wedgwood, Minton, Coalport or Copeland. For the pine-stripped, Welsh dresser of today, or any other brand of dresser to put in a modern kitchen or dining-area, a collection of Victorian plates in china or pressed glass could not be bettered.

There are few antique shops in small country towns or villages that do not have a wooden stand put out by their door on which, among other assorted treasures, there will not be found at least one, or two, attractive plates marked down for a modest sum. In one such a shop, I found recently a much begrimed and tiny plate shell $3\frac{1}{4}$ by 3 inches, flushed white and pale-pink, delicately fragile which turned out to be marked Chamberlain's Worcester. Another find was a shallow, round plate, French in origin, decorated with a transfer-printing in fawns, browns and greens, of a stage-set taken from Adolf Adam's opera *Le Chalet* first produced in Paris in 1834 and later in London, when it was called *The Swiss Cottage*. Reputed to be Queen Victoria's favourite opera, it proved so popular that its name was given to the district of Swiss Cottage then in the process of being laid out. This plate marked *Terre de Fer, Sujets musicaux* is one of a run of plates featuring operatic scenes. Bird plates are varied in design and attracted Charlotte Brontë, who wrote how '. . . a certain brightly painted china plate whose bird of Paradise, nestling in a wreath of convolvuli and rosebuds, has been wont to stir in me a most enthusiastic sense of admiration.'

Botanical Plates with their fine and correctly-drawn groups of plants, ferns, flowers and grasses have their names sometimes affixed on a tiny scroll such as Minton's.

Both Bird and Botanical plates can be hand-painted or decorated by transfer-prints, when of course they are much cheaper. Nineteenth-century transfer-printing offered an excellent means of decorating both china and earthenware. When successfully adapted to mass-production there was no obvious decline in artistic standards. Large china or earthenware platters and chargers used for

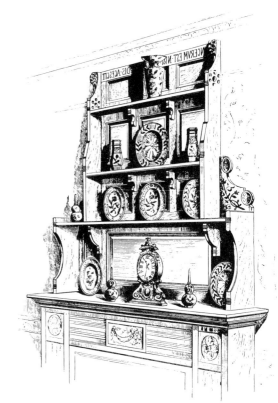

155 *Mantel shelves equipped with suitable period furnishings, designed by Charles L. Eastlake*

dishing up whole joints, etc., are at their most handsome when showing historic scenes, picturesque views, notable buildings, churches and bridges, etc., besides a series of country seats (some no more), and they can form an interesting collection. So can those featuring marine subjects with appropriate sentimental verses which were a feature of the local pottery works round Newcastle and Sunderland from about 1780 till the last decades of the nineteenth century.

Lastly come Portrait Plates, which include that unrivalled charmer 'The Gibson Girl' who became a best-seller in the ceramic world when created by the genius of Charles Dana Gibson (1867–1944), a leading American pen-and-ink illustrator of the '90s. 'The Gibson Girl' was not only seen on plates and plaques but on buttons, brooches and buckles, etc. Quick to take advantage of her popular public image, the Royal Doulton Potteries at Lambeth produced a series of twenty-four plates which depicted in black on a white ground different episodes of the Gibson Girl, under the title of 'A Widow and Her Friends'.

In a group of notable nineteenth century ceramic artists come the names of William Stephen Coleman (1829–1904); William J. Goode (1831–1892); and Louis Marc Solon (1835–1913), a Frenchman who worked at Minton's for 34 years.

It was not until the end almost of the 1860s that Coleman, a well-known illustrator and water-colourist turned his attention to painting on earthenware. After a brief period working for Copeland he accepted an offer to go to Minton's at Stoke, where his special talent for a completely new style of decoration was quickly appreciated.

In 1871, Mintons established an Art Pottery Studio at Kensington Gore, London, under the direction of William Coleman who put it on the map as one of *the* artistic show places of London. Painting on china was fashionable and being taken up by professionals and amateurs alike. At the Art Pottery Studio students decorated a vast quantity of plain white china ware (plates, plaques, vases, etc.) supplied by Minton. Here, too, Coleman produced his plaques, initiating his own individual style that embraced most naturalistic subjects besides some studies of nude children. Of these, one critic in 1876 wrote: 'The figures are perhaps too nude but so good in drawing and so innocently rendered that they could scarcely fail to please.'

But after four short years from 1869–73, Coleman's interest in painting on china ceased. It was, perhaps, just as well for Minton's Art Pottery was destroyed by fire in 1875 and never rebuilt, although another centre appears to have taken its place. This was the Old Pottery Galleries at 203 Oxford Street and 31 Orchard Street run by John Mortlock who advertised how in his studio, 'Ladies can learn to decorate their own rooms under the guidance of Young Ladies from South Kensington.'

It can be added that both Coleman's sisters, Helen Coleman (Mrs. Angell) and Rebecca Coleman painted Minton earthenware in a successful and attractive manner as did many other nameless ladies.

William J. Goode was the son of Mr. Thomas Goode, the founder of the famous firm of china retailers still established in South Audley Street, Mayfair. When William Goode succeeded his father in the family business he was particularly interested in designing pottery and porcelain and decorating Minton ware, which was returned to be fired at their factory. Although Goode treated his work only as a hobby, he did exhibit some four to five pieces a year at International Exhibitions. At one, the Parish Universal Exhibition of 1878, a writer in the *Pottery Gazette* had this to say of him: 'His own etchings continue to attract the notice of French critics as being among the most original and artistic objects of decoration in the porcelain.'

William Goode also painted in full colours and some of his work is fully signed and dated; others carry a monogram of his initials, W. J. G.

Louis Marc Solon was born at Montauban, France in 1835, and received his training early in life at Monsieur Lecoq de Boisbaudran's studio, where he chose rather to work in the field of design and free creative expression than in painting.

On going to work at the Royal Manufactory of Sèvres, he concentrated on research work for the process known as *pâte-sur-pâte* which had recently been introduced. It was now that Solon tried his hand at producing a few small plaques in *pâte-sur-pâte*, signing them 'Miles', a name containing his initials.

To his delight, Solon discovered that the *pâte-sur-pâte* process was singularly adapted to his own style and form of ceramic expression. For 12 years he worked at Sèvres, and then on going to England became associated for the rest of his working life with Minton. As has been said, Solon's art was most successful when applied to the flat surface of plaques. On them his classic and delicately draped figures, his playful cupids, appear at their poetic best. The most typical pictures on his plaques include *Cupid's Fireworks, The Webs of Venus, Cupid's Prison-House* and other similar titles. He never duplicated his scenes, having an abundance of new ideas. Colours used as backgrounds for the reliefs (white usually) are celadon, olive and sage green, bright chocolate, a ferruginous brown, and peacock blue; very occasionally black. After each cameo picture was finished, a glaze was put over it. The delicate semi-translucency of his draped figures caused a sensation in the ceramic world of the '70s and '80s.

It is interesting to note through a circular published by Messrs. Howell & James, London (1880) addressed to those competing in their spring exhibition that the subject chosen was *Plaques*.

Moreover, they recommended that for their entries

'Dark-coloured grounds should be adopted – sage greens, bronze, browns and blues in graduated tints; when flowers are painted, they should be confined to one sort and all designs arranged so as to cover the whole plaque as far as possible. Subjects should be well and faithfully drawn from Nature where possible and broadly and artistically treated. Plaques from twelve to sixteen inches in diameter are the most saleable and the following subjects the most readily disposed of: pretty rural scenes with children after the style of Birket Foster; graceful figures in pairs on oblong panels from eight to fifteen inches in length; artistic

grouping of single flowers; picturesque heads (female heads in particular) with ornamental backgrounds and sober colouring in the drapery; landscapes'.

Messrs. Howell & James also drew attention to long panels decorated with tall-growing plants (i.e. hollyhocks, sunflowers, iris, etc.) and tinted backgrounds for which 'there is a growing demand'.

There was, indeed, so much so that many ladies of the impoverished spinster-type took up their production, adding a range of hand-painted, plush-framed china plaques of their own which can still be come across but which have only period value.

OVERMANTEL-SHELVING

Like many another good decorative idea, Charles Eastlake's 'Overmantel-shelving', by which means he hoped to lure ladies away from crowding their whatnots and plate-rail with sentimental gifts and family keepsakes, was soon carried to excess;

for it bred a plethora of corner cabinets and brackets far removed from the early charm of an eighteenth-century 'Chinese Chippendale' wall bracket that is so difficult to come by now. Very soon, to overmantel-shelving was added a multitude of: 'Tiny shelves either connected like bookshelves or independent on which plates of

157 *A richly carved, dark mahogany Louis XV-styled overmantel, 1870*

156 *Fireplace shown with overmantel-shelving, artistically dressed*

158 (right) *A fashionable overdoor in bamboo with shelf displaying a Japanese decorated panel and oriental china*

74

peculiar and dainty ware can be placed to look safer than when suspended by cord or wire.'

This extract comes from Mrs. Orrinsmith's *The Drawing Room and Boudoir* published in an amusing series of little books edited by Mr. William Loftie, F.S.A., under the title of *Art at Home*, 1878. For this was the heyday of the first so-called professional lady decorators headed by Mrs. Haweis (1858–1898), their doyenne, a noted arbiter of domestic taste. Others included Mrs. Panton (*A Gentlewoman's Home,* 1896)', Mrs. C. S. Peel (*The New Home,* 1898) and Mrs. Talbot Coke. Each lady had her own ideas on home decoration and gave earnest expression to them in women's journals and magazines of the period.

The one-time small, pretty 'chiffonier' beloved by Mrs. Danvers and Jane Loudon, which had once graced the early Victorian drawing-room and boudoir, was now described as 'entirely unsuitable and dangerous, being inaccessible with its shelves and cupboard so close to the floor for valuable and interesting ware.'

So the 'Hanging Cabinet' of hardwood stained black and French-polished with bevelled plate-glass doors and mirror-lined shelves above, below and all around, became as crowded with Venetian glass, Indian painted pots and pipkins, green-glazed vases from the Aures mountains and even Spanish and Tunisian common clay water bottles as 'The Whatnot' had once been with Spangled and Spatter glass, a Parian hand or flower-encrusted little china watering-pots. In *Art and the Foundation of Formation of Taste*, published after her death, Lucy Crane (1841–1882) attacked early Victorian fashions when lecturing to her contemporaries. 'Why', she declared, 'should candlesticks be preserved like exotics under glass bells. Curtain poles be so gilded that their real work must be done with iron ones hidden below? Cushions and foot-stools meant for repose studded with hard cold beads?'

In spite, though, of Lucy Crane's efforts to try and explain contemporary art-forms to her sex and to analyse the word 'Art' in relation to its application in the domestic realm of house décor and house furnishings, her words fell for the most part on deaf ears. Leading their lives of sheltered ease behind portières of clattering strands of beads or tiny sections of bamboo, would-be artistic boudoir ladies continued to reduce art to the most absurd levels of what can only be des-

· A FIREPLACE · IN SUMMER ·

159 *A summer fireplace with tiles and potted plants, charmingly designed for a lady, by Lucy Crane*

160 *Portrait of Lucy Crane (1841–82) drawn by her brother Walter Crane*

cribed as purely trumpery, decorative domesticities. For instance, a whole afternoon might be taken up by carefuly gilding a palm-leaf, stuck with ostrich feather tips, to hang up as a new wall-decoration, while an ear of corn, equally bedizened, and tied with a flaunting bow of scarlet ribbon did strange duty as a thermometer stand on their writing table instead of one delicately carved in ivory.

When stained wood furniture came in, Mrs. Panton was its firm supporter, declaring 'how it could be so easily renovated and altered while the *unmoving* surface of rosewood, walnut and mahogany remains the same year *after* year.'

So it was that the Victorian boudoir of the '70s, '80s and '90s lost all sense of direction in regard to its decoration and furnishings. Very few things that it contained at this period appeal to collectors. As for the word itself, *boudoir*, who uses it today? And where does this room, with its elegant occupant dressed in a flowing Liberty silk gown dispensing tea to a group of ladies or, better still, to a tall, frock-coated figure of the opposite sex, calling so discreetly, survive?

5 The Library or Writing Room

161 *Library mantelpiece showing artistic arrangement of book shelves, tiled fire-place, patterned dado and Morris wallpaper. Designer Robert W. Edis*

The library was one of the best rooms in the house. It had been built early in the 18th century for a ball-room, a long narrow room with five tall windows; but James Dalbrook had improved it out of its original character by throwing out a large bay with three windows opening on to a semi-circular terrace. . . . It was too large a room to be warmed by a fire of ordinary dimensions but the fireplace added by James Dalbrook was of abnormal width and grandeur while the chimney piece was rich in coloured marbles and massive sculpture. The room was lined from floor to ceiling. Clusters of wax candles burned on the mantel-piece and two large moderator lamps stood on a massive carved oak table in the centre of the room – a table spacious enough to hold all the magazines, reviews and periodicals in three languages that were worth reading as well as guide-books, peerages, clergy and army lists.

Miss Braddon, *The Day Will Come*

James Dalbrook's library at Cheriton Manor followed much the same traditional lines laid down for the decor and furnishings of any gentleman's library in Victorian times. By and large, they were rooms usually 'dark with wood and leather' and often connected to a Gothic-styled conservatory with stained glass panes and a tiled, or mosaic inlaid, floor. The tiles were usually supplied by Minton.

Ceilings on the whole were high and cornices richly moulded with an outsize marble or serpentine mantel-piece or one in carved wood on whose broad ledge stood bronze candelabra, a French gilt clock under a glass shade and a pair of handsome Oriental vases or urns in Derby spar – it depended on the choice of the owner. The curtains, made either of dark-crimson, bottle-green or rich brown velvet or rep were long and thickly lined with heavy drapes. Careful attention was given to what we now call *door furniture* (i.e. door handles and plates, key-hole shields, etc.) which were of ivory or bronzed gilt.

Nearly always, the book-cases which lined the walls were free-standing. On their tops stood a marble or plaster bust as it might be of William Shakespeare, Dante or Sir Walter Scott. Every book-shelf was filled with handsomely bound books whose authors and subject-matter differed little in one library or another, while reference books included: *The Annual Register; The Racing Calendar*; and *The Gentleman's Magazine* with bound copies of *Punch* and *The Illustrated London News*. Nearly always, too, a door was contrived in one book-case, the library side of which was covered with sham volumes whose titles followed a traditional but amusing pattern. Ralph Nevill, an authoritative writer on Victorian social manners and customs, has recorded in *English Country House Life* (1925) that the poet Thomas Hood (1799–1845) invented the titles for the sham library books at Chatsworth. Among these were *Annual Parliaments: a Plan for Short Commons* and *Debrett on Chain Piers*. Ralph Nevill has testified also to the high literary standard of nineteenth-century libraries:

'The well-selected contents of which, now for the most part dispersed, bore testimony to the wide and practical mental outlook which those who formed it then must have possessed.

A good family library was considered an indispensable adjunct of a country house, and many a country gentleman who cut a good figure at Westminster owed his culture and learning to the well-bound books amongst which he had been taught as a child to browse . . . they might indeed have been called the mental nurseries of many distinguished soldiers, sailors and ambassadors as well as the forcing-houses where bishops and judges were trained.'

As a room, then, given over either to the carrying-out of estate duties and business or used for long hours of enjoyable reading and quiet meditation, it was deemed necessary to provide furniture conducive to male comfort. Thus chairs were of quite a different design to those belonging to the drawing-room and dining-room. Upholstered in leather, buttoned or stamped for the most part, they were low in the leg with a 'horse-shoe' back for support and short, padded arms. Or again, they were Gothic or Elizabethan in style with a tall, straight back and some carving. Library chairs can be found with a small, reading-desk attached on one side or with a useful, pull-out ledge on which to rest a book. In the 1840s, a so-called 'library' chair was actually designed which became very popular. Originally, its back and arms had formed one single unit repeating the shape of the old 'horse-shoe' chair. But by 1870, the inevitable row of turned balusters had been worked into the over-all design to give further comfort. A portable reading-desk that could be moved about for better light has survived and so have pairs of solid mahogany library steps which are now prized.

Small display cabinets to hold collections of ancient coins, seals, fossils, semi-precious stones, butterflies and stamps abounded in the Victorian library while oil lamps stood about with their inevitable green-glass shade, gilt-rimmed, to throw a benign circle of soft light on an opened book or writing-pad. Today, these same lamps have been adapted by the score for electric light and reappear in modern homes – at a price.

But the two most important items in a library over whose purchase care and attention were given was a large round mahogany or rosewood 'loo' table on a pedestal base and even more important, an equally large, flat-topped and often knee-holed writing desk or one with a roll-top or fall-front.

Early examples of a Victorian 'loo' table (a name derived from an eighteenth-century card game) have a central column in the form of a truncated cone standing on a triangular base supported by four, little lions' paws in brass. Such tables are in great demand today as they are just the right size to place in a modern living room or to use as a dinner table.

About 1854, the central column of a 'loo' table underwent a change, the base block being either partially or completely absorbed in the curves of the legs. By 1860, their old circular tops were made oval and often inlaid while their single, central column was broken down into a cage of four to five, small functional columns. Walnut was more popular than rosewood. This type of Victorian 'loo' table less elegant in design than its earlier prototype is not so popular and so less expensive to buy.

As Victorian men and women were compulsive letter writers, while many kept diaries, a writing-table played an important role in their lives. They were equipped with many desk accessories discarded now. To name but a few, there were bronzed metal letter racks, Gothic-styled, and envelope clips shaped in the form of a bird's head with its beak the clip; stationery cabinets of papier mâché, brass or mahogany with silver ornamentation; quill trays and quill cutters; pens and pen-wipers; inkpots and ink-stands of every shape and size; a taper-stick

163 (above) *Dead pigeon carved in limewood by James Minns, Norwich artist, 1877. Considered a suitable library embellishment*

164 (top right) *Brass paper-clip in shape of a duck's head, c. 1860*

165 (right) *Elaborate engraved and chased silver pen tray with matching candle snuffer and trimmer to stand on it, 1865*

and paper-knife. There were charming little round paperweights in heavy clear glass, handsome blotters and small boxes in carved wood from Switzerland or in mosaic work from Florence bought as souvenirs to hold seals for sealing wax on envelopes or for the new steel nibs and stamps when they came in.

Complete and often expensive 'Writing-sets' in papier mâché or irridescent pearl shell-ware were considered an important desk adjunct. In fact they were almost a status symbol, as they reflected the social position of their owner in an era when to write 'an elegant hand' was an upper class accomplishment and of primary importance. These 'Writing-sets' were composed usually of a matching stationery cabinet, an ink-stand, blotter and pen tray and belonged to the library or stood on a spare table in the drawing-room or boudoir. Bedroom sets were also available but they were not so grand in appearance being made of some pretty light wood like olive or sandalwood or in Tunbridge ware.

For a lady a slender pen of silver, ivory or agate was considered a suitable present. Indeed, the finer they were the better. Some figured in wills. For instance, in 1853, on the death of Amelia Opie (1769–1853) it was found that she had left her elaborate 'beadwork' pen to a friend. Seals came into this category, favourite stones for them being lapis lazuli, bloodstone, onyx, cornelian and amethyst. They were in constant use till 1840 when the appearance of the 'gummed' envelope put them out of action.

WRITING TABLES

'Mary Anne cast longing glances at the solitaire board, with its variety of glass marbles, which she liked to run round the edge of it. But she did not dare to venture in its vicinity. Instead, she sidled up to the table where Aunt Anna was writing and began to examine the contents of the handsome silver inkstand with its tray of quill pens, its bowl of shot and the wafer box, and the sticks of red and black ceiling wax. She attempted to remove the silver candlestick with the miniature red wax candle from its pedestal between the inkpots. This action disturbed her aunt who looked up.'   *A Book With Seven Seals* (Anon)

This is merely one of numerous descriptions in Victorian fiction when a lady is found seated at her writing-table like Aunt Anna. But in this case, attention is drawn to the actual equipment of her writing-table which might have been a small *bonheur du jour* inherited from a Regency mother or a Davenport.

A Davenport on account of its small, compact size and elegant design was most comfortable to sit at (and still is), hence its popularity in Victorian times. Usually made of rosewood or walnut, it is best described as having a long, sloping lid with ample knee space provided below and a longish deep drawer (sometimes more) on its right-hand side that is pulled out by a small knob or knobs. The name 'Davenport' is derived from its designer's name (a naval captain) and early examples that date from about 1800 are high and square with a top brass rail.

Some Davenports have boldly curving and carved leg supports with compartments for stationery, one small one having a lid to contain an ink-pot; others possess, even, a secret drawer which can be released by a hidden spring. Others, again, like one in my possession are decorated by a panel on either side showing bouquets of flowers inlaid in ivory and different, pale-coloured woods. Besides the Davenport of elegant appearance, others square and of a sturdier build were produced for the school-room. On account of its compact size and general practicability, the Davenport retains its place in the world of period writing-tables by still being in demand today. Prices for them vary in relation to their condition, when found, or the quality of workmanship shown. But as small distinctive pieces of Victorian furniture, their value tends to rise and not fall.

When bamboo furniture became fashionable from the 1860s, much of this cane material became incorporated in the design of both library and drawing-room writing tables by way of legs for lightness, and for up-to-date decoration. Another type of writing-table of this time imitated the Queen Anne style of kidney-shaped table with walnut veneer and a brass rail. Others, again, were small, square and sturdy with a roll top or fall-front and featured brass handles. Still later, towards the close of the century, the writing-table

166 (left) *Davenport with side drawers, 1878*
167 *Davenport with railed top and inlaid Escritoire*

168 *Solid and firm 'pedestal' library table with drawers and raised flap on top*

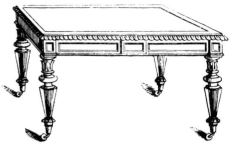

169 *Another table with carved legs and carved moulded edge*

was subjected to fresh treatment by designers leading the Art Nouveau movement. One notable example of cabinet work at this time can be studied at the William Morris Gallery at Walthamstow where A. H. Mackmurdo's writing-desk is on view. Another example in oak with copper hinges (1896) which has a matching writing chair is in the Victoria and Albert Museum, South Kensington. It is by C. F. A. Voysey.

But of all writing-tables, known and unknown, surely the most famous and repeatedly photographed for illustration in books on Victorian furniture, were those used by her late Majesty, Queen Victoria, at Windsor, Osborne and Balmoral. Take the one at Windsor, beginning with the room itself, a private writing-room which lay on the first floor and presented an amazing spectacle of multitudinous and incongruous objects ranging from the ridiculous to the sublime almost. Dominated by a large oriel window, the enormous marble mantel-piece was rich in carved mythological figures, while below lurked a cheap

brass fender from Birmingham. In the grate, birch logs were burnt, no other kind of wood being permissible. On the mantelpiece itself was a large Empire clock flanked on either side by a Chinese vase enclosed in a glass shade. There were several bronze statuettes and a pair of heavy candelabra. Displayed all round the room, on small tables, were animal figurines, plaster busts and a motley collection of sentimental and often cheap souvenirs, some in glass cases; others not. A large circular table bore a perfect forest of framed photographs while plush drapes almost concealed the piano and more plush, buttoned and padded, covered chairs and couches.

Two flimsy bamboo tables stood on each side of Her Majesty's actual writing-table, whose top 'resembled a stall in some Fancy Bazaar', it has been said, so littered was it with desk paraphernalia like quill pens in gold trays, paperweights, etc., and to crown all, a cockerel's head in gold flaunting a bright scarlet comb doing duty as a pen-wiper.

PORTABLE WRITING DESKS

A small portable writing desk that could be moved about from room to room or taken away when travelling was a necessary and important item in a Victorian lady's or gentleman's life. At Chawton Cottage, Chawton in Hampshire, one time home of the Austen family, Jane Austen's portable writing desk still lies on the sofa table in the drawing-room. Another of later date, can be seen at Haworth Parsonage Museum which once belonged to Charlotte Brontë. Hers is a typical example of

early Victorian cabinet work being veneered with mahogany and decorated with a narrow line of brass inlay. It has a brass lock-plate while another small brass plate on the lid is engraved with the name: 'C. Brontë'.

But Victorian portable writing-desks were made in other mediums besides rosewood and mahogany. There were some very handsome ones in papier mâché, glossy-black and gleaming with 'pearl' ornament; others in pearl shell-ware. After a little girl had learnt to write and compose a letter, it was her dream to have a little writing-desk of her own. Miss Braddon, the well-known Victorian lady novelist, has described the one given to her on her eighth birthday:

'It was a beautiful brand-new mahogany desk with a red velvet slope and a glass ink-bottle; such a desk as might be bought now (*c.* 1890) for three-and-sixpence but in the 1840s cost at least half-a-guinea.'

Miss Braddon tells how she kept in her desk sticks of variegated sealing-wax, speckled with gold, and a tiny seal with an intaglio showing Pliny's Doves. But who Pliny was and why he kept doves she was never told.

Today a small portable Victorian writing-desk in mahogany with a red velvet slope would cost more than half a guinea, particularly if it had literary associations. But quite apart from these, they are well worth tracking down as attractive examples of Victorian cabinet work in miniature.

VICTORIAN STATIONERY

While on the subject of writing-desks, attention must be drawn to the different kinds of writing-sheets and envelopes, besides wedding and funeral cards that were in everyday use in the Victorian era. For it was the time when news, mournful or happy, of a birth, death, wedding or christening was announced through the medium of writing in a family and not through the press.

The field of Victorian paper ephemera is a fascinating one that is still largely undocumented, so the collector is offered much interest in it added to the fun of original research. As we know, a saying has been handed down from mother to daughter, governess to pupil that as in the case of her gloves and shoes 'One can always tell a lady by her writing-paper'. At no other time, possibly, was this saying so well-observed, as when the Queen herself was maintaining almost a daily correspondence with her enormous number of relatives, at home or abroad, on paper deeply-edged in black and headed by her initials V.I.R. in black, too. For during the greater part of her long reign, her life was passed in mourning, not only for Prince Albert, but for some other close or distant relative.

In *Cranford* published in 1853, Mrs. Gaskell describes how Miss Jenkyn favoured 'a square sheet' which was then considered unfashionable. Equally in poor taste was the large round red wafer with which she sealed her envelopes. For these had been 'banished from polite society after the publication of Miss Edgeworth's *Patronage.*' Charming little coloured wafers in pale-pink, Wedgwood blue, lilac, celadon green and grey embossed in white relief with the minute figure of a deer, greyhound, dove, or floral sprig were favoured. Many were marked, too, with a girlish name of the period like Lucy or Caroline. When in mourning a black-and-white wafer decorated by a black cross, an ivy leaf or anchor was considered most suitable. Recently a whole collection of little decorated wafers turned up in mint condition in a box picked up in the Bermondsey Market for a few shillings.

From an early age, a Victorian child learnt his, or her, letters on writing-sheets with hand-coloured borders on much the same principle that little girls learnt how to do various forms of stitchery with their needle on a sampler. Then, as today, children had their own stationery decorated by suitable coloured motifs on sheets and envelopes. In the adult world, small single or double sheets of cream-smooth paper is found headed by the most entrancing little vignettes in sepia or black engraving. These vignettes show famous houses like Haddon Hall or Abbotsford along with others not so well-known to the public. Many of these charmingly depicted houses have long crumbled into dust. This kind of early decorated writing paper was put out by various printing firms, to name two, Messrs. Newman and Co. of 48 Watling Street and London and Messrs. Rock and Co. also of London.

When staying away at a popular sea-side resort like Hastings or Brighton or a spa town like Tunbridge Wells, a local stationer had writing-sheets headed by an engraving of a local picturesque view or historic building for sale. These sheets were bought by visitors. Today this writing paper has the same topographical interest as small glass paperweights. Not to be outdone by local stationers trading in attractive paper ware, hotels catered for their rich clients' 'writing activities' by providing free writing sheets and envelopes. These carried an engraved picture of the hotel in question: hotels of baronial style with embattled facades pepper-pot towers from one of which fluttered a flag so often.

In the 1860s, when 'Illumination' came in and

the Gothic style was fashionable, ladies took to designing their own monograms or initials for their writing-paper. Before me, as I type, lies a double sheet of faded and thin, smooth paper headed by the kneeling figure of a Pre-Raphaelite angel encircled by rosy garlands and gilt swags and curlicues. This sheet, dated 17 November, 1847, was the work of Lady Murray, artistic wife of Sir John Murray of Philiphaugh who was an early illuminator.

About this time, too, there was an odd vogue for decorating with pen-and-ink or in watercolours the outside of an envelope, a hobby no doubt inspired by the introduction of 'The Mulready Envelope' which is of much interest to stamp collectors.

On 10 January, 1840, the Penny Post, brainchild of Rowland Hill, was inaugurated in the United Kingdom and in honour of the occasion, the P. O. conceived the idea of approaching the well-known Royal Academician, William Mulready, to design a special envelope for 'franking' letters. This he did. However, Mulready's envelope, which shows the figure of Britannia sending forth her winged messengers to all corners of the earth, was not in use for long, giving way to a more practical plain envelope embossed with the now long defunct red penny stamp and gummed as well. After writing-sheets headed by vignettes of country houses or seaside views, came 'illuminated' monograms, crests and initials followed, an engraved and full postal address with the tiny reproduction of a puffing steam-engine and the name of the nearest station. Charming little boxes of extremely ornate writing paper and matching envelopes were also obtainable. They were sold for some special purpose like the sending of happy birthday wishes or to express pleasure at receiving a present. With their embossed surrounds or exquisitely fine paper-lace borders, painted with sprays of flowers and other suitable motifs, these fairy-like sheets and tiny envelopes are redolent of the sentiment and the highly romantic tone of the period. In every way, they are near relations to valentines; in fact, at times, they did duty for them, when discreetly worded messages of love under cover of an innocent missive was dispatched by young girls to their male admirers. Those same young gentlemen who had called earlier, top hat in hand, and in lavender trousers, to leave prettily decorated cards on them.

Today, in coarsened form and not nearly so attractive, an ornate type of floral stationery has been revived that is sold under the name of 'Notelets': much favoured by the younger generation. The well-known papermaking firm of John Dickinson and Company have recently put out not only a new range of writing paper with flowery envelopes and linings, but what they call 'Lyric Wallets' and 'Love Notes'. These take the form of tiny, heart-shaped, pink sheets with envelopes to match. What could be more Victorian?

MEMORIAL CARDS

No self-respecting Victorian family could be without a large quantity of writing-sheets deeply edged in black with envelopes to match to use when in mourning. Envelopes were sealed always with a blob of black wax or a small black wafer that was embossed in white relief with a marble cross, an anchor or an ivy leaf. After the conventional period for mourning had elapsed, black-edged sheets were exchanged for violet ones. Apart from mourning paper, an enormous number of memorial cards to announce a death or give notice of a forthcoming funeral were despatched by Victorians. This custom has long fallen into complete disuse.

At the recent 'Death, Heaven and Victorians' staged in Brighton, a large selection of memorial cards (1855–1895) from various museums was on view. There was one card issued on the death of Queen Victoria which was elaborately edged in black-and-silver that bore the solemn words:

'The entire World mourns her Loss.'

Weeping willows, classic urns, cast-iron tombstone fencing, desolate broken pillars, a screen of ivy tendrils, sometimes even that sacred floral emblem, the *passion-flower*, were all considered suitable motifs to appear on funeral cards. These cards belong to the world of cut-paper work; to the infinite delicate skill wielded by an amateur, or professional, with a sharp pair of scissors. At first, the special paper dedicated to their work was imported from France, but during the 1790s English paper-makers so improved the quality of

170   *Gothic-inspired memorial card in loving memory of Mr. Joseph Nuttle, died 5 December 1896. In its original maplewood frame. Printed by J. Hannaford, Undertaker*

their goods that they produced a far tougher paper than that made in France and so took over the market. Throughout the Victorian era, all material for 'Cut-outs' cards with finely-pierced borders and pin-pricked ornament was English in make and origin. Today, the collector of paper ephemera is faced with a fascinating variety of embossed cards for all kinds of celebrations, ranging from private invitations to Christenings, Weddings and Funerals to those more public such as City Banquets, Royal Balls and State Dinners.

Funeral cards range from those with black flock and silver decorations made by Wood, 1871, to some in paper embossed with a tomb, the figures of mourners and weeping willows on a black ground or hand-coloured, even, and mounted on black velvet for framing. The latter type sometimes incorporated a tinted photograph of the deceased with his name and date of death inscribed in the space below. Suitable verses were often included. (Chapter X: Cottage Art).

INKPOTS

During the nineteenth century, inkpots were produced in their thousands to meet the enormous demand. For it was not only the educated classes that needed them, but those poor and humble now being taught at last how to read and write.

The collector is faced then with myriad examples of Victorian inkpots, ornate or plain, fantastical and comic, in every kind of medium, too, from gold to pewter, and fine porcelain to common earthenware. He has only to make up his mind what type he wishes to concentrate on and then follow his fancy from china inkpots modelled in the shape of a blackamoor's head to one, made in wood, like a miniature writing-desk complete with drawers for stamps and rubber bands, etc. and two little glass ink wells for red and black ink.

From about the 1830s, a distinct touch of fantasy became noticeable in the fashioning of an inkpot and many small-scale ones in silver-gilt were modelled in the form of animals. A donkey carrying panniers of which each contains an ink-well on either side of his flanks was made by J. & J. Aldous, 1836; another, a be-hatted and jacketted monkey gaily beating a drum with ink-well con-

cealed inside, by Messrs. Rawlins & Sumner, 1850.

In her book, *Notable Women Authors,* describing interviews she had had with celebrated lady Victorian novelists Helen Black was much struck by 'the great solid silver donkey with panniers which must have held at least a pint of ink and which stands on a table close to an oval Venetian

171–2   *Unusual brass inkwell shaped like a miniature sea-chest made by the House of Leuchars, London in 1864, engraved regimental crest is of the Berkshire Volunteers; (right) Lady's bronzed metal inkpot with ivy-leaf and robin adornment has a pink glass trumpet-vase for flowers, 1870*

glass framed in gold and silver' that belonged to Helen Mathers (Mrs. Reeves) author of that Victorian tear-jerker *Comin' Thro' the Rye* (1875). Obviously it was one of Mr. Aldous's. At the Great Exhibition, and later at the Crystal Palace, many curious novelties bloomed in what was designated as 'the natural imitative style'. From now on, as one advertisement read: 'An ink-stand instead of being literally a glass bottle set in fine bronze, may be fashioned to represent anything from a fountain with a muse inspiring its flow to a metal reproduction of Petrach's ink-stand brought from Italy by Miss Edgeworth.'

This reproduction appears to have been put out by the metal firm of Messrs. Messinger & Sons.

So the Victorian ink-pot broke away finally from the earlier Regency 'standish', as it was called, complete with its two sunken ink-wells, pounce or 'sandaric' pot containing sand to scatter over wet ink and dry it, plus of course, a little taper stick and quill vase. Methods of writing were altering and new aids appearing such as blotting paper and steel nibs. Though blotting paper was invented as early as the fifteenth century, it was of such a coarse nature and grey to look at, that it stayed in the counting-house, being considered unfit to grace a lady's home.

The 'Gillott' steel pen was patented about 1820 by Joseph Gillott of Birmingham and by the end of the 1850s was in full production, revolutionising writing techniques for ladies and gentlemen.

173   *Massive 'Berlin black' inkstand, 1845*

174   *Carefully modelled mahogany inkstand in shape of a little writing-desk, with a tiny pyramid form of glass inkwell, 1865*

Hand-writing, indeed, was never to be so elegant and stylised again. For the age of 'The Pickwick, the Owl and the Waverley Pen' had come but whether as 'a boon and blessing to men' remains a debateable point.

PENS AND PAPER KNIVES, BLOTTERS AND TAPERSTICKS

Until the widespread use of steel pens and nibs the number and variety of small pen knives kept on the writing-table for 'the mending of a quill', a crow-quill or otherwise, was legion. With shining blades and handles of mother of pearl, ivory or horn, or in the case of luxury trifles in gold, silver and tortoiseshell, both pen and paper knives were considered worthy of a cutler's and a turner's best skill. Today, however, they have left their old traditional place beside a quill-tray as they are no longer needed. Nor do they sharpen a pencil when so many foolproof kinds of pencil-sharpeners abound. On the other hand, an attractive paper knife skilfully 'turned' in ivory, agate or Whitby

175   *Small square lady's papier mâché blotting book with tassel*
176   *Metal quill holder in form of a squirrel, 1865*

jet, in serpentine or wood, can still be used on the writing-table and with a blotter to match, most collectable. Victorian blotters cannot be more handsome with their ornate papier mâché, pearl shell and brass covers. Some blotters are inlaid with small mosaic motifs of Italian origin on their front cover.

Before the arrival of gummed envelopes much time and patience was required before despatching a letter by way of folding, addressing and sealing it. For sealing, a small candle or taperstick was essential on a writing-table. The latter object wound round with waxed wick can be found in silver, plate, china or bronzed brass. The model of an elaborate taperstick is illustrated in *The Connoisseur's Complete Guides* (page 1385). It was produced by Messrs. Elkington in 1844 to the design of the Chevalier Benjamin Schlick, a Danish architect who was in their employ and much influenced by Greek, Roman and Etruscan modes. His taperstick follows the form of a foot in a Roman sandal.

Elaborately embroidered pen-wipers in beadwork or Berlin woolwork that were largely the handiwork of Victorian ladies for Fancy Fairs,

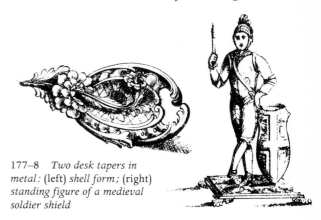

177–8 *Two desk tapers in metal:* (left) *shell form;* (right) *standing figure of a medieval soldier shield*

Charitable Bazaars and birthday gifts form another group of attractive desk items to be collected. They can be picked up together with slim, bead-worked pens or those made from the fine quills of the porcupine. So too can intricately carved intaglio signets which have been in use since the days of the Pharaohs and stamp boxes in Tunbridge ware. Many of these have a real penny stamp on the lid, varnished over, or a stamp made in mosaic.

BOOK-MARKERS

'"This is the last day of the year", said the Parson impressively as they began to find their places in their Bibles by the aid of blue ribbon book-markers, made and presented by their aunts and embellished with strips of perforated cardboard and texts worked thereon.'

Anon, *A Book with Seven Seals*

This quotation pinpoints the widespread use of book-markers during mid-Victorian days when they were given as birthday presents to little girls or made by young ladies as sentimental souvenirs for their beaux. Nearly everyone going to Church on Sunday carried in their prayer books a book-marker made from a watered-silk blue or purple ribbon if rich or from cardboard if poor.

Book-markers have been the companion of Bibles and prayer-books for centuries. Theirs is an ancient history dating back to before the reign of Henry VIII, when specially designed and embroidered panels first came to be used in the bindings of devotional books.

At the Bodleian Library, Oxford, Queen Elizabeth I's Bible has been preserved complete with its heavily fringed silk marker. It was a New Year's gift, presented to her in 1584 by Christopher Barker, the printer. Another book-marker of this day was formed by attaching a number of different coloured ribbons to a pad, or cushion, at the top and then tying these ribbons in knots at the end. Yet another kind belonging to a Bible printed in 1632 that is owned by the British and Foreign Bible Society has a contemporary marker consisting of 12 plaited silk cords attached to a small roll at the top and ending in silver knots and small silk tassels.

In the long production line of Victorian parlour pastimes for ladies, book-markers were almost top favourites because they were so easily and quickly made and lent themselves so well to all kinds of extra ornamentation.

Book-markers can be divided into three distinct groups: the religious; the sentimental; and the commercial. The number, and kind, of religious book-markers are legion and the earliest feature for the most part holy texts and sacred symbols like a cross or funeral wreath. These motifs were embroidered with floss silks on ribbon in ivory-white, deep crimson, purple or ecclesiastical blue colours. Those for the poor and pious folk of rural England were made of strips of perforated board or canvas, worked in cross-stitch with coloured wool. 'God is Love'; 'Faith'; 'I shall pass through this World'; and 'Christ is my Saviour' are typical among the hundreds of texts chosen to decorate religious book-markers.

The sentimental book-marker represents those made for souvenir presents or love tokens; for children's birthdays and festive occasions like Christmas and Easter; or, and this constitutes a large class, to commemorate Coronations, Royal Weddings, Jubilees and other events of national importance and interest. Woven in silks on the Jacquard looms of Coventry, they were on show at the Great Exhibitions of 1851 and 1862.

It was Thomas Stevens who gave his name (Chapter X: Cottage Art) to a particular kind of small, loom-woven picture reproduced on ribbon of which no less than 500 different subjects were listed for display on his 'Illuminated Pure Silk Woven Book-Markers' by the year 1870. Some of these book-markers are decorated with bead-trim and tassels; others mounted on ivory were for those large Bibles used on the altar or lectern; others, again, appealed to a music-hall loving public by having bars of music and lines from popular songs imprinted, while some even bore quotations from Shakespeare and other celebrated authors as well as favourite lines from hymns.

The Commercial book-marker was produced for ordinary people who bought branded goods in grocery shops or departmental stores. Nearly all of a comic character, they reflect contemporary taste. Today, in the supermarket, we are often given a free sample of some household commodity like soap powder with a plastic rose too gaudy by half. In Victorian times, this practice was also carried out but it was a book-marker – and not an imitation flower – that was found tucked up inside a box of Pears' Soap or Messrs. Huntley & Palmer's biscuits. A highly entertaining collection of commercial book-markers could be made for they are genuine joke-makers. What about 'The Nun Book Mark' once given away to a buyer of Cherry Blossom Boot Polish in 1889? Printed on it are the following words which tell how in the High Court of Justice:

'Gosnell V Durrant on Jan 28th, 1887, Mr. Justice Chitty granted a Perpetual Injunction with Costs restraining Mr. George Reynolds Durrant from enfringing Messrs. John Gosnell & Co.'s registered Trade Mark CHERRY BLOSSOM.'

Collectors of Victorian book-markers might be interested to learn how a book-marker was made from instructions that appeared in *The Girl's Own Book of Amusements, Studies and Employments* of 1876:

'Take a piece of perforated cardboard and cut it about 6 inches long and 2 inches wide, work on it in cross-stitch with coloured sewing-silk any text, motto or name that you may choose, then work a border round, and stitch on the back of the cardboard a piece of ribbon two inches wide, twelve inches long, fringe the end of the ribbon. The sewing-silk and ribbon must match in colour.'

179–80 Pair of domed glass 'souvenir' paperwights, showing coloured print of The Paragon & Fort Crescent, Margate, and The Tower at Blackpool, c. 1860

GLASS PAPERWEIGHTS

Glass paperweights, the products of Stourbridge, Baccarat, Clichy and Apsley Pellat fetch astronomical sums in the sale-rooms. But as they belong to the millionaire class of collectors they will not be dealt with here. Instead, I will take another type of Victorian glass paperweight; those small, round, engaging little objects made of heavy clear glass under whose domed tops a coloured print, or engraving, was stuck. These miniature pictures usually show some picturesque building or site, now vanished of the place where they were once sold for a few shillings as souvenirs of travel. Topographically, then, they are interesting because they depict the world once known to Victorian tourists. Possess one and there in retrospect is the sea front, of some South Coast town like Ramsgate or Brighton. Or it may be the Pantiles at Tunbridge Wells with elegant figures in bonnet and shawl strolled down them. In these days of wholesale demolition, these once so cheap but decorative souvenirs of a happy holiday visit have a modest charm, all their own. Acquire them and one acquires part of lost, Victorian England.

Another type of paperweight produced in different mediums such as marble, brass, slag and serpentine was the work of individual craftsmen. But they are too widely divergent in subject-matter to be placed in one particular group. For instance, at a recent 'Death, Heaven and the Victorians' Exhibition at Brighton, a paperweight made in white marble with the date 'May 24th, 1861' was on view. This paperweight, whose top

181   *Small square marble paperweight with inlaid flower spray (pietra dura)*

182   *An essentially comic example of Victorian taste, metal be-hatted goat paperweight*

was adorned with painted pansies and an angel standing beside a cross, is supposed to have been the work of Queen Victoria's eldest daughter (Vicky), then the Crown Princess of Prussia, to commemorate the death of her beloved father, the Prince Consort. It is now at Osborne House, Isle of Wight.

IVORY DESK THERMOMETERS

Ivory is at once the most durable yet yielding of substances, yielding that is to the skill of the carver's knife. Since time immemorial the smooth pale surface of ivory has preserved not only the first scratchings of primitive man but the most delicate and intricate carvings as well. The best or *true* ivory comes from the tusk of an elephant, which can belong either to the large African species or to its smaller Indian counterpart.

At the Great Exhibition of 1851, several monster tusks were on view, including one pair which weighed some 325 pounds! As an artistic substance capable of being rendered into many desirable objects ivory, in Victorian times, was made into brooches, bracelets and lockets; buttons and snuff-boxes; toilet accessories; knife-handles, billiard balls and caskets. Ivory can be turned, too, very successfully, on the lathe. About 1830, a sculptor, Benjamin Cheverton, invented a small-scale machine with which he reproduced marble statuettes, then very much in vogue, in ivory. But these ivory figurines were not commercial when done in any number as materials were so expensive.

One of the most interesting objects 'turned' in

ivory from about the 1870s were ivory desk thermometers. The making of them was sponsored by a family called Holzapffel whose head came over from Germany, possibly from Nuremberg, a centre of the turning trade, in 1787. After settling in London as a worker in tools and lathes Holzapffel's eldest son, Charles, (1806–1847) was born an Englishman. Receiving a good education, Charles became a highly skilled mechanician and the author of *Turning and Mechanical Manipulation,* a work in five volumes, the first volume being published in 1856 after his death. As this mammoth tome had not been fully completed by Charles Holzapffel his son, John Jacob, who followed the family profession and became a Master of the Worshipful Company of Turners finished it for him.

John Jacob Holzapffel was an even more influential figure than his father in the revival of the ancient trade of Turnery in all its branches in mid-Victorian times. For some time, now, the effective control of many an old-established City Company over their respective trade had been almost abandoned. This was particularly true of the Worshipful Company of Turners. But it was a matter soon to be remedied by John Jacob Holzapffel who conceived the brilliant idea of offering an Annual

183–4 *Two intricately cut ivory desk thermometers. One imitating a gothic spire; the other minaret form, 1878*

185 *Three Tunbridge-ware desk thermometers: tombstone shape; Cleopatra's Needle and Pillar, c. 1878*

Prize of £5 for the best example of turnery executed by a member of the Company during the final year of his apprenticeship.

To begin with, results for the setting up of this annual award were disappointing as only two entries for the first competition were received. In consequence, the Prize money had to be divided between the two contestants for two fishing-rods submitted. However, under the vigorous direction of John Jacob Holzapffel, a new class for amateurs 'in ornamental turning in ivory and hardwood' was formed in 1878 and added to that of turning in wood.

After being widely advertised in the Press, the new class for ivory workers created great interest and when the Exhibition of their submitted work was opened on October 7th at the Egyptian Hall, London, the public flocked in.

In the eighteenth century, a gentleman and, for that matter, a lady too, as in the case of the original, clever and witty Duchess of Portland, were much addicted to 'turning in ivory and jet' as a home pastime. After 1878, this same amateur hobby was taken up by many Victorians with similar enthusiasm. And there, at hand, to give them expert advice on this new accomplishment was John Jacob Holzapffel who had just seen the last volume of his father's by now classic manual through the press.

It is in this volume, Volume V of the series, that the illustration of a Clock Tower in Ivory (Fig. 486, Plate XLX, page 464) with others of a similar character can be seen; from them derives the over-

all design for an ivory desk thermometer so popular in the Victorian library.

The many processes involved in making an ivory thermometer are far too technical and complicated to go into here, but the finished model, Gothic nearly always in style, with slender rising columns and rounded pillars building up to support a graceful, church-like spire is fascinating.

It was at Number 64, Charing Cross and at 127, Long Acre that the family firm of Holzapffel & Co. was established. Here amateur turners could call and be supplied with every kind of tool and lathe for their hobby and be instructed too if they wished. Leading figures who 'turned' in ivory and thoroughly enjoyed this agreeable pastime were Leopold, King of the Belgians and, like the eighteenth-century Duchess of Portland before her, the Lady Amherst of Hackney.

But Victorian desk thermometers come in other mediums besides ivory. A 'Cleopatra's needle' thermometer and other 'obelisk' types which date roughly from 1878 can be found in heavy glass and Tunbridge ware, the latter examples featuring cube mosaic work. Both small and large monolith thermometers in glass are sometimes engraved or painted in floral motifs. They are pretty objects for a writing-table, besides being collecting specimens. In the Pinto Collection of Wooden Bygones at Birmingham Museum and Art Gallery, a rare, combined Thermometer-and-Compass, octagonal stand can be seen. The price for antique ivory thermometers vary according to quality of workmanship.

6 The Best Bedroom

186 'The Best Bedroom': lady regarding her suite of cream furniture with pink
decoration. Exhibited in the Suffolk Street Galleries, 1882

Maria Godolphin turned on her uneasy couch and lay with eyes open; anything for a change in the monotonous hours. The dressing-table, its large glass, its costly ornaments, stood between the windows; she could trace its outlines, almost the pattern of its white lace drapery over the pink silk. The white window-curtains were looped with pink; some of the pretty white chairs were finished off with pink beading. A large cheval glass swung in a corner. On a console of white marble, its frettings of gilt, stood Maria's Prayer-book and Bible with 'Wilson's Supper and Sacra Privata.'

A small ornamental bookcase was on the opposite side, containing some choice works culled from the literature of the day. On the table, in the centre of the room, lay a small travelling desk.

Mrs. Henry Wood, *The Shadow of Ashlydyat*

Maria Godolphin's charming bedroom in her home at Prior's Ash was typical of many another which, like the boudoir, reflected a lady's taste and contained her most intimate possessions.

Time dealt lightly with the Victorian bedroom and it changed little until the International Exhibition of 1862 introduced many new modes in furniture and colour-schemes besides the cult for Oriental fashions.

Whereas the Victorian drawing-room was showy and crowded with as many objects as possible, bedrooms were mainly kept light in treatment of colour with pretty rose-and-ribbon types of wall papers and muslin drapes to windows. What furniture there was, like a wardrobe, chest of drawers, wash stand and chairs, etc. was admirably made on simple lines. A low comfortable sofa was allowed on which a lady could recline and a chintz-covered ottoman was usually found at the bottom of the bed in which spare blankets were kept. Sometimes, an ottoman claimed special attention, such as the one made of papier mâché in 1840 for the Duchess of Sutherland which was described as 'Beautiful and Novel.'

At first, beds were of the four-poster family left over from earlier times, but these gave way to the half-tester in wood or iron with two posts from which hung chintz or cretonne curtains. Charles Eastlake favoured the tester-style and designed an 'Iron Bedstead with Canopy' (1878). In *The Bedroom and Boudoir* published this same year, Lady Barker described some wooden beds with plain rails at foot and head, made low, and having a spring frame with one thick mattress laid on top which were being patronised. Bed curtains seemed to be going out except where a lofty-ceilinged room necessitated a more formal and furnished style of bed. Then Lady Barker recommended 'Sweeping curtains of silk or satin gathered up quite or almost at the ceiling to fall in ample folds on either side of a wide low bedstead.' A fashion being revived today.

Brass beds, much ornamented with curlicues, knobs and scrollwork now staging a happy come-back began to appear and soon were popular. A shop catalogue of the time lists: 'Brass bedsteads in Stock. From 8/9 to 55 Guineas'. Similar brass beds would be many times this price today. Pictures considered most suitable to hang in a bedroom were contributed by gifted members of the family. So Swiss and Italian landscapes in chalk or water-colour reminiscent

92

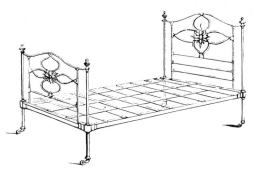

189 *Example of brass bed, 1851, with light, graceful lines at head and bottom*

188 *Suggested design for a small single bed in wood by Lady Barker, 1878, showing corner of period bedroom*

190 *A tent bedstead complete with draped curtains and frilled base to bed*

of a trip abroad were proudly exhibited; for sketching was rated high as a genteel accomplishment. Besides landscapes there were portrait heads in ink or pencil, silhouettes and copies, possibly, of well-known masterpieces inspired by lessons with a drawing-master. For good measure 'Shanklin Chine: Drawn in Alum Bay Sands' bought as a holiday souvenir in the Isle of Wight or a romantic 'Castle in Cork' when touring Scotland were included also. Today all such pictures find a ready market.

An early Victorian bedroom of much charm and character belonged to Mrs. Dulcimer who lived in an old country parsonage.

'They went up to Mrs. Dulcimer's bedroom, a large old-fashioned chamber with an immense four-post bedstead and flowery chintz curtains, a muslin-draped dressing-table adorned with a great many china pots and a pincushion that was a noteworthy feature. Mrs. Dulcimer's devotional books with a great many markers in them, were arranged on either side of the looking-glass . . .

'There was a bright fire and the chintz-covered sofa was wheeled in front of it. Between the fire and the sofa was Mrs. Dulcimer's work-table and on the table the missionary basket full of ingenious trifles, useful or useless. Babies' socks, muffatees, pincushions of every shape and design and a variety of the aggravating family of mats.'

191   *Long dressing table between windows;* (right) *toilet table, c. 1870*

192   *'La Duchesse' dressing table, 1870–80*

THE DRESSING-TABLE

The most important feature in the Victorian bedroom was the Dressing-Table, which stood usually before a window. Though late eighteenth-century Sheraton and Hepplewhite dressing-tables were elegant and graceful, they lacked certain practical

193   *A chest-of-drawers toilet table with unusual brass handles shaped like swans. Separate small swing mirror*

advantages demanded by a generation who came to possess more and more toilet and dressing accessories.

Today, we have only to remember the solid, country-house style of dressing-table used by our grandmothers and great-grandmothers to envy them the comfort and amplitude of space afforded by their broad tops and firm wooden frames made, more often than not, by the estate or village carpenter. In spite, though, of their solid nature they were essentially feminine on account of their draped or pleated muslin skirts, often ribboned and be-laced, which were placed over an under-skirt of pale-blue, pink or lilac baptiste. As for their imposing array of gold, silver or ivory combs and brushes, their deeply-cut glass scent bottles, pin boxes and hatpin holders, little china ring-stands and paper and shell-decorated glove boxes, never had such a number of miscellaneous objects been seen on a lady's dressing-table nor would again; what is more, there are few of these items which are not being collected today.

Lady Barker supported 'the old-fashioned dressing-table of deal with muslin draperies over soft-hued muslin or baptiste as nothing else afforded a prettier spot of colour so long as a skimpy and coarse muslin flounce over a tight-fitting skirt of pink calico was not added with its hideous crackle.'

She drew attention also to another type of dressing-table making its debut. This was called

'La Duchesse' and it was an adaptation really of an étagère complete with its brass rail and ormolu decoration but with a toilet mirror added. This essentially feminine 'Duchesse' type of dressing-table was followed by others which looked more like a chest of drawers (the drawers fitted with brass handles), and with a toilet mirror either rectangular or shield-shaped that swung between two supports with little trinket drawers below. These dressing-tables of mahogany or Victorian pine when stripped of their paint, varnished and polished are well worth buying.

Victorian toilet mirrors vary very much in size when found separated from the tables they once stood on. The familiar 'cheval' type of mahogany swing-mirror, so long in use, were once known by the pretty name of 'Psyches'. Others were called 'Skeleton' glasses and these had straight or gracefully curved feet and brackets. Some more were bow-fronted or serpentine in shape like the dressing-table-cum-chest of drawers that supported them. Lady Barker liked both the style and frame of a lady's toilet mirror to harmonise with her dressing-table and vetoed the use of 'draped' looking-glasses on account of their being able to catch on fire from a lighted candle put too close to them.

Many Victorian toilet mirrors that imitate the form of Georgian oval and shield ones are made in deal veneered with walnut, an eighteenth-century habit. Later examples come in mahogany and can be lined or bordered with contrasting woods. They carry, too, brass ornamentation by way of handles and key-plates and stand usually on a base of small drawers. On the whole, prices now being asked for Victorian toilet mirrors are not at all disapproportionate to their pleasing shapes and good looks.

TOILET EQUIPAGES

This rather pompous name was given by leading makers of fine porcelain who produced elaborate china toilet sets for the dressing-table.

One of the most magnificent of these 'toilet-equipages' is preserved today at Osborne House, Isle of Wight. It is still laid out on Queen Victoria's dressing-table which stands in the window of her dressing-room. It was given to her as a Christmas present in 1853 by Prince Albert and was made by Minton. It consists of an oval looking-glass, mounted in porcelain coloured blue and gilt on white, and furnished with candelabra for two lights on each side. Furthermore, it is decorated with little white porcelain angels and carries the V.R. motif surmounted by a coloured and gilt crown. Other pieces in this handsome toilet service include a tray, covered dishes for soap, powder, pins and other items, besides a matching pair of scent bottles. All these objects show a floral-and-ribbon design in pink, blue and gold with the neat V.R. motif and crown. Incidentally, this dressing-table is not muslin-draped. Made of fine mahogany it has a knee-hole front and a smaller version of it with mirror stands in Queen Victoria's dressing-room at Balmoral.

Many charming and small toilet china sets, as opposed to toilet equipages, were put out during

194 *Heart-shaped silver trinket box;* (centre) *Oblong box with velvet lid marked in silver 'Hairpins';* (right) *Traditional silver ring stand showing coral raised twig at centre, c. 1890*

195 *Small china (Worcester) dressing-table candlestick;* (centre) *Typical hatpin holder of the period, c. 1890;* (right) *trinket box (unmarked) white china with black lid having applied flower decoration and pink frill round base;*

196 *Ruby-red glass dressing table set with white scalloped decoration. Presented as a wedding gift, 1875*
197 *Complete china, moss-rose sprigged dressing table set, very pretty, 1860s*

198 (below) *Shell-decorated round ribbon box and glove box with 'scrap' picture and two padded green-silk hearts inset on lid, possible Valentine gift*

the last decades of the nineteenth century; still moderately priced, they have their uses today. They consist usually of a flat tray for brush and comb, a little ring-stand, powder box, a scent bottle or two, and candlesticks. Patterned with moss-roses, violets or lily-of-valley sprigs, they could not be prettier. Enchanting little china pin and hairpin boxes – boxes, indeed, of every shape and size – abound from this time. They have such absurdities on their lids as a small china dog, cat, swan or deer. Others are hand-painted with a spray of heather, a moss-rose or lily-of-the-valley; later, ferns and seaweed fronds appear. Small porcelain caskets for trinkets are still available. They are not too costly and eminently collectable. They stand usually on small scroll or shell feet and are decorated, sometimes, by a china flounce.

China hatpin holders are attracting American collectors and can be recognised by the cork stopper at their base into which long, be-jewelled pins could be stuck to keep them in a safe, upright position. Another type of box found on the dressing-table were glove and ribbon boxes. They are very pretty though fragile, being covered with embossed paper and edged with lace paper, the kind familiar on Valentines.

In this same category come oval-shaped ornamental boxes known as band or 'brides boxes' which were filled with ribbons at a time when ribbons were the rage and seen on everything.

Another range of boxes for the dressing-table was made in stamped, red sealing wax, together with visiting card-cases, by ladies in imitation of the small red lacquer Chinese and Japanese boxes then fashionable. Yet another type of toilet box was made of box or yew, varnished and painted, or transfer-printed like pottery was, with charming little pictures and views. One in my possession is inscribed 'For Toothpowder' and painted with a lily-of-the-valley spray.

Many dressing-table accessories, such as scent bottles, small candle-sticks, and pomade pots were also produced in clear or opaque glass. In fact, any trifle, fanciful and rare, to be used as a toilet aid was considered to be a bride's suitable present. When Miss Bella Scratchell, daughter of a poor small country town solicitor married rich but parvenu Mr. Piper, a widower who had set himself up with his children in the 'big' house of the district, she was sent:

'Scaly golden snakes with emerald or ruby eyes,

199–202   Ladies' visiting-card cases: Tortoiseshell and pearl; black sealing wax; japanned with eastern inlay work; silver on tortoiseshell

mother-o'-pearl envelope boxes, filigree bouquet holders, lockets, fans and personal finery. To the bride of a gentleman in Mr. Piper's position, no one could think of offering butter dishes and dessert knives, claret jugs and carvers, pickle bottles and biscuit boxes which are presented to modest young couples just setting up in domestic business. Bella's presents were all of an expensive character. Beatrix gave her a set of pearl ornaments and Mrs. Dulcimer a dressing-case.'

Miss Braddon, *An Open Verdict*

A Victorian lady's dressing-case could weigh up to 20 lbs when sold, ready to take away, with its full complement of fittings. As always, Miss Braddon gives a full description of one:

'He (Colonel Deverill) took up the travelling-bag which was large and heavy, made of crocodile leather, clamped with brass, and provided with all the latest improvements. He had reason to know the bag for it was his only wedding gift to his daughter. . . .

He opened it and looked dreamily at the silver-gilt stoppers, the ivory brushes and glove stretchers, and shining cutlery. All her little luxuries of the toilet had been packed in this receptacle. White rose, eau-de-cologne, lavande ambrée, attar of roses. A cloud of perfume came out of the bag as he opened it. . . . He turned out all the treasures, the bottles, and brushes, and thimble-cases, and brooches and bracelets in their morocco boxes, treasures of ivory, crystal and gold, of agate and silver. These he flung ruthlessly on the dressing-table. . . .'

Miss Braddon, *Like and Unlike*

DRESSING-TABLE SILVER

What the 'silver table' was to a lady in the drawing-room, so was the dressing-table in her bedroom, i.e. the traditional place to display her own intimate collection of silver toilet accessories, her pin trays and boxes, her photograph frames, hand-mirror, brushes and combs. The latter objects, sold in sets to fit her dressing-bag were heavily embossed with popular contemporary designs. Very much favoured was one of cherubs' heads after Sir Joshua Reynolds' painting. A typical hairpin box of this time was made of rich, dark-blue velvet mounted in silver with the word 'Hairpins' inscribed in silver letters on its velvet lid. Silver boxes more often than not were heart-shaped and ring-stands modelled like sprigs of coral. These are all delightful objects.

PEARL SHELL WARE

Next in popularity to gold, silver or ivory ware for the dressing-table came pearl shell ware, which had its heyday from 1851 till the '60s and which is now collected.

Irrespective of their social background, both rich and humble Victorians like their eighteenth

203 (top left) *Pearl-ware tea caddy and small photograph album with 'turbo' shell shown in foreground*
204 (right) *Composite group of mother-of-pearl shell objects. These comprise two pocket knives; a quizzing glass; some pierced and decorated fan sticks; a bouquet holder; and a large engraved shell showing (in relief) figures of Christ and saints. To hang up as a religious plaque*
205–6 (bottom left) *Richly worked visiting card case in pearl shell with desk box in tortoiseshell and pearl*

century forebears, were deeply drawn to shells. But with this difference, that theirs was a more sentimental than scholarly approach. For instance, they did not wish to be collectors of shells paying vast sums for them to display properly classified and catalogued in library cabinets, but rather to make an everyday, even commercial, use of their shimmering linings, colours and shapes which so attracted them.

One definite use of pearl shell (i.e. the lining of oyster, nautilus and omer shells) had already come about through the popularity of the papier mâché furniture which it decorated. As early as 1825, the leading Birmingham firm of papier mâché, Jensens & Bettridge, had obtained the first patent for the use of pearl-shell, followed by another, in 1847, for what was described as 'gem inlaying' with it. Both these processes of pearl shell decoration was applied not only to papier mâché but also to stained and painted wood. So everything was to

hand, it might be said, for a third use of pearl shell as a profitable side-line. This soon got under way through the production of a whole new range of shimmering luxury goods such as work boxes, small writing-desks, trinket caskets, fan-sticks, album covers and visiting card cases, that all came to be covered with irridescent and lovely gleaming flakes of pearl shell for ladies' use.

It is difficult to attribute the names of individual firms to the pearl shell ware which was first displayed at The Great Exhibition, but they were nearly all Birmingham-based and producers already of papier mâché and mother-of-pearl buttons. Among these firms were Jensens & Bettridge, of course, Henry Clay, Loveridge, Thomas Farmer, Dean & Benson and Walton of Wolverhampton.

In Cassell's *Household Guide* of 1875, an article on the actual making of pearl-shell ware lists three kinds of shell used: firstly, there was *aurora pearl* notable for its lovely iridescency but obtained only in small pieces of an inch square; then, *snail* or *Scotch pearl* which came in larger sized pieces than *aurora pearl* and with more gradual changes of colour; and lastly, *green pearl* which changed from blue to green but was liable to crack when worked.

Both professional and amateur shell workers could obtain cheaply small sheets of these trade-named flakes of pearl. From firms dealing with pearl shell ware a variety of ornaments already stamped out like flowers, bells, stars and dots, etc., could be obtained.

Flakes of pearl were cut with a pair of small but strong sharp scissors; rectilinear figures were best cut with a fine bow-saw as used for 'Fret-work'. A number of flake-patterns could be glued together and then sawn through at the same time. The article which was to be decorated with pearl shell was known to the trade as a 'blank'; amateurs were advised to begin work on a chess-board as the easiest kind of object to decorate.

The late Mrs. Frederick Beddington, whom I knew, was an early collector of pearl shell ware and kept a magnificent assembly of lovely shimmering examples like work-boxes, trinket caskets, hand-mirrors, glove boxes, etc., in her bedroom. The overall effect was quite magical.

Incidentally, for collectors of the minutiae, many exquisite small tools of needlework such as spools for winding silk on, stilettos for embroidery work, needle cases and etuis, etc. can be found in gleaming mother-of-pearl besides bouquet holders, album covers, elaborately carved buttons, spectacle cases and pen-knives.

PORCELAIN BIRD'S EGG SCENT BOTTLES

Another striking feature of the Victorian dressing-table was the number of scent-bottles on it; bottles in china, decorated or plain, in clear or opaque glass, coloured apple-green, rose-pink, turquoise-blue or vaseline.

Among the many charming and costly trifles owned by eighteenth-century ladies were those miniature objects known as 'Chelsea toys'. These included tiny china figures into which thimbles, etuis, bonbonnières and scent bottles were put. A century later (c. 1860) a china firm, James Macintyre of the Washington Works, Waterloo Road, Birmingham, had the brilliant idea of issuing a variety of both large and small scent bottles made in the identical shape and colouring of eggs laid by British birds. These little bottles could be easily carried about in a handbag as well as being put on the dressing-table.

Not so long ago I was put in touch with the owner of a fascinating collection of Bird's Egg Scent Bottles. Kept in a large basket, there were quite 40 different examples, from a swan's to a robin's egg. Some bottles had plain silver stoppers; others ornamental ones. But all bore this registration mark: 'Design No. 20771 registered on January 20th, 1885.'

Unfortunately, no factory records have been preserved about these delicious little scent-bottles, but from James Macintyre & Co., a firm that still survives, I have learned that the production of

207 *Row of porcelain bird's egg scent bottles including a moorhen's and starling's and one flower-splashed with different silver designed stoppers*

fancy and domestic ware (Chapter II: The Dining Room) was given up many years ago, in favour of Electrical Ceramics.

Victorian scent bottles in china and glass have long been collected, but more recently attention has been drawn to those double-ended and more unusual scent bottles which took the place of Vinaigrettes in the 1870s. The use of ammonia had replaced aromatic vinegars and the shape best suited for its use was a new, double type of bottle, about $3\frac{1}{2}$ inches long. Extremely well-made, the earliest hallmarks are about 1851 (Birmingham) and some bottles can still be found in their original leather cases. In *More Small Decorative Antiques*, Miss Therle Hughes has devoted a whole chapter to the history of scent bottles through the ages which collectors should consult.

BEDROOM ELEGANCIES

Besides the luxury trifles displayed on her dressing-table, there were the fancy fitments in her bedroom which had to be coped with and which were a lady's sole concern. These 'elegancies', as they were called, were more often than not supplied by the skill of her needle. They included bead-and-silk embroidered watch-pockets, or stands, an important item; elaborate comb cases and sachets; hair-tidies of satin or plush, a-glitter with beads and fringed; bedspreads and covers; besides a splash-back for the washstand. Last but not least, a pincushion and lamp mats, indeed, mats and catch-alls by the score.

The making of these fitments was done in leisure hours, and was considered one of the most genteel of activities. When a bedroom was thought to have reached its full complement of elegancies, others were contrived, to go on the stalls of an impending Church Fete or Fancy Bazaar.

Watch pockets and catch-alls

There is no doubt that the most celebrated watch-pocket which no self-respecting Victorian husband could be without, was the one owned by Prince Albert which his faithful widow, the Queen, kept pinned above her pillow every night at Osborne.

A Victorian watch-pocket, or stand, which was placed on a marble-topped commode, (one being on each side of the marital bed) was made in rich velvet, leather or fretwork. When produced in fretwork, a popular hobby of the 1870s and 80s, the frame might either be home-made or bought and then hung with its velvet pocket richly embroidered.

Catch-alls, subjected to different kinds of embroidery, were hung on the wall to accommodate anything from the morning paper to a duster or feather broom. Hair-tidies swung on a cord from the toilet mirror, and hair-combings were put in them till removed by the housemaid. No bedroom was without one and the more fanciful the better. Heavily decorated in beads and pearls, tasselled and fringed, they swung till another, equally fanciful, was made to take its place.

Victorian Pincushions

The pincushion has a long and ancient history, fulfilling an urgent dressing-need for men and women which began with the earliest fastener of all – a common or garden thorn!

In her long dramatic poem 'Aurora Leigh', Elizabeth Browning records how seven men must be employed 'to make the perfect pin' and that was not a man too many. Today steel pins are mass-produced by machinery and then boxed. They are rarely found stuck in elaborate patterns on a pincushion.

Pin-sticking, as it was once called, was a pretty pastime considered to give little girls in the Victorian school-room good training in finger-dexterity, so necessary for playing the piano. In her diary, Princess Victoria recorded how she had made 'a white and gold pincushion' for *dear Lehzen*, her governess.

Early Victorian pincushions still resembled their Regency counterparts, being of a flat thin shape easily carried about in a reticule. Sometimes, they are found made in the shape of a heart, a bellows, a swan or a lyre. The tube of one pincushion made like a bellows has inscribed on it 'Victoria, born

208–10   *Three ornamental pincushions: Flower Embroidery on satin; (centre) ornamental, octagonal-pointed 'Christmas' pincushion made up of silk-woven little pictures with Robin inset wishing recipient 'A Merry Christmas'; (right) Shell-shaped patches with velvet centre, lace-trimmed, and bows of ribbons at each corner*

24th May, crowned 28th June, 1838'. It survives to this day, as do many others made by juvenile workers on canvas. These carry cross-stitch slogans, pious or sentimental, like 'Dieu me voit' or 'Bless the Lord O my Soul'. When chairs became more and more padded and buttoned, the pincushion followed suit and swelled to vast proportions. They dominated the dressing-table, plump and heavy with bead and pearl incrustations. Or they were made of muslin, ruched and flounced and threaded with blue or pink ribbon to match the table skirt below them. Or, again, they were made in patchwork, in silk materials featuring the Box or Star or Diamond patterns. Mounted on the top of a 'Roundabout' reel holder, the pincushion becomes a most charming and 'collectable object' of the dressing-table for which quite a lot of money is now asked. In Tunbridge ware, in tortoiseshell, pearl shell, ivory or papier mâché, the range of mounts for a pincushion is endless.

For Victorian elaborations of dress demanded an abundance of pins to be handy and few ladies moved about the house or went travelling without a small, stuffed pincushion kept hidden away in a pocket of their voluminous skirts.

A charming custom of the day was to send an expectant mother or one whose baby had arrived safely an exquisite white satin and silver pincushion with the words 'Bless the Babe' inscribed across it in shining silver pins. There were ornamental 'Bachelors' pincushions, too, made by his sweetheart or inamorata for a birthday or souvenir gift.

Collectors wishing to form a collection of Victorian pincushions or one even more representative of pincushions used through the centuries, should consult E. D. Longman and S. Loch's *Pins and Pincushions*, for it is not only a splendid authorative book on the subject, but a charming one too with many unusual illustrations.

Bedspreads

Bedspreads were of some importance in the bedroom and included often a separate loose muslin cover to keep them spotless and fresh. For summer use, bedspreads were made of fine white linen, delicately embroidered or done in drawn-thread work. There were others crocheted in heavy mercerized cotton-thread in elaborate patterns or in rich, jewel-like shades of wool featuring the popular 'shell' or 'star' crochet design. These have now become very fashionable but are expensive

when found. Another type of crochet bedspread came from Irish convents or from peasant homes in Ireland where crochet work was a cottage industry. Worked in a fine white thread, they featured raised, petalled flowers like the marguerite and rose; others had bands, or squares, of filet lace from Carrickmacrosse or Limerick inserted. For all such bedspreads there is a heavy demand, as those which have survived have become collector's pieces and are always being advertised for.

Authentic Victorian patchwork bedspreads in velvet have their admirers too. There is one particular design, 'The Log Cabin', which consists of long narrow strips of velvet and bright-coloured silks which are made up into graduated crosses on a black ground; these always have a market. The best Victorian patchwork dates from about 1850 to 1870 and when it is found in good condition, or has historic interest, it can command a high price rising even to three figures.

In a country-house inventory of this time, at least half a dozen different types of bedspread can be found listed for each bedroom (designated as the Blue Bed room, say, or the Pink.) From these same inventories, we learn that at least six pairs of sheets and pillow cases were allocated to each bedroom with a set of summer and winter blankets which were kept, lavender-scented, in the ottoman that stood at the foot of the bed.

About the 1880s, a fashion for Maltese and Teneriffe lace used in large medallions with bands of insertion between on a bedcover came in. This lace, no doubt, was brought home from a happy winter spent in Malta or the Canary Islands. Though delicate and fragile, many of these bedspreads have survived.

Twill bedspreads worked in crewel wools can be found. On their natural-coloured background, a few birds are usually depicted in both long and short stitches not unlike satin stitch but bolder. Or trails of honeysuckle are shown. I have such a

bedspread done in the olive greens, yellows and soft browns of the new 'Art Shades' that the Royal School of Needlework in South Kensington were sponsoring during the '90s. At the time of the Boxer Rising (1900) there arrived in England a number of Chinese satin bedspreads from the sack of Pekin which were exquisitely embroidered with flowers, birds and butterflies. They were heavily fringed and about 200 years old. These satin bedspreads can still be seen decorating the four-poster beds of those historic homes now open to the public.

However, by the turn of the century, feminine attention was being turned to more serious occupations than the making of a Hair Tidy in plush or a Candle-Stand in momie-cloth edged with tufted crewel and embroidered with blue periwinkles. Large department stores like Maples and James Shoolbred in the Tottenham Court Road were taking over the sale of machine-made bedspreads and household linen. Only the rich could now afford to buy finely embroidered sheets and pillow-cases trimmed with hand-made crochet.

Today what few Victorian bedroom 'elegancies' – absurd, gay and trivial – remain behind, interest only collectors of needlework or the social historian intent on recording the nineteenth-century domestic scene.

VICTORIAN DRESS ACCESSORIES

From the crown of her demure little bonneted head to the toe of her small, silver-buckled shoe, the dress accessories of a Victorian lady's wardrobe were many and various. What is more, as they all have their appointed place in the history of costume through the ages, they are zealously collected. Even such a small and minor dress-item as a silver buckle or an enamel clasp can focus attention on account of the skill and artistry that went into its making.

Take buttons, for instance. What the zip is for us, so were buttons to the Victorians. Buttons were

seen on everything, from boots and shoes to children's clothes, and those of adults. Victorian buttons belong to a world of their own: over their creation jewellers, silversmiths and button makers gave endless care and attention.

In America, button history or *buttony* as it is called there, has long been studied and examples from every century collected. Clubs have been established where button collectors meet to discuss the merits, or not, of their different specimens. Equally sought after now, are buckles and belt clasps, bouquet holders, skirt holders and visiting card cases.

Bouquet holders

A lady could not go to a dinner party or ball *en grand tenue* without carrying a bouquet. This was

gracefully held in her gloved right hand in a holder or *porte-bouquet* as it was called and which was made in silver or silver-gilt by a fashionable jeweller.

211   *'Making A Posy', by William Frith,* RA, *1856*

212   (top right) *Two mother-of-pearl and gilt bouquet holders, c. 1850*

213   *Dyed feather flowers in a plaited straw holder for a lady*

These entrancing little objects have long been collected. Among their admirers was her late Majesty, Queen Mary, some of whose bouquet holders are now at the London Museum in Kensington Palace, London. No one knows exactly when the bouquet holder first made its appearance, though it is thought to have been during the eighteenth century. Some fashion plates of this time show a bouquet carried in silver filigree paper and not a holder.

A collection of *porte-bouquets* were on display at the Great Exhibition of 1851, each one complete with its guard chain and finger-ring. Some bouquet-holders are found in the shape of a brooch modelled after a calla lily with a little glass vase concealed in its stem to keep a miniature bouquet from wilting. These baby holders were placed as a boutonnière in the lapel of a coat; for button-holes were much favoured. *Vice versa*, they could be fastened in the hair as a decoration.

There were some ladies who always preferred to carry a bouquet made of flowers of feather and wax, flowers that never faded. These were arranged in a small rustic holder made of plaited straw. As bouquets grew larger and larger, they were known as 'cartwheels' and ceased to be carried. With their demise, the *porte-bouquet* vanished.

Skirt holders

Besides the bouquet holder a novel kind of clip was produced when skirts became longer and longer towards the late '80s and '90s. Fitting close round a lady's hips then flaring out into a wide be-ruffled hem that trailed along the ground, a skirt, if not upheld by a dainty gloved hand encountered many dangers. So a skirt clip was invented to help ladies from having continually to hitch up their skirts when crossing a street or to avoid getting them wet on meeting a puddle. These little objects took the form of a lucky horse-shoe or a fan, a shell or brass butterfly.

It has been said, though, that a skirt clip however pretty would *not* have been used by 'carriage' ladies or by any lady of the upper-class world. She would have disdained them, preferring to bend down gracefully and *pick up* her skirt with one hand. Be that as it may, Victorian skirt clips in brass or silver remain to be picked up in a different sense by the collector.

Buckles, belt clasps and hair combs

Buckles can be as diverse in make, size and decoration, as buttons, though possibly they are not as old. One of the earliest recorded owners of a handsome pair of buckles was Samuel Pepys (1633–1703) who wrote in his diary in the year 1659, 'This day I began to put Buckles on my shoes.' This was, indeed, a very smart step forward in society for him. For buckles were, then, aristocratic wear only and made of silver.

Buckles, together with buckle-clasps for belts and hair combs, too, have been in and out of fashion for centuries. When more masculine clothes for sport like long skirts and Garibaldi shirts arrived for ladies, a slender waist-span of about 18 to 22 inches was something that every pretty Victorian girl and young matron aspired to, either by natural or artificial means like tight-lacing, with dire results to their health. Nothing was calculated to show off a tiny waist so well as a belt of ribbon, velvet or leather fastened by a buckle, and the prettier the buckle, the better. Victorian buckles can still be found in the trays of both first-class and second-hand jeweller's shops or the pawnbroker's in a sleazy neighbourhood. Handsome in silver, chased or embossed, fragile in jet and coral, sparkling in paste and striking in cut-steel, a collection of period buckles and belt clasps would be fascinating to make, along with other dress items of their day.

Recently, I read that one collection of buckles made by Lady Maufe, wife of the eminent architect, Sir Edward Maufe who designed Guildford Cathedral, numbers about 2,000 examples. One pair made by the silversmith, John Wilks are dated 1722.

At one time many of Scotland's famous regi-

214   *Belt clasp of a butterfly in jet and two intertwined coral-designed buckles in obsidian*

ments, like the Black Watch, the Seaforth and Cameron Highlanders wore buckles, each regiment having its own pattern that is sealed and kept at a Government office. At the present moment of writing metal buckles, plus small metal chains, are decorating most of our out-of-door shoes and genuine old paste, jet and painted china buckles being tracked down to wear for best occasions.

During the 1840s, hair styles necessitated the use of large, high-backed combs to set off the hair when dressed to its best advantage and to keep every curl and puff in place. Fancy combs in every kind of material, in silver, ivory, jet, coral, tortoiseshell and carved wood appeared. Some of the finest combs of this time are in tortoiseshell so intricately carved that they look like stiffened lace, emulating Spanish combs, long famed for their workmanship. At this time, too, the teeth of combs will be found to be made of brass wire which, again, was superseded by lead. A tortoiseshell comb requires all the skill of which a craftsman is capable. Some examples are often inlaid with silver or gold or even artificial gems with great effect. Later, in 1863 when hair styles again demanded the need of combs, paste was much employed.

Buttons

Button history, or *Buttony* as it was once called, makes fascinating reading, though no one knows who made the first button or when and where that was. In England, the word button, once spelt 'Botoun', goes back to the sixteenth century when it was recorded that Queen Elizabeth was given two gold buttons shaped like acorns at Eastertide. Buttons were rare possessions in her day and only owned by the gentry and then rarely by ladies. When seeing that fascinating exhibition *The Elizabethan Image* at the Tate Gallery I made a point to look for, and make notes on, the buttons I saw on the costumes shown in the Tudor and Jacobean portraits. There were plenty to be seen sewn in a row down the richly embroidered doublets sported by the Queen's handsome Court gallants. But a lady's stiff, long, pointed bodice only showed very occasionally a few odd, knob-like objects worked over in braid, or silk, similar to old Dorset buttons, the making of which was once a thriving cottage industry and about which I shall write here.

But before I do, it must be said that the first buttons in pewter, brass and silver costing from a few pence to shillings per dozen began to appear early in the seventeenth century. Gold-wire buttons are first listed in a contemporary dress-maker's bill and priced at 9/- for 12. *Points*, as these knots of material were called which tied together parts of a lady's bodice when needed, disappear about 1745.

By now a button industry, one of the first in England, was flourishing in Somerset and Wilt-shire and this survived till about 1850 when the first machine-made buttons were put out by Midland factories, thus ending the manufacture of the much-prized old Dorset buttons.

Dorset buttons come in two distinct types. There is the solid clothwork button, and the flat one which was probably produced later when another cottage industry (lace-making) began to decline in the West Country. For it was Flanders lace-thread which was employed to make flat buttons on a metal ring. Its older, more solid and round, brother was made on a disc of horn supplied by Dorset sheep, a wad of rag first being pulled through a hole in the centre of the disc and then moulded into a firm convex, or cylindrical, shape held in place by a network of delicate

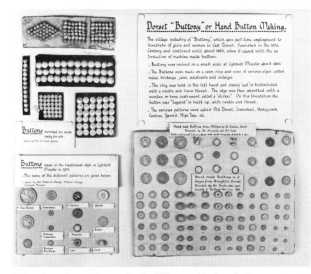

215 *Sample trade card of different kinds of Dorset 'hand-made' buttons available during the first half of the nineteenth-century*

stitchery resembling a spider's web. Convex Dorset buttons went by the name of 'High tops' and were used on a gentleman's hunting waist-coat.

The town of Blandford, which was famed for its button industry had, for its chief pattern, the 'Cartwheel' which was made in all sizes from one-eighth of an inch across to one inch. There were others known as a 'Cross-wheel', 'Basket', and 'Honeycomb'. But all these patterns have com-pletely vanished.

Men, women and even children were employed in making Dorset buttons in early Victorian times, an expert hand (a man's) being able to produce as many as a gross of buttons per day for which he was paid 3/6d. Meagre pay indeed! In the button trade there were people called 'finishers' and 'paperers'. To them the duty fell of first boiling, then polishing each finished button and finally, mounting them on pink, yellow and navy-blue cards, ready for sale.

At one time, Dorset buttons were sent out all over England, some being exported to America and Canada, till disaster befell this remarkable cottage industry. Left without local work and so the means to support themselves, whole families packed up and emigrated.

So much for Dorset buttons, not to be seen now outside a valued collection. What of other buttons: those hundreds, thousands and millions of buttons

that were made in the Midland factories of England and which are still being produced, for the most part in new materials including plastic? Buttons in horn, in hand-painted porcelain, in jet, mother-of-pearl, ivory, agate and silver; buttons of every shape and design in paste, onyx and diamond; the collector is faced with an endless choice.

Old sporting buttons worn by various Hunt Clubs during the last century afford an amusing line. From 1848 to 1851, these were the rage and the market was flooded by those produced by Messrs. Allen & Moore, famed button-makers. Buttons of this kind feature silver animal figures which stand out in high relief against a plain or lined background. In my possession are a complete set of buttons, big and small, in this genre that show on a smoky pearl ground a boar, a wolf, a shooting dog and other animals of the chase. They have survived the wear and tear of being used for four generations in my family.

Mother-of-pearl buttons can form an entire collection on their own. As early as 1778, two Birmingham button makers, Henry Clay and Obadiah Westwood applied for the use of pearl shell as a button patent. Since then till today mother-of-pearl buttons have been in constant use on clothes. They have also been used by the costermonger fraternity as a means of highly decorative dress-ornamentation, individual to themselves alone. The Pearl Kings and Queens of London are world-famous and their costumes are handed down from one generation to the next.

The evolution of even an ordinary pearl button in Victorian times, beginning with its natural habitat, the seabed, and ending with its final cutting and polishing in a Birmingham factory is long and involved. To start with, the gathering of pearl shell from Australia, Ceylon and South Sea islands was an arduous and dangerous business done by expert, deep-diving natives armed with a sharp knife and a fibre sack. White pearl shell comes best from Australia or Panama; yellow from the Philippines and South Pacific Islands; black shell from Tahiti. Till about 1885–1890 all pearl buttons were cut from real mother-of-pearl or ocean shells. Today, on account of high production costs, plastic or imitation form of shell is used instead. In Birmingham's City Museum a splendid collection of eighteenth-century and nineteenth-century pearl shell buttons can be studied. They are the most delicate and fragile of objects, hand-

216 *Seventeen different sorts of buttons dating from about 1840 to 1900 include silver, mosaic, paste, cut-steel, bronze, cat's-eye and old sporting buttons*

carved and the finest examples embellished with paste jewels, metallic foils, gilded pieces of metal and 'steel' mirrors.

Other types of buttons to collect are those made of staghorn, enamel, steel, silver, china or glass. Small glass buttons very much worn from about 1825 to 1875 were tiny reproductions of small glass Victorian paperweights and are enchanting. Black glass buttons, in the trade traditionally called 'Jet' buttons, are still plentiful and popular for specialised collecting. Needleworked buttons come into this category too, some worked with stitches so fine and small that they look as if covered with lace!

To help place the date of an old button when found, it is best to study the fashion plates of ladies' magazines from the 1850s onwards, or to stroll through a picture gallery like the Tate or National Gallery and note the kinds of button being worn on the clothes shown in portraits of men and women. In 1877, for instance, large plate-like porcelain buttons, hand-painted in the flowery style of the Louis XV styles in furniture then so popular, were much seen. Set in a long row down a lady's dress, they looked like oval, miniature plates. Cuff-buttons and ear-rings could be bought to match. The following year, 1878, tiny steel bell-shaped buttons appeared and small, jet buttons from Paris like balls cut in facets with a shank.

The 1880s saw the vogue for buttons à la Kate Greenaway, whose enchanting illustrations were setting the fashion for a new way of dressing little girls and boys. Insect buttons have enormous appeal, too. Made of tortoiseshell they have little beetles or butterflies done in pearl shell on them. Their date is about 1882. About this time, a small enamelled or bronze type of button was *de rigueur* on ladies' riding habits instead of earlier silver and gilt buttons. Old coins were mounted, too, as buttons and worn on dresses.

Although in 1890 image and object buttons were still being worn, buttons of a more conventional design were appearing in ever-increasing numbers. For instance, though a young lady's 'Reefer' or 'Sailor's' jacket of blue serge featured white pearl buttons still being 'used for garniture' were no longer the elegant and costly kind of earlier times. Metal picture buttons were replaced by conventional patterned ones and the one-time genuine mother-of-pearl beauties from Ceylon had been dropped in favour of more cheaply acquired fresh-water pearl ones. The button industry, in fact, was being taken over at last by big business and thoroughly commercialised.

Today, to meet the demand for period buttons of every size, material and design there exists in Christopher's Place, off Wigmore Street, London, a fascinating little shop given over entirely to the sale of buttons. Buttons go to Christie's, too, and fetch high prices. A good reference book on this subject is *The Complete Button Book* by Lilian Smith Albert and Kathryn Kent. There is also a fully detailed chapter on 'Buttons' illustrated with lovely coloured plates by Jane Ford Adams, Editorial Consultant to the 'National Button Bulletin', in *Antiques International*, 1966.

THE WASH STAND

At a time when even a well-to-do Victorian home boasted rarely of more than one bathroom and that situated at the end of a long draughty passage, the Wash Stand occupied a prominent position in the bedroom. For here it was that daily ablutions were performed.

Many Early Victorian wash stands were nothing, more or less, than those small, pretty, three-cornered stands, Chippendale or Sheraton-styled, with bow fronts and a cavity to contain a china basin. Such stands are eagerly sought after by any-one living in flats or country cottages where room-space is restricted. They can even be utilised as plant containers.

217 *A so-called 'modern gothic' washstand with two china jugs and basins and matching soap dishes*

218 (left) *Superior washstand with lid to close and full set of china washing utensils, 1878*

219 *Bedroom washstand with complimentary matching china fittings by Charles Eastlake, 1864*

As the nineteenth century advanced, Chippendale or Sheraton-styled 'Bason Stands' as they were called could not possibly house the many different toilet accessories demanded by Victorian ladies.

In her book *The Bedroom and Boudoir*, Lady Barker advised her readers to provide themselves with a wash stand 'to take not only a basin as large as possible but a jug, too, of a convenient form to hold and pour from.' A smaller jug and basin to match was also a necessity, besides a lidded sponge and soap bowl. To accommodate all these items, a wash stand became quite a solid piece of furniture, complete with a towel horse or towel rack. To prevent splashes from staining the wall behind it,

a marble slab came to be attached to the wooden back of the stand, or, if not marble, a piece of Indian matting or a length of embroidered linen cloth known as 'a splash-back' was put up. More often than not, a lightly-patterned Indian or Japanese paper screen was placed round the washstand to give its user complete privacy.

However, on the arrival of more than one bathroom in a house, the Victorian old-time wash stand became redundant and disappeared into the attic or junk yard. Here, stripped of their marble slabs which are sold now separately for paving-stones in sun rooms and patios or for a pastry board, old-fashioned wash-stands are still good buys.

SHAVING MUGS AND MOUSTACHE CUPS

Imposing and very prettily patterned Victorian wash-stand sets by Minton and other leading china firms which consisted of one large and one small basin with jugs to match besides a slop pail, chamber-pot, soap bowl, etc. could be picked up once for very little. But of recent years, largely

220 (left) *A white china moustache cup with 'Remember Me'. in gilt;* (right) *a blue-banded and flower-painted china shaving mug,* c. *1885*

to meet the increasing demand of American china hunters, these toilet sets have been broken up and pieces sold separately for any purpose except the one for which it was made! In this same category, one can place shaving mugs and moustache-cups which do duty now as flower-vases.

The grooming of a Victorian gentleman's moustache needed time and patience. According to Mrs. Beeton, if a valet was kept: 'He must be a good hairdresser. He has to brush the hair, beard and moustaches, arranging the whole simply and gracefully according to the style preferred.'

This was the era, then, of the 'moustache cup', one of the most period of toilet items which stood on the wash-stand. A certain number have survived and interest in them has revived on account of the more hirsute fashions of today. Prices vary on their condition when found. Primarily, moustache cups were produced by leading china firms to assist a gentleman suffering discomfort while sipping tea or when, of course, attending to his own moustache and beard. Across the mouth of a moustache cup lies a curly little china bar on which a luxuriant handlebar moustache could rest. These cups came into the category of sentimental, or souvenir, gifts presented from a doting wife to her husband; or from a young maiden to her 'intended'. Some cups are inscribed in gilt letters with the words 'Remember Me' or 'Happy Christmas'. Recently, I came across a very good specimen made in fine white china with a gilt border decorated by crimson stars. On one side it carried the coloured transfer print of St. Issey's, Cornwall. Another, dated 1860, was rose-pink and stood on a gilt-striped pink saucer. The base of the cup, itself, was formed in the shape of a cockleshell. A genuine and pretty collector's piece!

Shaving mugs are simplified forms of moustache cups, but more solid in weight so that they are not easily overturned. The inside of a mug may be divided into two compartments; the one to hold soap; the other warm water. They came into commercial production about 1840 and often carry their owner's initials and date.

A recent survey of men's shaving habits showed that there are still many die-hard Britons alive who shave themselves traditionally, seated before a mirror with brush, soap, a strop and cut-throat razor to hand. This breed of man, though disappearing would, no doubt, require the office of a shaving mirror, or stand, which have become

221–2 *Two shaving mirrors and stands. Left-hand is c. 1850, and right is walnut c. 1815*

collectors' pieces and whose antique value continues to rise.

Victorian shaving stands are usually made of mahogany and are mounted on a tripod base with ball-and-claw feet. Their small swing-mirrors, circular in shape, and wooden-framed can be detached and used as a wall-mirror. At one time a Victorian shaving-stand in good condition was relatively cheap but today it has become much more expensive.

In conclusion, the Victorian best bedroom which has been under survey in this chapter did not change character much before the International Exhibition of 1862. This Exhibition, however, like its more important prototype, the Great Exhibition of 1851, brought about many new changes in the Victorian home. By and large, these changes in regard to furniture styles, colour schemes and fancy fitments were towards the rich, heavy, dull and pompous. There is not much about them which is attractive. The Victorian bedroom thus maintained its solid character till the last decades of the century when another look, a new-look, came in expressed by leaders of the Nouveau Art Movement. The mid-Victorian bedroom finds its best description, I think, in the following passage from a novel, little known, by Miss Braddon:

'Everything in the room dated from the International Exhibition of 1862. All the furniture was of polished mahogany, the best in material and in manufacture that money could buy. The bedstead was Arabian with a lofty canopy and a footboard of colossal size, rich in scrolls and mouldings. A 'Duchesse' dressing-table occupied the central space in a vast bay with three long windows opening on to a balcony. For people who could appreciate the furniture of 1862, the room was perfection. Sofa, easy chairs, writing-table and a huge wardrobe with looking-glass, a French clock on the broad marble mantelpiece, an Axminster carpet and hearth rug to order and gas brackets jutting out wherever a lamp could be needed, all that makes for comfort was provided in the best spare room at Vale Hall, near Skipton, Derbyshire, the home of Matthew Rayner.'

Miss Braddon, *The White House*

7 The Nursery

223 *The nursery scene. Coloured frontispiece to* Girl's Own Toymaker, c. *1850*

It was the last Sunday in Advent. Nurse was bustling about in the night nursery preparing for the children's bed-time by the light of the fire and a tallow candle stuck in a large tin candlestick, which was set on the tall chest of drawers.

The baby was asleep in her wicker cradle in the corner and Sarah Turke had gone downstairs to fetch a can of hot water from the kitchen. Three little nightgowns were hanging in a row on the high fireguard to air. A bath shaped like a coffin was in front of the fire with sponges, soap and towels. Nurse's low wooden chair stood near it, all ready for action.

A Book with Seven Seals (Anon.)

The nursery quarters in a Victorian house lay on the top floor reached by at least three flights of stairs. Across the landing at the top was a little wicket gate kept closed to prevent small figures in holland overalls or pinafores from straying, more often tumbling, downstairs.

In a country house, the convention of keeping children segregated from the world of their elders and betters also prevailed. But instead of a small barred gate, there was a green baize door usually at the end of a long corridor. This door shut off the nursery quarters.

Those of us who knew the safe security of a fully-staffed Edwardian nursery that included Nanny with a nursemaid or two to assist her, may possess memories too of the Victorian one that preceded it. For it was not so different from the one we knew; moreover, many of the toys and games belonging to it had been handed down by parents to be played with again. Today, however, all this is changed for both kinds of nurseries have been swept away by the domestic upheaval following two World Wars.

225 *Historical teetotums: A nursery game, c. 1840. Master cards are hand-coloured engravings*

226 *Three kinds of Victorian top, cut-out from a nursery book, c. 1885*

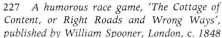

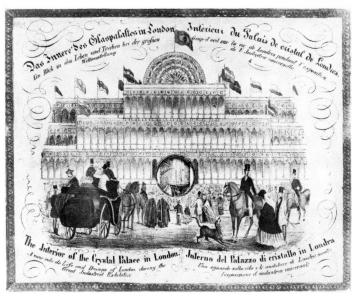

227 *A humorous race game, 'The Cottage of Content, or Right Roads and Wrong Ways', published by William Spooner, London, c. 1848*

228 *Peepshow: interior of the Crystal Palace, 1851*

To return, though, to the nursery of vanished days; to the high brass fender that guarded the flying sparks of a well built-up coal fire; to the rag rug spread in front of that fender and the comforting creak of Nanny's rocking chair complete with its patchwork cushion that broke the warm silence of a wintery afternoon; to the strong, square nursery deal table laid for tea with gaily patterned china mugs and plates and silver-plated spoons marked 'N' for nursery; to the rocking-horse standing with scarlet, flaring nostrils and scarlet saddle-cloth and shining stirrups in one corner and Lucy's tall red-brick dolls-house in another; to an entrancing scrapwork screen by the door and the picture of a golden-haired little boy in a velvet suit over the mantel-piece known as 'Bubbles'. To everything, in fact, which was once part and parcel of the Victorian nursery-scene and which has been so often recorded by notable Victorian authors remembering their childhood.

For some time now, Juvenilia, as it is termed, has attracted many collectors and prices for old dolls, rocking-horses, period dolls-houses and first editions of well-known nineteenth-century children's books have appreciated as much as anything else in the sale-room. In particular old Victorian dolls change hands for vast sums. In England many exhibitions are now held for displaying old Nursery Games and Toys. Collections of them, too, have recently been given to Museums such as the Raymond Barnett Collection of Instructional Toys and Schoolroom and Parlour Games to the Victoria and Albert Museum.

An extremely interesting exhibition has recently taken place at this same Museum on Children's Books that were published during the nineteenth century primarily to lure children into 'Learning without Tears' by the aid of pictures. There is also a permanent exhibition of period Toys, Old Games, Musical Boxes, Thermatropes and Kaleidoscopes, etc. besides the Juvenile Theatre at the Toy Museum, London.

229 *Example of a large fine 'alley' glass marble with wavy coloured threads inside, 1866*

MARBLES

'There was the floor on which I played at marbles, the pattern in the carpet serving as the ring.'

So wrote Robert Chambers in 1866, recalling his nursery days. But how many small boys spin a top now or play at marbles either at home, in a school-yard, or on the pavement? Instead, marbles are collected by adult men to display in the drawers of a cabinet or on the glass shelves of an alcove, illuminated by concealed strip-lighting. One such collector is Mr. Robert Graves, the poet, whose collection has been valued at £5,000.

A game of marbles was common to all classes in Victorian England. In fact, it is one of the oldest children's games in the world and one, too, played by adults. An interesting reference to its popularity during the 1870s and '80s in rural England comes in *Lark Rise to Candleford*, that enchanting trilogy by Flora Thompson first published in 1945.

'Even marbles, at twenty a penny, were seldom bought although there were a good many in circulation, for the hamlet boys were champion marble players and thought nothing of walking five or six miles on a Saturday afternoon to play with the boys of other villages and replenish their own store with their winnings. Some of them owned as trophies the scarce and valued glass marbles called 'alleys'. These were of clear glass enclosing bright, wavy, multi-coloured threads and they looked very handsome among the dingy clay ones.'

Marbles measure from 2″ down to $\frac{1}{4}$″ down in diameter and are made in china, glass, marble, agate or baked clay. They are the most endearing objects, easy to handle and display. They possess much the same fascination in their different elaborate patternings as those price-stealers of the sale-room – glass paperweights. Like them, too, they form a specialised branch of the glass-maker's art.

The first hand-blown marbles were produced by Venetian craftsmen in glass. Later Bavarian artisans 'blew' them with delicate spirals and bands of coloured glass threads imprisoned within their transparent hearts. During the nineteenth century an enormous number of glass marbles were imported into England to meet the heavy demand for them. The largest number came from Nuremberg which had long been a world centre for the toymaking industry.

It has been recorded that in the year 1877 over 100 different types of marbles were manufactured. Not only were various kinds of material used in their making but they were also decorated in numerous ways. The painting, glazing and polishing contributed to the beauty of the final product. Materials employed included crystalline, limestone or marble, besides different kinds of clay and stone. When not containing exciting bands and whorls of coloured glass inside them, glass marbles hold enchanting little objects such as a silvery-white miniature bird or doll. Others – in particular green glass marbles – have silvery flakes in their heart while yellow and orange glass marbles sport golden threads inside that shine. Another type of marble is made of crackle glass.

To produce marbles with objects inside, the glass-blower placed his silvery image of bird or child at the end of an iron rod which he then dipped into molten glass, imprisoning it inside the glass. Although the outer case of a glass marble is clear and transparent, it often has a bluish, yellow, green or amethyst tinge due to certain imperfections in the mixing of the batch of glass under production, or to the various types of ingredients used in different glass-making districts. The collector will find there is usually a small roughened spot at one point where the pontil rod was broken from the glass and this spot can be utilised when mounting a marble for display, as I do, on a suitable small flat stone found on a beach.

Today, marbles made of variegated stone like onyx and agate are highly prized. They were fashioned by two methods. Either small pieces were placed between two heavy millstones and then rolled round and round until they were worn down into smooth little balls, or they were placed in a barrel which revolved on an axis. This barrel was put in a brook where the water turned it over and over till the stones rubbing against one another were ground down smooth and round.

Common crockery-ware or clay marbles are as old as Time. For not only have Egyptian, Greek and Roman children played with them but they have made them, themselves, by rolling little bits of wet clay into balls and then leaving them to dry in the open air. Later, they were rolled again between the palm and placed in a small oven, or kiln, to bake hard. For this process, a clay marble was put on a tiny, three-legged stool, or tripod, so that on some specimens of clay marbles three little dark spots can be seen made by the tripod. Many clay marbles are decorated with circles, stars and other formal designs in bright colours. These colours were burnt in.

From the age-old game of playing marbles a store of superstitious lore has gathered. For instance, at one time children thought it unlucky to play with green marbles. Charms, too, have been attached to the game that vary in different parts of England. From Stoke-on-Trent in the Midlands comes the cry of:

> One, two, three
> Lucky, lucky, lucky,
> Four, five, six.

as small figures crouch, huddled, over their marbles in some secluded alley-way. In *The Lore and Language of Schoolchildren*, by Iona and Peter Opie, a ten-year-old Birmingham boy has supplied

230   *Group of small pretty marbles containing one cat's-eye and one of onyx, 1880s.*

231   *Crystal glass salt cellar filled with an assorted number of variously coloured opaque and clear glass marbles, 1860*

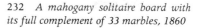

232   *A mahogany solitaire board with its full complement of 33 marbles, 1860*

this saying: 'If you are playing marbles and want to win, put a cross in front of the hole with red chalk and shout "Bad luck!" Then the person playing with you gets confused and misses the hole!'

Not so far away from Birmingham, in Nottinghamshire, comes a piece of advice for the hag-ridden marble player. 'When another boy is near your marble and it is his shot, draw a ring round it and he will miss you.' In Swansea, if a child is near to losing the game, he will cry out to some invisible presence: 'Black Cat, follow me, not you!'

Marbles have been given nicknames. In the north of England, they are often referred to as *potties* (clay ones) or *glassies*. At Bishop Auckland, Durham, they are collectively called *migs*. In my own district of Essex, which was a pretty remote one till quite recently, an old village woman told me that she had called her marbles *poppers*. Actually they were the small round greenish-glass balls found inside the neck of an old-fashioned lemonade bottle. Her mother could not afford to buy her proper marbles.

In a more sophisticated way, adults have played with marbles through the ages as well as children, and several games have been evolved in which they take a leading part, such as in Chinese checkers and solitaire.

Solitaire was popular in the eighteenth century as well as during the reign of Queen Victoria. Horace Walpole refers to his game in a letter. He writes: 'Has Miss Harriet found any more ways at solitaire?' For there were many cunning and devious ways of eliminating one marble after another on a round wooden board pierced by holes in which sat each glass marble till all but one was left and the player awarded his prize. Solitaire marbles are usually made of glass and are among the most decorative.

Although marble-playing is recorded as slowly losing its popularity among children and grown-ups from about 1885, there is one small village in England, the tiny hamlet of Tinsley Green, north of Three Bridges in Sussex, where it is still played at the Greyhound Inn. Here, on Good Friday, for 300 years and this in spite of all attempts by the Church to have this event deferred to Easter Monday, a local marbles championship takes place. Recently, with American participation, this meeting has gained almost international fame and status. Handsome cups and glittering medals are presented, not to speak of free beer. Asking how this local game was played, one participant told me:

'For the team championship 49 marbles are played in the centre of the ring. Two teams armed with tollies aim to knock them out. The first team to knock out 25 marbles wins the contest.'

233 *Early jigsaw: 'Life of Napoleon', c. 1860 typical instruction puzzle*

EARLY JIGSAWS

By the time that Queen Victoria came to the throne in 1837, jigsaw puzzles were available on most subjects suitable for study in the school-room. When crude prints of 'Queen Victoria's Dinner at the Guildhall with the Lord Mayor and Citizens of London, November 9th, 1837,' appeared, followed by 'The Grand Coronation' and then by her 'Marriage' 1840, these colourful souvenirs were cut up into jigsaw puzzles. But they are not nearly so interesting or of as much value today as those depicting everyday scenes from contemporary life. For instance, one jigsaw called 'The History of the Sabbath' (c. 1840), which shows the interior of a contemporary church with high pews, a three-decker pulpit and a congregation of pious Victorian churchgoers, is highly illuminating.

The word 'jigsaw' did not come into general use

until the end of the nineteenth century. It was named from the actual instrument that cut wood into irregular pieces, known as a 'jigsaw', by American puzzle-makers to differentiate it from a fret-saw.

Owing to the difficulty at first of producing irregular-shaped pieces of wood, early jigsaws are much larger and more coarsely-shaped than those cut later. Inter-locking pieces, too, found round the border of the first puzzles are mounted on a thin sheet of mahogany to ensure rigidity and form. Jigsaws were sold in solid boxes with a sliding lid which carried a descriptive label of the puzzle inside and their maker's name.

After 1850, these mahogany boxes gave way to ones produced in varnished whitewood, the lids of which were stuck with a brightly-coloured label. Then, with improved techniques in the industry and lowered costs of production, the hand-coloured engraving that first decorated all jigsaw puzzles came to be used less and less until they vanished. By 1900, in fact, all jigsaws were printed in colour and the word 'jigsaw' established as their trade-name.

234   *Typical family jigsaw: 'The Juvenile Party' depicting charming arrival of little guests, c. 1840*

NURSERY CARD GAMES

Although card games were being played as long ago as in the days of the Pharaohs, from which time the oldest pack of cards (i.e. the Tarot or Taroc) derive, children's card games did not appear in Europe till the nineteenth century when the nursery, proper, as we know it, was established.

It was only then that those first, happy Victorian nursery card games like 'Snap'; 'Old Maid'; 'Happy Families'; and 'Jack Drew the Well' were played by children filling a room with delighted cries.

'Happy Families' still survives, but an original pack is quite hard to come by as they have been reproduced in their thousands. The game derives from an earlier one called 'Spade the Gardener'. But this game is played with the aces, tens and court cards of an ordinary pack, with this difference, that each of the four kings of the four suits, Clubs, Diamonds, Hearts and Spades have a special name, while the remaining court cards of the same suit are regarded as members of his family. Thus there is Spade, the Gardener (the King of Spades); Spade the Gardener's Wife (Queen of Spades); his son the Knave; his Servant the Ace; and the Dog of the Ten of Spades. In turn, Club the Constable is the King of Clubs; The Good-natured Man the King of Hearts; and Vicar Denn, the King of Diamonds. Each of these characters has a wife, son, servant and dog.

It was the famous illustrator of *Alice in the Wonderland*, Sir John Tenniel (1820–1914) who was called upon to create the immortal families of Mr. Chips the Carpenter and Mr. Bones the Butcher, etc. by drawing them on each card. Cards that were destined to enchant and entertain succeeding generations of juvenile players to the end, perhaps, of Time. 'Happy Families', we know, was played by Queen Victoria's children and a delightful scene is described by Mrs. Malet, one of the Queen's ladies-in-waiting, when her little son, Victor, came to stay with her at Windsor Castle. For a game of 'Happy Families' was organised for him and those who took part were Mr. Tufnell (the Tutor) Princess Helena (Princess Christian) and her daughter, Victoria, and the Honourable Rose Hood, a Maid of Honour. On being asked by Mr.

Tufnell for Mr. Potts the Painter, little Victor Malet replied: 'Yes, he *is* at home, but he is *not* going out of his house today for I am collecting the Potts family myself.' (Windsor, Dec. 2nd, 1897).

The game of 'Kings and Queens of England' (each card 5″×6″) published by the Religious Tract Society, London, *c.* 1865 was one of the most popular Victorian card games. Others which have vanished more or less into limbo are listed as 'Historical Tetotums' (*c.* 1840), and 'Historical Amusements. A new Game.' Each card was 1⅜″×2¼″ (*c.* 1840). There were also pictorial cards dealing with the subject of geography. These were known as 'Geographical Groups' (*c.* 1835). But the prettiest cards, surely, were those produced when botany was being taught to every little Victorian school-room miss.

This game, 'Botanical Lotto' (*c.* 1850), was played as much in the drawing-room and parlour as in the nursery. For it had sentimental links with that most popular language, beloved by young people – 'The Language of Flowers'. A pack of 'Floral Cards' numbered about 64 in all and the game was played like 'Happy Families'. On each card a flower was represented with its meaning printed above; its name below. Thus TIGER LILY symbolised this sentiment: 'For once may Pride befriend Me'. The MOSS ROSE: 'A Confession of Love'. The MONKEY FLOWER: 'Mischievousness'. The HEARTEASE: 'Think of Me'.

The collector of nursery playing cards can collect also the pretty ivory, bone or mother-of-pearl counters, that went with them. Those in the form of fishes are the prettiest. Nursery counters date from about the end of the eighteenth century and are becoming increasingly difficult to find. There are some made in the shape of ivory letters (*c.* 1840s) which are as pleasing to handle in our own gambling games of today as they were once by children endeavouring to learn their letters.

236   *'The Language of Flowers'; five representative playing cards from a floral pack, c. 1845*

PIGGY BANKS

'A money box made of potters' clay wherein boyes put their money to keepe, such as they hang in shops, etc. towards Christmas.'

Higins, *Junius Nomenci,* 1685.

So reads an early reference to a child's clay money box which were traditionally made in the form of a gay little pig – hence the name, *Piggy Bank.* What is more, such little money boxes are universal to children in different countries all over the world.

In England, the first money boxes were made of earthenware. The origin of that familiar phrase 'Christmas box' is directly associated with the pig-shaped boxes given with a tip inside to Elizabethan apprentices.

Much later, of course, genuine children's money boxes were evolved to encourage thrift and an understanding of money. They were produced in their hundreds in glass and china, decorated or plain; in silver, brass, wood and other materials. They took all manner of shapes, too, from a bees-kip to a dog's kennel in shellwork and could be seen on many a Victorian nursery mantel-piece. In the cottages of England, a money-box was always prized by a village child and easily obtained from an itinerant pedlar coming to the door, or it was bought on the stall of a nearby market.

During the nineteenth century a pottery firm at Gorsty Hill, Worcestershire, produced what was to become a very popular model. This came to be known as a 'Hen and Chick' money pot. Measuring almost 8″ across by 6¾″ high and splashed often with manganese brown under a yellow glaze,

some money pots were formed of the hen, herself, with a slot in her back through which a penny was inserted. As copper coinage tended to increase in size, money boxes became larger and gaudier. Many looking like toy cottages appeared, modelled in earthenware or china and mounted on a square base. Even the copy of a circular toll-house can be found or a miniature cottage guarded by the crudely modelled figures of a boy and girl outside. Figure busts, too, of contemporary celebrities were provided by the potter, or, anything else that took his fancy to produce.

The traditional Sussex 'Piggy-bank' associated since the eighteenth century with the potters of Brede and Rye can be identified by their colouring and the slot that runs along the back of the pig. Produced in mottled brown, brilliant green or speckled yellow glazes, they carry, sometimes, a potter's name. Another type of money box known as 'Lion' money boxes has been attributed to Thomas Rathbone of Portobello, Scotland, who started the fashion for them. He produced them singly or in pairs about 1820.

That familiar term 'Penny Bank' refers to the first saving banks in which so small and modest a sum as one penny could be deposited for safe keeping. These banks inspired the fashion for money boxes to be made in their own image! Recently, I was shown a splendid example of one, superbly made and complete in every detail down to two little brass hitching-posts placed by the entrance door to accommodate a horse.

For a child, the fascination of owning a money box centres round the exciting moment when a coin is put into it. To enhance this thrill an en-

237 *Three traditional earthenware piggy-banks, Chilean*

238–40 *Beehive moneybox with raised white figures and dogs on blue ground, initialled 'W.B.', c. 1860;* (centre) *cardboard kennel with plaster dog moneybox, shell-decorated, 1870;* (right) *Cast-iron penny bank, with hitching-posts and brass decorations, 1860*

trancing blackamoor figure came to be modelled who stood with one dark hand, outstretched, and scarlet mouth open. When a child put his penny on the hand, it immediately jerked up to the mouth and hey-presto! the penny was swallowed. A piece of pure magic. At one time, these black-amoor money boxes stood on the counter of a tobacconist's shop with the word 'Eat a Penny' inscribed on them. Possibly they were inspired by those earlier 'blackamoor' wooden figures which were the traditional sign for Georgian shops selling tobacco and snuff – 'At the sign of the Blackamoor.'

During the middle of the nineteenth century there was a vogue for a mechanical type of money box which found its most popular form in the one that embodied the historic story of William Tell. A metal figure of Tell can be found with his Child, standing before him, apple on head. When the coin shot from William Tell's bow neatly strikes off the apple, it disappears with apple and all, into the slot behind the child's head. On pulling his arm that has jerked up, down to his side again, the apple reappears on his head and the whole perfor-mance can be repeated.

The slit, or opening, on a money box can help the collector to fix its date providing he knows something of the shape and size of small coins in use at various times. For instance, eighteenth-century gold and silver coins were almost paper-thin. A silver two-penny piece or half-groat that was the most popular coin to hoard, measured only about $\frac{3}{4}''$ across. Copper half-pennies did not appear till after 1770. After this date, there came a veritable flood of copper coins which increased in size and weight so that the slits on money-boxes had to be made bigger to take them. The engaging story of 'Piggy Banks' from earliest times has been charmingly told by Miss Therle Hughes in *More Decorative Antiques.*

NURSERY MUGS AND PLATES

In the nineteenth century, as it has been said, a new and happier life began for children in the nursery. This was soon reflected in the wearing of more appropriate clothes, eating healthier food and in having fresh equipment of a more decora-tive and suitable nature made for the nursery. To begin with nursery china was designed expressly to serve both an ornamental and instructive purpose like toys in general. For if children were to learn in future 'without tears' why not let them eat and drink on the same principle?

It was a felicitous moment to advance any new ideas in china production, as the Staffordshire potters were busily engaged in concentrating on transfer-printing as a cheaper form of decoration than that hand-drawn and hand-painted.

So the transfer-printed pictures now seen on children's mugs and plates echoed the high moral tone of the day set by contemporary educationalists. Or if pictures were not of this sort, they were frankly sentimental. This was how wise sayings, proverbs and religious texts came to be inscribed on numberless little nursery plates: plates that were strongly reminiscent of the lustre wall plaques which might be hung above little beds at night. On one little plate ran these words: 'Accept this Small Reward For Your Diligence'. On another: 'Silks and Satins, Scarlet and Velvets, Put Out The Kitchen Fire'. A simple verse pointing out some necessary virtue such as POLITENESS was also highlighted.

241   *Child's cream earthenware mug with brown transfer-printing of cow, farmer and boy marked FODDERING, c. 1850*

> *If little boys and girls were wise*
> *They'd always be polite,*
> *For sweet behaviour in a child*
> *Is a delightful sight.*

This type of nursery mug and plate was turned out by innumerable Midland potteries or those centred round Newcastle and Sunderland. Another kind carried charming naive illustrations of old nursery rhymes like 'The Cat and the Fiddle' or 'Little Bo-Beep'. One pottery at North Shields (*c.* 1850) added the letters of the alphabet for good measure round the rim of their plates.

From Swansea comes a little plate impressed with raised daisy heads, while Davenport was responsible for an attractive 'Zoological Gardens' series. As nursery china ware was comparatively cheap some of it found its way into humble homes where it was much appreciated. Flora Thompson, whose mother had been in domestic service with the gentry, has written of the pleasure of village children when given some pretty china mug, or plate, marked with their name and date. There is a charming story told of Thomas Chatterton, how when he was taken as a small boy of six to a

pottery works and asked what he would like as decoration on a Delft mug of his own, he gave a great shriek of joy and cried: 'An Angel! An angel carrying a great trumpet through which he will cry to the whole world my name – THOMAS CHATTERTON!' And this was accordingly done by the potter in charge.

About the 1870s, some full-sized children's meat plates were issued by Brownfields who named the series 'Pastimes'. Decoration took the form of children playing various games in a style reminiscent of Birket Foster, a popular illustrator of the day. Later designs after the style of Kate Greenaway (1846–1901) were great nursery favourites and one of her tea services in its original box can be seen at the Museum of Childhood in Edinburgh. I have a couple of plates each one of which shows a different scene from Bertha and Florence K. Upton's entrancing Golliwog books. They are on a green ground.

DOLL DISHES AND TOY TEA SETS

Children's small tea sets and tiny doll dishes will both appeal to the collector of minutiae as they form an attractive side-line in this field of Juvenilia. Between 1843 to 1867, when Copeland and Garret were in control of Spode's, one of their specialities was dolls' tea sets. Cups were only $1\frac{1}{4}''$ high with matching saucers of blue and gold, bearing the Spode mark. A tea pot, covered sugar bowl and

cream jug completed the set. Incidentally, Spode made miniature china candlesticks too only $1'' - 1\frac{1}{2}''$ high.

Another very attractive little girls' tea set can be found in the well-known Tea Leaf pattern of ironstone china which reached its peak of popularity during the 1890s. One set shown was marked 'Mellor, Taylor and Company, England'. Miniature sets, too, come in the Moss Rose design, also of ironstone.

Little china soup tureens, long parted from their soup plates, have much charm on account of their small prim patterns. Then there are little dishes, bowls and jugs that can be picked up in pressed glass. One little jug seen recently was in the shape of an owl, while a round dish had a lid on which a glass cow sat, munching. Tiny creamware jelly moulds can also be very attractive.

Of a much later date, but now being collected and steadily rising in price are nursery china pieces decorated with characters from the *Tales* of Beatrix Potter.

DECORATED EGGS

In the North of England there has long been a custom of giving a prettily painted china egg, a pinch of salt and a piece of bread to a new baby when it goes out for the first time held, tenderly, in a mother's arms or pushed in a pram.

Many of these decorated china eggs, seen once on a nursery mantelshelf or in a cottage parlour, were produced by Sunderland potters and can form a fascinating collection. To begin with, there are the quaint and long-forgotten names to note on them like SAMUEL TULIP, 1887; or, a more ordinary one, WILLIAM THOMPSON, 1852. For the most part, these decorated eggs, unmarked, were sold from door to door by itinerant hawkers who also took orders for them in the North. But two potters who did impress their names on what were known as 'Gift' eggs were William Walley (1785–1842), who had his workshop in Marsh Street, Shelton, Staffordshire; and John Dawson, who set up his pottery works at South Hylton, three miles west of Sunderland, County Durham in 1836. Among the many novelty items that Dawson produced were not only painted birthday eggs for children but ones in lustre for adults.

Wherever Her Majesty Queen Victoria happened to be the sentimental and age-old practise of giving an egg or some other appropriate gift at Easter was observed by the Queen. For instance, in her charming and well-recorded account of the years she spent at Court, first as Maid of Honour, then as a Woman of the Bedchamber, Marie Malet tells how, one Easter, the Easter of 1899, she was given a little lapis lazuli egg tied on to a small bunch of pink roses from the Queen besides a similar one in green enamel from Princess Mary.

For many years, Victorian mothers and housewives laboriously prepared, dyed and decorated hard-boiled eggs for Easter Sunday and some have survived. The eggs were first wrapped round in a frame of green ferns and crocus petals; then came a layer of onion peel after which the whole was put in a cloth and firmly tied with string. The eggs were then boiled in a solution of coffee grounds till hard-boiled.

When lifted and unwrapped, each egg was found to be amazingly coloured and patterned. The coffee grounds gave them a brown colour, the onion peel various yellow tints and the ferns their pattern. Finally, a rub of butter added gloss. In the north-east districts of England, Easter eggs were bowled on a lawn or field until they cracked, when they were eaten in the open, symbolical of an age-old fertility rite.

242 *North Country gift eggs: One with ship, one with rose, one with horses found at horse fairs for use as a love token, c. 1860*

8 Pictures without Paint

243 *Fine example of 'Skeletonising'. Transparent leaves and dried seed pods on black velvet ground. Original cruciform wooden frame, c. 1860*

244 *Cork Castle on embossed paper surround in oval gilt frame, c. 1830*

There was nothing that prosperous Victorians of good social standing liked more than to clutter the walls of their homes with large paintings by well-known Royal Academicians of the day, together with mezzotints, steel engravings, family silhouettes and water-colours; the last-named often being the amateur work of a talented son or daughter who were ardent and often very good sketchers. Their work was usually relegated to bedrooms.

In every category of subject, from landscapes to portraiture, from genre to problem, Victorian paintings have reached an astronomical price when sent to salerooms whereas some 20 years ago, and more, it was only the discerning who collected them. Re-assessed as to their present-day value and status in the art world by such authoritive historians as Mr. Graham Reynolds in his *Painters of the Victorian Scene*, 1956, and more recently by Mr. Jeremy Maas in *Victorian Painters*, 1970, there is no need here to draw attention to the pictures found in the Victorian home.

Instead, a small gallery that lies somewhat apart from the one which has been so brilliantly illuminated by modern art historians will come under inspection. But the pictures it contains carry few signatures. For they were done by women for the most part; by ladies denied the right to become professional painters by a strict convention ruling in their day. This convention barred them from entering a professional studio to work with men students drawing and painting from the nude because of their sex and gentle birth. When this barrier was at last removed by the combined efforts of a pressure group of nineteenth century women artists led by Lady Butler, the way was made open for women painters of the calibre of Frances Hodgkins, Ethel Walker and Gwen John to have their work accepted on equal terms with their peers and to be judged by them, impartially, with no reference made to their sex or social standing.

Since earliest times, then, portraiture was not for women nor was it rated as a genteel accomplishment. Allowed only to draw and paint flowers and plants to help them in their needlework designs, ladies copied these largely from the plates of illustrated herbals. However in 1606, Henry Peachman published his significant *Graphic,* a manual to encourage a taste among ladies for artistic pursuits other than needlework and to instruct them, generally 'or drawing and limning in water-colours'.

His book was an instantaneous success and was soon followed by others. From now on, a steady stream of pictures, but pictures still done in the most odd materials, in scraps of silk, satin and felt rifled from the work-box with additional touches in paint, began to appear. This early form of pictorial collage or appliqué work, now recognised as a true artistic medium, owes much of its originality of materials to women.

During Queen Victoria's long reign there was nothing they did not attempt by way of new materials like hair, cork, and tinsel for their pictures. But one of the most successful mediums remained as always the *fabric* picture now thoroughly Victorianised.

FABRIC PICTURES

During the seventeenth to eighteenth centuries, by way of convent education or through instruction given to them by emigrée governesses (all convent-bred), upper-class Englishwomen were initiated into the art of making elaborate pictures in fabric. One form of them took expression in Carolean stump-work. What Stuart and Georgian ladies began, their Regency and Victorian female descendants carried on with and perfected. Taking endless trouble they home-dyed individual samples of silk, satin, chiffon, velvet, muslin and cotton materials to the exact shade required by them to cut-out, and make the leaves and petals of the flowers they knew best and loved. Flowers depicted in Victorian fabric pictures are usually luscious-looking roses, dahlias, peonies, tulips and auriculas. Sometimes, a spray of honeysuckle or forget-me-not is introduced. When not arranged in a formal vase, or cornucopia of plenty, Victorian flowers in fabric are presented in a rustic basket. Extremely decorative, these pictures lend themselves well to be hung in a modern interior.

But women have not been the only creators of fabric pictures. Men have executed them as well and, in particular, one man with great brilliance. He was G. Smart, Artist in Cloth and Velvet Pictures to H.R.H. the Duke of Sussex. Mr. Smart was a country tailor who lived at Frant in East Sussex during the opening years of the nineteenth century. He became the subject of a fascinating article by R. F. Johnson that appeared in *Country Life* on September 15th, 1960, under the title of 'A Rag-Bag Rowlandson'. Today his pictures are preserved in the Town Museum of Royal Tunbridge Wells and enchanting they are, too, expressive of a lively rustic wit and extremely colourful.

With snippets of cloth and fragments of lace, linen, buckram and kid, Smart pierced together his compositions, making good use of all the left-over bits he had from making suits for the gentry.

245 *Bouquet of Felt Flowers in vase on black velvet ground,* c. 1820

246 *Portrait of Mr. Bright, Postman of Tunbridge Wells by G. Smart, 'Artist in Cloth and Velvet', c. 1830*

As for subjects, they were all to hand. So he did portraits in the simplified and naive style of the itinerant artist of old Bright, the Tunbridge Wells postman, and of Goody Betty the Goose-woman always met with on the road near Eridge-Castle. In her chintz gown, hooded cloak and with an inverted scuttle-shaped bonnet on her head, Goody Betty remains an unforgettable figure in fabric.

But this highly imaginative tailor did not concentrate on doing regulation portraits alone. He contrived to make some moving! To quote from Mr. Johnson's article:

'Against a background derived, perhaps, from the not-far-distant seascape of Upnor on the Medway, he contrived a magnificent hussar, who, by a simple mechanism at the back of the picture, can be made to pull off his head-dress in salute as Lord Charles Hay had done at Fontenoy.'

DRESSED PRINTS AND AMELIAS

Moved by the sentimental appeal of the engravings of Bartolozzi, Francis Wheatley and Angelica Kaufmann and thinking how happily they might hang on the walls of their boudoirs, nineteenth-century ladies proceeded to 'dress' them further with tiny scraps of silken materials superimposed on their painted clothes and draperies. In this way the seprints were given substantial body while faces were treated to make-up by tinting them delicately in water-colour. In time, these embellished engravings came to be known as 'Dressed Prints'. A whole collection of them that featured certain period beauties once passed through my hands. There was a 'dressed' engraving, I remember, of Elizabeth, Duchess of York, who had been given a marvellous stole of spotted flannel while some handsome bands of beadwork had been added to her three-cornered, Tudor head-dress. A brown silk curtain was looped behind her figure, tied back by a piece of golden cord. Another of the Duchess of Monmouth (Charles II's own sweet mistress, Nell Gwyn) showed her to have real

247 *An 'Amelia' or dressed print, c. 1850*

126

lace ruffles, while the most enchanting little pink silk bows tied up her curls. The engravings themselves which had been so richly 'embellished' were of eighteenth century origin but the actual 'dressing' of them from the kind of materials used dated them as *c.* 1850.

About this time, Dressed Prints were also known as 'Amelias', taking their new name from an artist who achieved considerable commercial success, it is said, in this medium. Her work can be identified by the use of real hair and the way she padded her figures. *The Young Lady's Book*, By a Lady (1829) gives detailed instructions on how to produce a Dressed Print.' Fine examples show the background to be usually hand-drawn but those sold in Victorian times were engraved only.

PIN-PRICK PICTURES

Pins have been put to both a familiar and odd use for centuries. At one time, for instance, to accept a pin from an old woman reputed to be a witch, put one in her power. William Cowper, the poet (1731–1800) owned a pin-pricked picture of which he was very fond and wrote these lines about it:

> *Could Time, his flight reversed, restore the hours*
> *When, laying with thy vestures' tissued flowers,*
> *The violet, the pink, the jessamine,*
> *I prick'd them into paper with a pin.*

Lines on the Receipt of My Mother's Picture.

A Pin-Pricked Picture is not easily come by as few have survived the rough passage of time, and little is really known about them except that they have been in existence in England for close on 200 years. An amazing variety of design is displayed in the making of them and those which include touches of water-colour have much charm. Watercolours occur when a border of flowers and foliage, partly pricked and partly coloured, appear as framework to figures shown. From the introduction to Andrew Tuer's *Old Fashioned Children's Books* comes the following passage referring to pin-pricked pictures:

'Pricking pictures with pins was another agreeable accomplishment. The pins were of several thicknesses, broad lines and heavy shadows being prickt with stout, and the finer work with thin pins. A toothed wheel with sharp points was used for outlines. For filling up large spaces two or more wheels were mounted on an axle. Without such labour-saving appliances the more ambitious and microscopically minute pin-prickt pictures, specimens of which survive, could not have been achieved.'

Another type of pin-pricked picture, Early

248   *Pin-pricked picture of 'Boy with Violin', c. 1820*

Victorian in date, that occasionally turns up shows men and women wearing what appears to be fancy dress. These pictures have been described in an article in *The Young Ladies' Book: a Manual of Elegant Recreations, Exercises and Pursuits* under the title of 'Piercing Costumes on Paper'.

'Turkish or other figures, in oriental costume or draperies, are produced by a combination of water-

127

colour painting for the features with a series of small punctures made with needles of various sizes for the dresses. The face, hands and feet being first drawn and coloured, the outline and folds of the drapery are marked with a tracing needle; the paper is laid then on a smooth cloth, or a few sheets of blotting-paper, and the punctures inserted in the folds of the dress from the front to the back of the paper; the drawing is then laid with its surface downwards, and the interior of the various outlines filled up with punctures made with a very fine needle, from the back to the front of the paper. It sometimes affords a pleasing variety if the costume be wholly or partially coloured, as it relieves the monotony of the white. Needles of various sizes should be used at discretion, and the whole of the background or body

of the paper painted in some sober opaque colour to throw up the figure.'

It will appear from this extract that needles were taking over from pins at this juncture to produce a new kind of pricked picture; also that more drawing and painting skill was required, which was all to the good where ladies were concerned.

In the Victorian nursery, many children were given pieces of paper on which designs had been traced with a pencil; these were placed upon a well-stuffed chair or sofa and the design pricked out with a pin, the pin going easily through the paper into the chair or sofa and then drawn out with a nice *plop*, a sound reminiscent of squeezing a fat fuchsia bud till it bursts, which delighted the child engaged on this work.

249 *Early form of Victorian paper collage with satirical verse relating to one, John, who 'drown'd himsel amang the nappy!', c. 1850*

Kings may be great but John was glorious!
Oer all the ills of life victorious,
Care mad to see a man sae happy, Een drown'd himsel amang the nappy.

CUT-PAPER PICTURES

It has been recorded that Mrs. Delany (1700–1788) first experimented in cut-paper work by making a little book on whose pages of stiff dark-blue paper, she pasted small miniature houses, groups of figures and animals cut with her scissors from fine white paper.

To begin with, the superior paper used for cutting by ladies was imported from France. But after 1800, English paper mills so improved the texture and quality of their paper that they completely took over the French market.

Professional English paper-cutters such as 'Nat Berminham, Scut', are recorded as practising their craft, commercially, from 1750. A century later, it was the turn of a Mr. F. Windsor whose cut-paper work was written up in *The Expositor* of July 26, 1851, under the heading of:

LANDSCAPES CUT IN PAPER

'At the Crystal Palace some beautiful specimens of cutting in paper, in imitation of nature have recently been placed on the walls of the stair-case. They are the production of Mr. F. Windsor, the profile artist at the Royal Polytechnic Institution. They consist of a cedar tree, a landscape, an elm tree in high relief and an imitation of an etching. They are of a large size, one being 2 ft. 10 in. by 3 ft. 3 in.'

The Victorians were as much enamoured of cut-paper work as the Georgians. Their love led to it being treated to new forms of expression. One form is found in the embellishment of Christmas cards, valentines and memorial cards; another in the art of the silhouettist. From him the Victorians ordered their profiles and those of their children to be cut and these were then framed in maplewood and hung in their parlours. But the art of the silhouettist has already been fully documented and so will not be dealt with here.

250 *Cut-paper picture of young girl seated at a spinning wheel. From a lady's album, c. 1850*
251 (right) *Amusing presentation of 'Lady Fishing' in cut-paper, white on red ground, c. 1825*

CASTLES IN CORK

From the subtlety of scissor-work, ladies moved on to experiment with a pen-knife, employing as their medium a very odd material indeed, Cork. The subject-matter taken for this new form of picture was largely inspired by Sir Walter Scott's Waverley novels, combined with the Romantic Revival – a movement which had engendered in delicately nurtured young womanhood a passionate interest in everything that smacked of the picturesque. So it was castles with pepperpot towers or crenellated mansions, ivied ruins, crumbling stone statues and fallen pillars that came to be reproduced by the cork artist in his pictures. Sometimes, these castles can be identified as being real, and not imaginary ones, by the name found written under them. But more often than not, they carry no identification tag nor the signature of the artist.

Full instructions on how to make a 'castle in cork' is given in *Enquire Within* as late as the 1865 edition. Equipment needed seems to have been a sharp-bladed little knife, scissors and glue. Should

decoration be needed to enhance a romantic and naturalistic note, it was necessary to have in hand some pieces of dried moss and bark, tiny ferns and powdered flour. This material was added in suitable places to the overall scene which was of a castle either rising in a wood or built beside a northern loch. *Enquire Within* recommends ladies

252 *Castellated mansion in cork, original black and gilt frame, c. 1830*

253 *Large scale cork landscape of Fribourg, Switzerland*

when travelling abroad, in Italy, say, to take all materials 'so easily come by and light to carry' to make a cork picture as a souvenir. So they could, and did, recreate a 'Ruins in Cork', reproducing part of the Coliseum in Rome or the temple at Paestum.

A cork picture showing either a castle or ruin can be the work of both an amateur or professional artist and their unusual colouring, ranging from a dead leaf-brown to a rich chestnut shade, gives them an individuality and charm, all their own. The best examples are worthy of survival and their price is steadily rising.

HAIR PICTURES

Pictures in hair were a by-product of that extra-ordinary obsession Victorians had in the suit-ability of hair to provide them with mournful souvenirs of their beloved dead. This was by way of hair jewellery (memorial rings, brooches, etc.) and by hair pictures. Although this vogue reached its zenith in the nineteenth century, hair-work stems back to Georgian days and even beyond.

A hair picture is composed of fine but ex-tremely tough threads of black, brown or gold hair, but rarely red, which were used for silks instead of silks embroidered on to a background fabric of pale-hued satin or watered silk. Subjects depicted can be a landscape in miniature; a house, real or imaginary, set in a tiny park; of some funereal scene like a pillared urn against which a slender black figure leans! Fragile and rare, pictures in hair are not easily come by, for they are mostly

130

preserved by old families still living in an ancestral home and thus fondly treasured.

During the 1860s and '70s, it was fashionable to devise a hair wreath as a pastime while mourning. This wreath was made either from the hair of the one dead, or from the combined locks of the entire family. Set within a recessed frame of ebonised wood it was hung up on the wall of a favourite room till replaced by another pictorial vagary of fashion.

254 *Country house in park embroidered in hair on white satin ground, c. 1825*

PICTURES IN FEATHER

Some of the prettiest examples of 'pictures without paint' are found in feather work. 'Painting with Feathers', as it was termed, had its heyday during the 1840s and '50s when feather flowers were preferred for a time to those reproduced in wax or shells. But again, like hair pictures, they stem from earlier times. For instance, 'Birds executed in their own Plumage' were extremely popular during the

Regency and the craft was given a prominent place in those listed at this time. Bird pictures of this date (*c.* 1820 or so) are treated far more delicately than those that followed. Each bird, as it might be a duck or jay, is usually placed within the framework of a tiny water-colour sketch suggesting its native habitat. The final result has the delicate charm and colouring of a Chinese print.

As far back as 1771, when Mrs. Hannah Robertson, a teacher in ornamental crafts, publish-

255 *A pair of birds in delicate feather-work, c. 1820. 'Jay with Young' and 'Drake', painted-touches to background*

257 *Swag of multi-coloured feather flowers and painted butterfly in gilt frame, c. 1840*

ed *The Ladies School of Art*, she advised on how 'To Preserve Birds with their Elegant Plumage Unhurt'. Later, in 1835, a Mrs. Kinglon carried on Mrs. Hannah's good work in her own manual *The Wreath*. She gives the full treatment for a bird picture in feather, her methods being as following:

'After the outline of the chosen bird has been drawn on a piece of fine white paper, the head, neck and body are filled in with feathers plucked from the dead model which, of course, is to hand. Every tiny feather must be put in its correct place with a minute pair of pliers after the surface of the paper has been prepared with gum. Great care has to be taken, also, to keep this gum from oozing through the feathers – a tricky operation requiring good eyesight and a very light touch. When every feather is in place, and secured, a round piece of paper is cut out, painted and varnished, in imitation of the natural eye or a small glass eye is used,

instead. The bill, legs and claws of the bird are drawn in and painted by hand.'

During the reign of Queen Victoria, pictures of birds in feather became coarser in outline and lacked their earlier delicate look of a Chinese print. But they still remained decorative and with the popularity of maintaining an aviary in the home, the parrot, macaw and canary were added to the more humble run of jays and robins.

About 1850, pictures of feathered birds came to be produced commercially. These were advertised as being made with feathers of authentic hues that had not been tinted or dyed. A few names of artists working in this medium have been preserved: Wilhelmina Randolph of 55 Marsham Street, Westminster; W. J. Maguire of 5 Chenies Street, Bedford Square; and Mary Hool whose address is unknown.

PRESSED FLOWER PICTURES

In the nineteenth century, both well-bred girls and those of humble parentage enjoyed 'rambling' about England's still lovely and unspoilt countryside. While rambling they pursued that most delightful hobby of all – botany. For botany had been put on the social map for Victorian ladies by Miss Anne Pratt (1806–1889) as successfully as gardening had by Jane Loudon.

Strolling down lanes or emerging slightly tousled from woods, girls, first in bonnets and shawls, then in a smart Inverness cape and Balmoral boots, could be seen complete with their black tin vasculums in which they took home the plants and flowers, ferns and mosses, they had collected so arduously. Some of this floral treasure was preserved, dried and tabulated, correctly, in an album or *hortus siccus*; some of it went into the making of a picture.

Though Victorian 'Pressed flower' pictures lack the more poetic appeal of those done in delicate water-colour, they still possess unusual charm and are extremely decorative. An early exponent of this craft appears to have been a little sewing-girl befriended by Princess Charlotte who rescued her from a London slum and placed her in healthier and more comfortable circumstances. So grateful was she that on every anniversary of her Royal

258 *Graceful arrangement of dried seaweeds, ferns, and mosses when botany was a 'must' in the Victorian schoolroom, c. 1845*

133

259   *Unusual composition of two ladies garbed in pressed moth's wings strolling through a dried fern grove, c. 1840*

260   *Specimen bouquet of pressed maidenhair ferns and flowers bound with coloured floral label marked 'My Hope'. From an album, 1850*

patroness's tragic death in 1816, she would take 'an ornamental composition of dried flowers' to Claremont, where Prince Leopold still lived, as a mark of her love and constant gratitude. Touched by this act and moved too by the delicacy of her work, Prince Leopold took these pictures (there were about 30) with him when he left England to be King of the Belgians. They were hung on the walls of his palace at Laeken.

Pressed flower pictures fall into two groups. One that shows small bouquets gracefully arranged when bouquet-making was a practised art and in these one can come across little pieces of maidenhair fern, seaweed fronds and dried berries; the other that depicts sacred symbols, as it might be a cross or wreath done in pressed flowers together

with ivy leaves. Again, there are some 'pressed flower' pictures which reveal that they were the outcome of 'botanising' while abroad, for these show the use of unfamiliar flora and fauna. One such picture has been described by Flora Thompson in *Over to Candleford*. In a cottage she saw – 'Some pressed flowers from the Holy Lane arranged in a frame made of olive wood from the Mount of Olives.'

Variations on the Victorian 'pressed flower' picture also exist, for in my collection I have one that shows two crinolined ladies, whose garments are done in moths' wings and flower-petals, strolling through a ferny grove. It is an enchanting little composition.

SKELETONISING OR NATURE PRINTING

In England, 'skeletonising' took the form of making Phantom Bouquets in Early Victorian times. These were bouquets composed of 'skeletonised' seed-pods and leaves placed against a background cloth of dark-blue paper or black velvet to show off their spectral charm. In a shallow recessed wooden frame they were hung up with great effect on a wall. As soon as the fern craze struck the

Victorian home and fernhouses, fern vases and fern-hunting became the order of the day, Spatterwork replaced Phantom Bouquets. This form of decorative art was given full treatment in *Cassell's Household Guide* for 1875. July, it seems, was the month of the year in which to gather leaf-specimens and poplar and aspen leaves figured high in the list for their beauty. Apple, pear, crab-apple, and ornamental ivies were the most easy to be treated. A maple leaf had to be picked 'young' and then 'cleaned with a hard brush and a soft, tapping motion', before being placed in a pan filled with rain-water. The pan was then exposed to the sun and air for about two weeks or more. The process of maceration must have been the most unpleasant part of this craft, for on removing the decayed, pulpy matter from the leaf to obtain the perfect skeleton, the smell must have been quite unbearable.

Another method for the making of attractive 'Wall Ornaments' was practised round 1870. It employed the use of dried ferns, leaves and mosses, arranged in devices like an anchor or the Prince of Wales' Feathers. These arrangements were pinned down on light-coloured paper then sprayed all over with Indian ink. On removing them, a well-defined silhouette of every fern and leaf was left behind on the paper which was then squared off, framed and hung up as a picture. Lady Dorothy Nevill, a brilliantly clever but somewhat eccentric personality in Victorian society much sought after, was recognised as an expert in 'skeletonising'; so much so that her friend, Sir William Hooker wrote from the Royal Gardens, Kew, on 9 April, 1861:

'You have excelled in preparing skeletonising leaves, I know, and I have seen some foliage in the early stage of the operation, in vessels of soft rain-water to remove by a putrefying process the pulpy matter. A lady friend of mine wants to know the further process for removing *ALL* the decaying matter and leaving the fern in a beautifully clean state when the operation is finished. Is it chloride of lime or some bleaching fluid?'

Enquire Within Upon Everything (1875) gives instructions, by the way, of how to skeletonise ferns and leaves, but by the end of the century little mention is found in any book of this minor artifact.

261 *Companion bouquet to figure 260, but featuring a skeletonised leaf and tied with blue ribbon, a paper rose and paper Cupid's head. From an Album, 1850*

262 *Phantom bouquet under glass shade, c. 1860*

TINSEL PORTRAITS

During the Regency, private theatricals were much *en vogue* and many titled families owned their own theatres attached or built inside the ancestral home. Such a house was Bentley Priory, Stanmore, Middlesex, country seat of the Abercorns, where plays were enacted regularly by amateurs and where too Queen Adelaide, widow of William IV lived in retirement for some years till her death.

From this aristocratic interest taken in the world of the stage, the Juvenile Theatre originated in the early days of the Regency as a kind of theatrical souvenir. From about 1808, portraits of famous actors and actresses of the time were sold for a *penny plain* or *tuppence coloured*. These portraits were the forerunners of our own 'pin-ups' today and soon after their appearance came to be embellished by tinsel, velvet or silk applications. J. K. Green claims to have been the 'original inventor and publisher of Juvenile Theatrical Prints' and to have been the first to publish all the characters in a play plus sheets of scenery and a simplified book of words.

In response to popular demand, toy theatre publishers began to produce and sell, stamped-out tinsel ornaments, in every shape and size which also included stars, dots and spangles and all the gleaming accessories of stage costume like Roman helmets, breast-plates, sweeping plumes, crowns, swords and poignards which were retailed by fancy stationers to stage-fans or ladies interested

in a new pastime. This took the form of 'dressing' up theatrical portraits of contemporary stage stars shown usually in their favourite roles, after the style of 'Dressed Prints' or *Amelias*.

It was generally considered that the stage costumes of actresses like Miss Grant in the role of Ophelia or Miss Sharpe as Columbine offered less scope for embellishment than their male counterparts. This is hard to believe, although, as a point in question, tinsel portraits of nineteenth-century stage heroines are more difficult to come by than those of leading actors like Mr. Freer or Charles

263 *Tinsel portraits showing the Princess Royal as a child, c. 1860*

Keen. The popularity of tinsel portraits continued till about 1830 when they came to be produced in dwindling numbers throughout the century till about 1900. Today, however, they are again much in demand and originals are sought after to form a collection such as some of our leading actors and film stars of today have already formed.

264   *Mr. Freer in the role of Richard III, c. 1860*

PYROGRAPHIC PANELS

Pokerwork (i.e. pyrography in its simplest and most naive form) was first listed as a period accomplishment in the English school room of the 1870s and '80s when shellwork, waxwork, etc. had been replaced by newer up-to-date ploys like playing on the banjo instead of the harp and piano, and old plantation songs were heard in the drawing-room instead of Thomas Moore's Irish ballads. *The Lady's Newspaper, The Girl's Annual* and *Parlour Recreations,* etc. all supplied articles from time to time on how effective pokerwork could be for decorating card and letter racks, leather portfolio cases and brackets.

Mr. Edward Pinto, the leading authority on wooden bygones has a unique collection of pyrographic panels, besides a self-portrait by Ralph Marshall whom he records as being probably the most versatile and skilful of nineteenth-century pyrographic artists, though he (Mr. Pinto) wonders if it is not a moot point whether pyrography should be classified as an art or craft.

It was in the Victoria era that pyrography reach-ed a high standard of craftsmanship when used for wall decoration. This took the form of reproducing well-known pictures and portraits of the day by burning them, exact line by line, with, first, the glowing, sizzling tip of a red-hot poker, then by one, gas-fired, on to smooth flat panels of fine grained hard wood as sycamore, birch and satin-wood but best of all, box. No pigments were allowed, but by burning to various depths a pleasing range of varying colours from light browns to sepia and black was arrived at – very pleasing to the eye as seen against a background of light-coloured wood.

Apart from Mrs. Ramey and her curious draw-ings with a poker, there were several distinguished artists who indulged in pyrography. One was Ralph Marshall, awarded a medal for his exhibits in this craft at the Great Exhibition of 1851. Since 1830, he had been experimenting in this medium by reproducing candle and lamplit scenes charac-teristic of Henry Moreland's work. Then he at-tempted others of a more romantic nature finally ending up with a series of copies of the Raphael Cartoons. Another pyrographic artist of this time

137

was John Smith, who specialised in copying full-length portraits of the nobility.

By the end of the century, though, that gallery for ornamental pictures came to be closed. Women who had once been its main contributors were now following men into the far more satisfying world of real art; that world of paint and oil and canvas. Today, however, an ever-increasing interest is being taken in the ornamental arts of the past. What is more, many old and long forgotten art-forms are being revived or re-created in a modern idiom. Fabric pictures, pictures in shells and pressed flowers, all have their admirers and are quickly snapped up wherever they appear. Recently, several London picture galleries have been staging exhibitions of artists working today in shells, gauze and pressed flowers. Even the pyrographic artist appears to be emerging, or so Mr. Edward Pinto has informed us. Only instead of creating pictorial panels on wood with a red-hot, sizzling poker, he uses now a heat-controlled electric needle.

⑨ Parlour Pastimes

265 *'Young Ladies Doing Shellwork' Aquatint, artist unknown, c. 1825*

Elegant Arts for Ladies comprise the making of Feather Flowers, Hair Ornaments, Porcupine Quill Work, Printing on Vellum, Velvet and Glass, Gilt Leatherwork, the Gilding of Plaster Casts, Bead & Bugle Work, Seaweed Pictures and the mysteries of Diaphanie and Potichomanie.

The Ladies' Magazine, 1850

England has long been unique for a kind of Imitative or Mock Art largely based on the suppressed artistic talents and inventive powers of first Stuart and then Georgian and Victorian ladies of leisure who because of their gentle birth and sex were denied the right to be professional artists and so remained merely gifted amateurs. As Louisa, Marchioness of Waterford wrote to her sister, summing up the situation:

'It is not considered desirable that ladies of gentle birth should possess artistic talent and it is actively undesirable that they should ever openly parade such talent.'

Augustus Hare, *Lives of Two Noble Ladies*

Through the centuries, then, except in some rare circumstances, when ladies modelled, they did so in bread and wax. Not for them the masculine medium of plaster and stone. In the same way, for bricks, they took shells and created the most enchanting floral trophies and grottoes in the eighteenth century. Later with feathers, tinted paper, gauze and lambswool, they contrived exquisite bouquets which were housed under imposing glass shades for posterity, adding pressed ferns and leaves with blackthorn twigs dipped in scarlet paint for coral if more decoration was needed.

During the reign of Queen Victoria, several factors not only increased the popularity but brought into being many new parlour pastimes for ladies. This age was, indeed, their heyday. To begin with: there was a superabundance of cheap, domestic labour which gave nearly all upper and middle-class young women, besides matrons, a great deal of time on their hands in which they could carry out their favourite accomplishments. Daughters of rich tradesmen who had received a genteel education wished to model wax flowers or design a shell box like the squire's daughter. But the biggest incentive of all came with the Oxford Movement, when church restoration took place throughout England. For this praiseworthy effort, funds had to be raised and Fancy Fairs and Summer Fêtes were the order of the day. No one has described these fairs and fêtes better in her novels than Miss Charlotte Yonge. Again and again, she tells us of the widespread and continuous demand for suitable articles to be sent to the nearest repository and sold there in the name of Charity. Amongst these articles were: 'Pincushions, watch-guards (knitted in beads or crotcheted), leather pen-wipers, netted purses and the like. The making of these became a craze which entirely upset the school-room routine . . . Even the governess descended so far as to countenance paste-board boxes being plastered with rice and sealing-wax, alum baskets, dressed dolls and every conceivable trumpery.'

In *The Long Vacation* (1895) a superb description is given by Charlotte Yonge of a monster Victorian Fête organised on the grand scale. Assembled on the stall were some very odd objects, indeed. They included, 'a fat red cushion like brick-dust enlivened by half an embroidered cauliflower, shawls, bags, drawings, screens, scrapbooks, photographs and a statue, half as large of life of *The Dirty Boy.*'

At the Castle Museum, Norwich, the replica of such a stall, complete with a miniature display of extraordinary wares has been preserved, the work of a lady skilled in needlecraft and blessed with infinite patience.

The Jew's-basket known to Charlotte Brontë and others provided yet another stimulus for the production of charity ornaments. It is described by her in *Shirley* (1849) as 'a willow repository of the capacity of a good-sized family clothes-basket dedicated to the purpose of conveying from house to house a monster collection of pincushions, needlebooks, card-racks, work bags, and articles of infant wear made by willing or reluctant hands of Christian ladies of the parish to be sold at prices unblushingly exorbitant.'

It was not surprising, then, that before the nineteenth century was far advanced, the publishing world took over from the resident family governess the task of instructing young English girlhood in a multitude of ornamental arts and crafts by printing a number of little books all about them. Typical of this genre of books is *The Artist: or, Young Ladies Instructor* by B. F. Gandee (1835), whose frontispiece and title page are printed in colours by George Baxter. Now a book collector's item, *The Artist* is sheer delight to dip into. Mr. Gandee, it seems, lived at Richmond in Surrey and lists a weird number of parlour arts such as Grecian Painting, Oriental Tinting, Inlaying, etc. which he taught besides other 'Manufactories of Ornamental Articles for Fancy Fairs which include Pier Baskets and Writing Folios.'

An odd mixture! Very soon, following Mr. Gandee's lead, ladies' magazines took to listing the names of yet more 'Parlour Pastimes', besides instructions on how to carry them out. There was Artistic Pithwork, for instance, that would appeal to lovers of nature as well as Cone and Moss work. There was Leekwork, an example of which I have yet to come across. Porcupine Quillwork, Montmellick Work and Jewelled Embroidery. This latter work employed the use of rose-beetles' wings and transparent fish-scales. Crinkled Paper and Bent Iron objects were also starred together with Fretwork and Leatherwork that came in towards the 1880s. Continually, *The Temple of Fancy, Rathbone Place, Oxford Street, London*, is given as the address where materials could be obtained for all types of ornamental work.

An amusing diatribe delivered against the gentry for their tiresome habit of pursuing odd hobbies in their leisure hours comes in Wilkie Collins' *The Moonstone* (1868). It is made by old Gabriel Betteridge, family butler and house steward, on the occasion of his young mistress's (Miss Julia Verinder) birthday, when she sets out to paint the door of her boudoir with griffins, birds, flowers and cupids in the Italian style of decoration then fashionable. As old Gabriel stands by watching her, assisted by her adoring cousin, Frank, he soliloquises on why it is that gentlefolk:

'Drift blindfold always into some nasty pursuit. I have seen them (ladies as well as gentlemen) go out day after day to catch newts, beetles, spiders and frogs and then come home to stick pins in them in the name of Natural History. Or, sometimes, again, spoiling a pretty flower with pointed instruments or staining their fingers doing photography.'

In spite, though, of old Gabriel's condemnation, young ladies like Julia Verinder continued happily to pursue whatever parlour pastime was fashionable at the moment. Among them could be counted the Misses Margery and Esther Manners living in a small Chelsea cottage whose windows overlooked the high, walled-in garden of Tudor House, Dante Gabriel Rossetti's home in Cheyne Walk. In their small neat parlour were:

'Wax flowers and fruit under glass shades on rainbow-coloured mats made of Berlin woolwork; boxes contrived out of numberless shells reposing on bead mats made by Miss Margery; and photograph albums containing groups of dead and gone relations, all of whom Hetty knew by heart and Molly was never tired of looking at because of their outlandish costumes. The walls were hung with stuffed birds and fishes in addition to a number of wonderful water-colours painted by Miss Margery and her sister in her youth. Gigantic shells adorned the mantelpiece, together with china ornaments and vases full of everlasting flowers.'

A Book With Seven Seals (Anon.)

But as the century advanced, genteel old maids like the Misses Manners began to disappear one by one. The spinsters who replaced them were busy, energetic women seeking the vote and becoming more and more emancipated. If they wished to express themselves, artistically, they did not decorate a glove box with shells or a vase in potichomanie but took up painting instead professionally. They entered other worlds too; the world of medicine and of science and horticulture. The narrow confines of the Victorian drawing-room and parlour were left behind them forever and the strangely diverse, sometimes beautiful, sometimes quite hideous objects, over whose creation the gentle sex had for so long laboured, were ignored and neglected till our day when they have come to be admired again and collected.

VICTORIAN SHELLWORK

To assist Georgian ladies with their shellwork, Mrs. Hannah Robertson, who ran a fancy goods shop in Grosvenor Square, published *The Ladies School of Arts* in 1806. In it, Mrs. Robertson described various techniques for shellwork. However by 1837, when Princess Victoria ascended the throne, shellwork was no longer the mad craze it had been. Under the new name of Conchology, it had become the subject of prim study in the Victorian school-room – 'For there is no cruelty in the pursuit and subjects are so clean and ornamental to a Boudoir', declared one writer in *The Ladies Magazine*. Grottoes were out and 'rambles' being taken along the sea-shore instead. This led, of course, to local shells being collected and taken home, where

267   *Trinket box with drawer in shape of a bed and small stuffed pincushion for a pillow. Shell decoration, c. 1860*

attempts were made to contrive some kind of easy shell-arrangement. These were very simple at first, taking the form of mere 'Cone' or 'Cairn' shapes in which shells were built up to form a small mound with dried grasses and ferns, sometimes intermixed. Known as 'Shell Trophies', two examples of this early form of Victorian shellwork can be seen at The House of Shells, Buckfast Abbey in Devon.

Another type of early Victorian shellwork comes in a 'Tree' or 'Arch' form when a tiny human figure is placed under the 'tree' variety and a miniature ship under the 'arch' kind. Set on an oval or circular plinth covered by a glass shade, many of these shell arrangements have been preserved and, in good condition, fetch high prices.

I have a water-colour sketch strongly reminiscent of Adam Buck's delicate line and colouring which shows the doll-like figures of two young girls with their raven-haired governess seated at a table, out of doors, doing shellwork. Round each frail little neck is a coral necklace; round each tiny waist, a tightly tied broad satin ribbon. No breeze will ever rise to ruffle the sleek set of their small, boyishly cropped heads nor raindrops fall to drive them indoors. There they remain, immobilised forever in paint, the quintessence of elegance and engaged in one of the most charming of occupations.

268 (right) *Example of 'arch' form of shellwork with miniature ship under the arch, c. 1840*

Baskets in Shell

Shell baskets are given a prominent place in a small attractively produced manual called *Parlour Recreations for Ladies* published in 1854. These little baskets were made of tiny 'rice' shells and had many uses. For instance, they could be used as card-holders, to decorate the top of a bride's cake at a wedding, or simply as pretty table ornaments. As card holders, shell baskets were made of millboard in an octagonal shape, their edges being glued together with long thin strips of linen after-

Shell Figurines

There are two shell-dressed dolls in early Victorian costume at the Shell Museum, Glandford, Norfolk

wards covered with green paper.

Another small and very delicate type of basket can be found made of elfin 'rice' shells. They were produced for a young girl to carry at a ball and often a small wreath or tiara for her head was included. Small rosettes of rice shells on silvered wire that 'tremble' at a touch and whose flower-petals are formed of transparent 'mussel' shells are characteristic of these baskets for a Victorian debutante. A fine example of one with a tiara to match is on view at The House of Shells, Buckfast Abbey, Devon.

and Mr. Thomas Higham has one of a boy who is dressed in jacket and trousers made of small black periwinkles except for a frontal strip of whitish bivalves on his jacket. He clasps a wicker-basket

269–70 Two shell-dressed dolls, c. 1830

of small, yellow sea-snails. This figurine – the creation of some lady's fancy – was found at Diss in Norfolk and is probably late Victorian shellwork.

Sometimes the collector of shellwork may be fortunate to come across a model of a Gothic Villa or Cottage ornée in shells. Such a house, Gothic in style, was made by a retired Isle of Wight sea captain in 1838 and is now preserved in fine condition, at the Shell House, Buckfast Abbey. Incorporated in the over-all picturesque design are coloured Alum Bay sands which adds to its interest and attraction.

Pictorial shell collage

This forms one of the largest groups of Victorian shellwork; a group to which I am indebted to Mr. Higham for supplying me with valuable information gathered by him during the many years he was establishing his unique shell collection. Mr. Higham divides pictorial shell-collage into two groups. One of which is the 'Framed' kind that could be hung on a wall; the other, the 'Encased' or 'Casketed' type usually put on a table.

Framed shellwork comes in specially constructed boxes known as 'shadow frames' or 'shadow boxes' that measure from $1\frac{1}{4}$ inches in depth to $5\frac{1}{2}$ inches. Their shape can be rectangular, circular or octagonal. Sometimes, two octagonal shadow frames of the same size, glazed or not, are found hinged together, side by side; others are placed occasionally one above the other. When opened out with the shellwork within, displayed, these octagonal 'shadow boxes' could either be hung up as wall plaques, left to stand upright, or laid down flat on a table or any other level place. Alternatively, these boxes could be shut up, face to face, and fastened with a hook-and-eye or by a lock and key. During their lifetime in the Victorian era many of these shell 'shadow boxes' must have been kept closed to account for the brilliant colours retained by their shells. It must be remembered, too, that during the eighteenth and early part of the nineteenth century cabinet-work reached a high level of workmanship and fine shellwork and fine woodwork were traditionally considered to be worthy of one another. Hence the handsome character and fine make of most 'shadow frames' or boxes.

The caskets to contain shell collage, which often comes in a mosaic form of design or sometimes of an even more elaborate pattern like Miss Musson (*c*. 1790) produced which showed a flowering tree on which a large bird sits, holding a twig in its beak, are usually fitted with a lock and key. A casket may contain (a) a single shell collage made on a ground or underlay fixed on its floor; (b) another, second collage mounted on a tray that slides or lifts out; or (c) with a collage fitted inside the lid behind glass to act, perhaps, as a model, plus three trays holding the very small specimen shells used for the work with sufficient floor-space left below the last tray to keep larger ones. This type of 'Casketed Shell Collage' made to contain shellwork is far more difficult to come by, says Mr. Higham, than the 'Framed' variety. He owns one example known as 'Mrs. Travers' Box for Ladies Shellwork' which is complete with three trays and a shell-collage for a model set in the underside of its lid. This box, found in a house at Bath in mint condition, is made of rosewood, ornamented with simple inlay. It carries the name of its maker, Miguel Sintes, a Spaniard whose firm, described as 'Makers of Marine Flower-pieces', was established at Port Mahon in Minorca, Balearic Isles. It is thought possible that this port, much used by British sailors in Victorian times, might have acted as a kind of clearing-house for the importation of Spanish shellwork which turns up in England from time to time. One means of identifying foreign shellwork is that shells were left in their natural colours by French and Spanish shell-artists (like Miguel Sintes), but in English shellwork local shells are generally used and are often painted over.

271–2   *Two examples of pictorial shell-collage in octagonal wooden boxes*

FLORAL SHELL GROUPS UNDER GLASS SHADES

Floral bouquets in shells were made first by Georgian and then by Victorian ladies. But Victorian examples do not reach the high standard of work achieved by Mrs. Delany and her eighteenth-century companions.

From the first simple Victorian 'Cone' or 'Cairn'-

shaped shell-groups ladies and their daughters advanced into making more complicated and picturesque arrangements of shell flowers when dried seaweed and coral sprigs might be added. All materials for making a Floral Shell Group to place under a shade were obtainable at dozens of little shops selling shells, madrepores, dried sea-weed, urchins, and mosses, etc. to visitors at popular South Cost towns like Weymouth, Sid-mouth, Torquay and others. Mary Wyatt of sea-weed fame (Chapter XII: Souvenirs from the Seaside) kept one at Torquay; another at Poole belonged to equally well-known Polly Perkins, a smuggler's daughter, who turned respectable and taught the craft of shellwork to many a West Country lady in the nineteenth century.

A Victorian Floral Shell Group will feature the garden flowers that were in fashion then, such as dahlias, geraniums, fat round roses, auriculas and the passion-flower – the latter flower always a favourite one as it was a sacred symbol. If it took a lady's fancy, she might also add for an appropriate touch a dried sea urchin or two and some fronds of seaweed. Floral Shell Groups made commercially were also on sale in South Coast shops to catch the eye of Victorian tourists.

As a skilled craft appealing to amateur and pro-fessional workers, shellwork is last-mentioned in *Cassell's Household Guide* for 1875 in an article entitled *A Basket of Shell Flowers*. The shells chosen to make this 'Basket' were those white, buff and pink-tinted ones found on the beach and the pretty wicker basket in which the bouquet was placed covered with strips of green tissue paper in width – half an inch. Flowers were: to the front, a large

273   *Floral shell group in straw basket*

passion-flower, lilies of the valley, May blossom, a dahlia, a moss rose damask and a small ranun-culus; at the back, China asters, snowdrops, crocuses, cineraria, a camellia, geranium and fuchsia.

By 1883 shellwork ceased to be listed either as a parlour pastime or as a commercial craft in maga-zines. In fact, *Sylvia's Home Journal* for this year recommends the 'use of coloured wools – not shells – worked over wire for making artificial flowers'.

MODELLING IN WAX

Queen Victoria had not been long on the throne when a young woman, the daughter of an Army surgeon who had left her in restricted circum-stances, called at Buckingham Palace with a superb bouquet of wax flowers. She made a humble request for this bouquet to be placed somewhere where it might catch Her Majesty's eye. Her request was granted and subsequently the Queen did notice the bouquet and, delighted by it, enquired who was the artist responsible. She was told that it was a Miss Emma Peachey.

A little while later, Emma wrote to the Palace, politely informing Her Gracious Majesty that she was going to take up modelling flowers in wax as a career. On hearing this, the Queen suggested to the Lord Chamberlain that Miss Peachey might be given a royal warrant and made her 'Artiste in Wax Flowers'. It was the first time such an appointment had been made.

From now on, Emma Peachey flourished as a wax flower-modeller, losing no opportunity to consolidate her career. For instance, on the oc-casion of the Queen's marriage to Prince Albert in 1840, she made thousands of white wax roses to be distributed as bridal favours. She produced also many of the wedding bouquets composed of white roses encircled by orange blossom and myrtle leaves tied with scented, white satin ribbon. Candle-power was strong in the rooms of the Palace and fresh flowers worn at long, crowded Court ceremonies were apt to wilt under the heat given off by hundreds of burning tapers. Mrs. Peachey scored an immediate success with her heat-proof wax flower bouquets and ornaments for a lady's hair or for the corsage of her ball dress and orders poured into her studio. To add to their novelty, her wax flower hair ornaments were sprinkled with a special powder made from arrow-root that prevented the edges of any petal clinging awkwardly to the head. The stems of her flowers, too, were covered in narrow green or brown China ribbon, never paper, and every flower was scented.

In 1851, the year of the Great Exhibition, Emma Peachey published her *Royal Guide to Wax Flower Modelling* dedicating it to the Princess Royal as a token of 'the spontaneous and fostering patronage of Her Royal Highness's August Parent, The Queen.'

Emma had two good reasons for publishing her book apart from wishing to instruct readers in her art. First, she wished to repudiate a rumour that she had fallen foul of the Great Exhibition's Executive Committee and so withdrawn her exhibits, one a mammoth bouquet of flowers; the other, a colossal vase of fruit which stood in a glass shade six feet high. She had removed her work, she wrote, simply because she had been alloted a stand too close under the glass roof, for the sun's rays not to penetrate on a hot day and possibly melt her amazing wax trophies! Her second reason to appear in print was that she needed to point out that there was absolutely no danger involved from lead poisoning where modelling in wax was concerned (the *Manchester Examiner* had alleged this in an article headed: 'The Danger of Modelling in Wax.')

By now hundreds of Victorian girls were enthusiastically making wax flowers and Mrs. Peachey wished to reassure them that no harm would come, particularly if they used her own specially prepared wax.

It has been recorded that the wax flower examples at the Great Exhibition reached such a high standard of skill that from this time, modelling in wax came to be recognised more as an art-form than a parlour-craft. For did it not combine the qualities of sculpting (modelling) and painting? What happened to either Mrs. Peachey's mammoth bouquet of wax flowers which was composed of almost every specimen known to the botanist, 'from the honeysuckle of the cottage garden to the rarest and most valuable exotic of the East,' or to her colossal Vase of Fruit, no one knows. But when they were shown to the public at her home, 33 Rathbone Place, Oxford Street, it has been recorded that she had over 50,000 visitors and the London Press were lyrical in their praise of them.

From modelling wax flower bouquets, women turned their attention next to producing colourful mounds of wax fruits to decorate (under a shade) a dining-room sideboard. Peaches, plums, pears, bunches of purple and white grapes arranged in a trellised basket or dish were considered to be the best arrangements. Great care was taken, too, to reproduce such natural blemishes as the bruise on the velvety cheek of a peach, say, or the pellucid gum drop found on a plum. When tackling grapes, ladies were advised to buy imitation glass ones and coat them over with purple wax.

274 *Mound of wax fruits in basket, c. 1845*

275–7 *Botanical wax models of* Camellia japonica *by Mrs. Chipperfield;* Hops *by James Mintorn* Odontoglossum crispem Lindi *by Miss Emmet (Mrs. Blackman)*

From fruit, eager modellers went on to make Wax Pastry, Cakes and Tarts and even more peculiar, Blancmanges. As early as 1835, Mrs. Kinglon in *The Wreath* gives instructions on how to make wax fruits and pastries. Many of the illustrations in Mrs. Beeton's cookery books show examples of such unreal-looking jellies, puddings and cakes in glorious technicolour that they might for all the world have been made in wax, I think.

Mrs. Andrew Lang has recorded her own memories in *Men, Women and Minxes*, when,

'Glass shades reigned supreme and in many mansions monumental structures of wax fruit and flowers reposed on little mats of beads or shaded wool; but these, it must truthfully be said, were only present when the family did not care for books or cover the table with them. In those days, the making of flowers was considered one of the elegant accomplishments of a 'finished' young lady and held the place that carving or brass repoussé work did later. The prompt answer of a young person desiring in 1889 to snub the curiosity of an aggressive female philanthropist was as follows, 'And what do *you* do with your time?' 'I make wax flowers', was the quick reply.

One interesting side-line in the professional wax-modeller's craft was to provide funeral souvenirs by way of spectral wax sprays and wreathes of pale ivory-white roses, passion-flowers and ivy that were placed against a sombre background of black velvet in a shallow recessed frame. Known as Phantom Bouquets, those which have survived are much prized by collectors, for they have a melancholy charm all their own.

But the most important contribution to the art of modelling wax flowers was made by the Mintorn family who lived at 36 Soho Square, London, and who owned a counter displaying their work in the Pantheon, Oxford Street.

The Mintorn family consisted of two brothers, James and Horatio, and one sister better known as Mrs. Mogridge. The talented children of a pictorial painter of the day, they were presented at an early age with a gold medal for their skill at modelling wax flowers. Some time later, they were appointed as 'Wax Modellers to Her Majesty'.

In 1844, they published their own little book on *Modelling Wax Flowers* which was dedicated to Her Grace the Duchess of Northumberland. It is not known exactly when imitation wax plants and their foliage came to provide realistic accessories to taxidermy studies but it *is* known that it was the Mintorns who first came into prominence in this line of waxwork after inventing an imperishable wax fabric called 'The Mintorn Art Fabric'.

For this prominence they were indebted to a Mr. Theodore Walker of Leicester, who first realised the potential importance of their indestructible 'Art Fabric' and commissioned them to do a Group of Pheasants picturesquely mounted against a background of wax primroses, ferns and roses: a strange habitat for these birds of field and woodland. But from this odd beginning, an entirely new approach to the presentation of Natural History studies in museums was established.

For when the Mintorns' 'Group of Pheasants' was finally given by Mr. Theodore Walker to the Natural History Museum, South Kensington, everyone there was struck with the possibilities latent in a craft not hitherto associated with taxidermy. In 1879, James Mintorn was asked by the Museum directors to re-mount some Birds' Groups in the Bird Gallery. He accomplished this task so successfully that it was duly noted by the writer of an article on 'Curiosities of Bird Life' (*Daily News*, 26 February, 1880), who complimented Mr. Mintorn on his work 'In the Bird Gallery where the birds are made to appear as in life with the minutest surroundings of foliage and ground faithfully reproduced'.

Wax primroses, ferns and roses were out and a new-look given by Mr. Mintorn to taxidermy. Lord Walsingham, a keen lepidopterist, now invited Horatio Mintorn and his sister, Mrs. Mogridge, to model a number of wax plants for him on which the larvae of certain butterflies in his collection fed. This led to an invitation for them to go to America to do similar work for three years at the Natural History Museum of New York City.

From New York, the Mintorn brother and sister travelled all over the United States and were received everywhere as 'The Two Artists who made Bogus Flowers and Plants which Deceive the Eye'. Modelling in wax had arrived and was no longer treated as a mere parlour hobby.

It was in Louisiana that Horatio Mintorn and Mrs. Mogridge studied the growth of the cotton-plant and its destruction by the ravages of the boll-worm with striking results. In the meanwhile, James Mintorn was deeply occupied at Kew making some fine botanical studies in wax which still remain on view. Among these exhibits is a magnificent study of crimson and pink roses; a cluster of hops; and a fine magnolia. Modelling wax plants for museum purposes was fully established and, as a craft, expanded rapidly under the stimulus of new techniques when applied in the years to come.

Later on in the century, Miss Emmett (Afterwards Mrs. Blackman) and Mrs. Chipperfield also produced botanical studies in wax in the true Mintorn tradition. In the Royal Botanic Gardens' Museums, Mrs. Blackman is represented by a striking collection of tropical orchids, meticulous in details, and Mrs. Chipperfield by a charming *Camellia japonica*.

FEATHERWORK

Second only in popularity to modelling wax
flowers was making them in feathers, not only for
ornamental display in the drawing-room housed
under a shade but also for the commercial market
connected with the trimming of bonnets. As a
trade millinery were associated very much with
female labour.

278   *Feather basket, c. 1876*

An ancient word in the Saxon language is
byrdicge, whose Latin equivalent is *plumaria,*
meaning a female worker in feather. This termin-
ology points to the existence of featherwork as a
very early English craft after its introduction by the
Romans when they settled down to civilise the
rude British. For the Romans were known to be
specialists in a kind of 'feather' embroidery.

At the Tate Gallery *Elizabethan Image* exhibition
(1969) I noted an enchanting plume made of
brightly coloured feather flowers which adorned
the velvet hat worn by Anne Hale, Mrs. Hoskins
(1629), in her portrait by Marcus Gheeraets the
Younger. Two hundred years later, from the
1840s, the demand for feather flowers by the
millinery trade was enormous, so much so that
they came to be almost mass-produced.

It was, of course, the era of the bonnet; of bonnets lavishly trimmed with bows of ribbon and
every kind of flower made with feathers or in
chiffon gauze and silk. In fact, milliners advised
ladies to wear flowers in their bonnets on all occasions including even a funeral 'mourning'
bonnet, trimmed with black flowers, bugles and
jet.

In competition with all the different kinds of
artificial flowers being imported from Paris, a
city which has been, and still is, the centre of the
artificial flower industry, English milliners now
employed hundreds of poor and often consump-
tive girls to make feather and chiffon flowers on a
near starvation wage. In the Burlington Arcade,
one fashionable milliner, Madame Marion, adver-
ised herself as an 'Artiste in Artificial Flowers'.
Like Emma Peachey, artiste in wax flowers,
Madame Marion won prizes for her work when
shown at the Crystal Palace Exhibition.

Many nineteenth-century ladies' magazines deal
with featherwork as a suitable parlour craft,
recommending that the best feathers to use are
those of geese and swans. Stress is laid on the
necessity of cutting them into 'exact petal-shapes'
and this is achieved by:

'Arranging the petals as near to Nature as
possible with the original living model placed
before you. If the flower is no longer in bloom, get
a cambric artificial one for imitation.'

The dying of feathers at home with special dyes
was obligatory. So was the making of the right kind
of paste with which to stick buds and calyxes. The
ingredients for this paste were common white
starch and gum water mixed together till it reached
the consistency of thick treacle.

In *The Girls' Own Book* (1876) instructions are
given for reviving what almost seems to be Roman
feather embroidery work. Feathers preferred for
this work were those of exotic birds in particular,
the parrot and macaw, now easily available, as so
many of them swung in their brass cages as drawing-room embellishments. After coating the back
of each feather chosen, they were laid flat on a
piece of black velvet cloth or satin in pretty patterns
and then stitched to the material with tiny stitches
in silk thread to match. Should a design of flowers
be attempted, their stems, centres and tendrils
were worked with these matching silks, while the
veins on petals were high-lighted with a little paint
put on with a fine camel's hair-brush.

Today, several gifted artists are reviving the
art of featherwork, giving new life and treatment
to this age-old craft that has survived for so long
in England.

279 *Beadworked tea cosy, ivy leaves on coral cross-stitch wool ground, 1860*

BEADWORK

The peak years for Victorian beadwork were 1845 to 1855, when it became largely allied to Berlin woolwork, then the rage. Immune to the ravages of moth, dust and time, drawing-room cushions, bell pulleys, stool tops, banner screens and lambrequins for the mantelpiece ornamented in bead-mosaic lasted a lifetime. It was tedious work, of course, very tough on delicate fingers, but the result, so enduring was worth all the trouble entailed in manipulating too fine a needle or receiving a sharp nip from scissors!

Victorian beadwork was largely based on the same patterns used in Berlin woolwork and these came from the German city of that name. Prior to the repeal of the glass tax in 1845, beads were imported from Venice and cost 5s. per ounce or more. Popular colours were opal, green, rose, amber and turquoise. But the beads used by Victorian workers in their glittering thousands were, after 1845, the rather coarse and sometimes ugly Bohemian type of bead supplied in roughly-cut, cylindrical sections $1\frac{1}{4}$ to $\frac{3}{8}$ of an inch long and costing far less than Venetian ones. Beads were sold at Gotto's Berlin Repository, 202 Regent Street, London, run by a lady of Germanic origin known as 'A. Gotto, Importer of Berlin wools and patterns'; of fringe and fancy trimmings; braids, tassels and cords; of all kinds of lamb's wools, worsteds, floss, netting and silks.' Mrs. Gotto's Berlin Repository must have been every Victorian lady's idea of a dream-shop, catering for all her needs.

To achieve an over-all effect of brilliance, beads were fastened to a fabric base of canvas, tammy-cloth or net by different methods. Beads could either be threaded on silk in chains and caught down at either end or each bead was sewn on separately to the canvas or tammy cloth in *gros point*. This was by far the best method. Yet another technique was to knit the beads in with silk or arrange them in a stranded pattern, picked up by a crochet hook. Many of the best pieces of beadwork will be found to be threaded on waxed silk; this type of work was used for decorating little wrist-bands mounted on velvet.

In the Victorian home, beadwork was used on table mats, urn rugs, the flat surface of a tea tray and on lambrequins. The sole purpose of a lambrequin – an object as Victorian as an antimacassar – was to provide a cover for anything considered to have too naked a look. Velvet, plush and damask

280 *Study of roses in Berlin work for a banner screen, 1855*

281–2 *Assembly of ladies' beadworked 'elegancies' that include pincushions, hair tidies, watch pockets, scissors holders and a pair of fancy girdles*

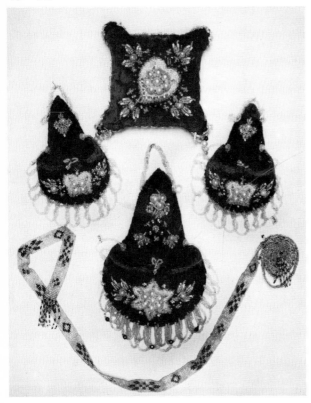

lambrequins hung in most rooms from anything that could give them support, and they were subjected to all kinds of ornamentation like beadwork, fringe and tassel or wool embroidery.

In the world of fashion intricate bands of fine, hand-made beadwork trimmed expensive dresses from a tea gown to a ball dress. A complete set of bead jewellery composed of a matching necklace, bracelet, hair ornament and brooch, could be ordered made from exquisitely coloured, tiny, glittering beads in floral designs. Bead nosegays, flashing bright, were carried in the hand by young girls as once they had carried little rice-shell bouquets! Or they were pinned on to the corsage as shoulder knots. An acceptable gift of the day was a little book of *Elegant patterns for lace, bead and other fancy work*.

For many years, a good bead bag or reticule was an essential dress-accessory like a Paisley shawl. Their shapes were many, including the obsequious 'miser' or 'stocking' purse large enough to hold 'a handkerchief, fan, card-case and an essence bottle'.

A long, slim type of knitted bead purse was considered to be 'a nice present for a gentleman' and was knitted either by his mother, sister or 'Intended'. Traditional colours are said to have been either blue or a dull crimson with steel-cut beads worked into every stitch. By all accounts the Victorian male did very well during the beadwork craze. For all over England, young women, including the redoubtable Miss Becky Sharp in *Vanity Fair* were set to turning out not only slim purses but beaded tobacco pouches, cigar cases, carpet slippers and a handsome watch-pocket. For themselves, ladies produced some quite lovely and some quite hideous, objects in beadwork like pincushions, hair-tidies, tiny sovereign purses, needle-holders, scissor cases, a dress girdle, tie-backs for curtains, napkin rings and quill pens. A beadworked quill pen was very much prized and was achieved by making a neat tight-fitting sheath of fine silk threaded with small beads, some being worked in to form the owner's initials.

The collector drawn to beadwork will be faced by a fascinating array of still available objects from which to make his choice. Pretty examples of different bead purses, for instance, in fancy shapes like a pair of boots or a jug can be found in good condition, pen-wipers and even a dumb-waiter. A beadworked banner screen or a pair of hand-screens have their appeal, as well as fender-stools worked in a design of fat cabbage roses and lilies on a scarlet ground. By and large, Victorian bead-work ranks high among the many ornamental crafts of its day and is extremely decorative when displayed as a collection.

BERLIN WOOLWORK

In her novel *An Open Verdict*, Miss Braddon tells how her young heroine, Beatrice Harefield, goes into the long-locked boudoir belonging to her dead mother to see how everything:

'Yes, everything was just as she had remembered it. There stood the Japanese cabinets with their rich raised work representing dragons, and birds, and fishes, and golden trees and golden bridges, all golden on a shining black ground. There stood the frame with the Berlin wool roses which she had watched slowly creeping into life under her mother's white hands. She lifted the tissue-paper covering and looked at the flowers. All the empty years had scarcely faded them.'

This was an asset of Berlin woolwork, that it rarely faded but when it did, it was only by the soft mellowing of its rather strident colours, which was all to the good.

It was Madame Wittich, a skilled embroideress, who made needlework easy for hundreds of mediocre young women by prevailing upon her husband, a print-seller, to reproduce hand-coloured, simple, cross-stitch designs after her own pattern and sell them complete with the right coloured wools and canvas. All Madame Wittich's designs were drawn out on squared paper in imitation of canvas (actually this had been the brain-child of an earlier Berlin print-seller called Philipson), so that each square represented an individual stitch. All that was required, then, of the worker was the ability to count her squares correctly. This done, she was well on her way to produce an adequate example of Berlin work without previous knowledge. Thus an entirely new race of needlewomen was born.

At one time, the demand for hand-coloured, cross-stitch patterns was so heavy that the monopoly for importing Berlin patterns and wools dyed specially at Gotha acquired by the firm of Acker-mann, London, no longer held good. A certain Mr. Wilks of Regent Street had begun to sell them in competition with others.

The stitches used in Berlin work were the cross-stitch and the tent-stitch, as well as *petit point*. But, these must lie in the same direction, otherwise the beauty of the work will be destroyed, declared a writer in *The What-Not* and this is an important point that might be remembered by collectors.

283–4   Pets on cushions. 'Piero' worked by Victorian Conroy, daughter of Sir John Conroy and 'Sleeping Cat' drawn and painted sample design for Berlin work

285–8 *Various kinds of Berlin work. In silks (but-*
terflies and house with deer) done on pierced board;
little girl with dog in fine wool cross-stitch; Bead
Flowers on red wool cross-stitch ground, 1850s

Other stitches found in Berlin woolwork are the Velvet, the German Diamond, the Victoria Pattern and the Algerine. From *Parlour Recreations* (1848) comes this excerpt:

'Berlin Work: canvas, bolting, chenille needles, cross needles, lambs wool, meshes of various sizes, cartridge and tissue paper, a piercer, camel's hair brush, pencil, gold thread, floss silk, soft cotton, strips of paste-board. For Pattern Marking: White lead and gum-water. This is used when the material for embroidery is black; when white, use stone-blue and gum-water. Wools: German, various shades, single and double; Hamburg, fleecy and of many shades. NOTE: Neatness and Order should characterise the arrangement of a lady's Work Table.'

When Victorian ladies became involved with the Oxford Movement, seeing to the restoration of dilapidated churches in their parish, Berlin wool-work was in great demand by way of supplying new kneelers, pew slips, altar frontals and bible and hymn bookmarkers. But this was to be the last triumphant phase of Berlin work. In their enthusiasm, ladies over-reached the bounds of propriety and were told that, 'although branches and flowers from Berlin patterns might be pretty

289–91 *Fox's head with moss-rose sprays on canvas and moss-rose bunch worked on black felt are typical Berlin woolwork patterns.* (right) *'Le Bouquet Charmant' pattern for Berlin work from The Englishwoman's Domestic Magazine, 1865*

for sofa cushions, they are out of place on a church kneeler'.

Pontings in Kensington High Street was the London centre for,

'Supplying everything for the practise of art needlework in its myriad branches, especially Church work; wools, silks, cottons, card mounts, plush goods, cloths and specimens of commenced work in toile-crosse, cross-stitch and Roman work . . . devices and designs for book marks, alm bags, pulpit hangings, altar clothes, etc., etc.' (Alison Adburgham, *Shops & Shopping*).

Pontings also ran their own school of needlework 'under the direction of a lady of high attainment and long experience.'

OTOLITH OR FISHSCALE EMBROIDERY

During the 1880s, when a new kind of Art Needlework began to sweep through the drawing-rooms and parlours of England it took in its stride several other types of embroidery done in the most up-to-date artistic (or what was then thought artistic) materials. First and foremost, executed by Mrs. Brightwen (1830–1906), a leading Victorian lady naturalist and botanist, was Otolith Embroidery which she herself has described in her *Rambles with Nature Students* as pretty work for the drawing-room.

And so it was, for it was done with the 'little snow-white bones found in the heads of haddock, whiting, gurnard and cod.' These little bones, transparent and shining when cleaned, boiled and dried, were used with rose-beetle wings for embroidering flowers and leaves on a panel of black velvet or other rich dark material. Rose-beetle wings were sold in Berlin-wool shops by the way.

Mrs. Brightwen made a banner screen in Otolith work by embroidering a flowing design of jasmine sprays on a piece of dark-green satin. She used sets of five otoliths, starwise; each star representing a jasmine flower while rose-beetle wings did duty for leaves.

Otolith work can still be found by collectors on the look-out for different examples of period embroidery. Recently, there came into my hands

155

an exquisite design of flowers and leaves on black velvet which might have been done by Mrs. Brightwen herself.

Another curious type of late Victorian needlework is listed in *The Girl's Own Book* for 1876 as 'Embroidery in Spangles and Cannetille'. Cannetille work included the use of bullion, frisure and cliquant. Bullion was composed of spirals of gold wire taken from the epaulettes of naval officers;

frisure was a smaller kind of bullion; and cliquant a flat gold ribbon. Leaf-shaped spangles for this work were called lamé. Both ivy and holly complete with their berries (formed of spangles secured in place with a jet or coral bead) were regarded as being suitable for leaf-patterns. The best form this fanciful handiwork took was a table-cloth bordered with a thick gold cord and with a gold tassel dangling from each corner.

CONEWORK

Conework manifested itself as an ornamental parlour craft about 1860, but being of a perishable nature owing to the materials employed, examples of it are difficult though not impossible to come by. The craft, was part and parcel of the Rustic Movement that introduced such fashions as bamboo and wicker furniture, fretwork objects and fern culture to the Victorian home.

It was in America, and not England, that articles decorated with fir cones and acorn cups were first shown at the Centennial Exhibition of 1875, followed in 1895 by the World's Fair. In the United States, conework is still regarded today as very much an expression of true folk-art and valued as such.

As its name implies, conework deals with the artistic treatment of pine, cedar and fir cones and acorns with, or without, their cups; white, red and purple-skinned beans; dark-brown apple and water-melon seeds; ivory-white rice grains; roasted coffee beans and dried twigs. All this material Nature provided free and what was more it had a natural affinity with wood when combined with it. So fir cones and acorn cups, dried seed-pods and various types of coloured beans came to be arranged in complicated floral-and-leaf patterns which had a beauty all their own, on such common or garden objects in deal like waste-paper baskets, utility boxes and picture frames.

293 (above) *Rustic needlebook decorated with dried cones;* (right) *thermometer framed in conework, 1875*

Occasionally, a striking composition of flower-heads made of seeds and beans arranged with the silvery discs of honesty plus moss, plus fir cones, plus bark and pressed leaves preserved in a shallow, recessed glass box may turn up to delight a collector. For these boxes are now highly valued. Conework may be said to have inspired the flower-arrangers of our day to try their own hand at composing elaborate 'set pieces' with pressed flowers and leaves, silvery plumed grasses, poppy seed-heads and ferns, etc. which are, again, as much in demand as Victorian ones.

ARTISTIC PITHWORK

A companion craft to conework, in so much as it makes use only of vegetable material, was Artistic Pithwork that aped carving in ivory. An extremely handsome example of this work was shown at the

Great Exhibition of 1851. This took the form of a small-scale model of the West Front of Exeter Cathedral which looked exactly as if it had been carved in ivory. Similar models of Indian temples had long been made by native workers from the pith of a plant called *Taccada*. But in England the

157

Close-up of Otolith or Fishscale embroidery, 1876

pith of an elder tree or, better still, of the common, round stemmed rush (*Juncus conglomeratus*) was substituted. This latter plant, when peeled, supplied a delicate white pith from which was carved the best examples of Irish and Cornish crosses, Gothic fronts and other religious emblems. When finished, these revered objects were placed under a glass shade to be admired far more as 'truly beautiful drawing-room ornaments' than their wax counterparts, declared Mrs. Brightwen. In her best-selling book *Inmates of My House and* *Garden* (1895), she gives clear instructions as to how they were made and what kind of implements were necessary for those drawn to Pithwork. The fashion for it was all part of the Oxford Movement, when ladies were bent on restoring order and beauty to their long-neglected local churches; when Gothic styles were *en vogue* and so many decorative objects like book-markers, wall texts and the frames of holy pictures featured crosses and other religious emblems.

MOSSWORK

During the '50s and '60s, which saw the height of the fern-cult, the Victorian world was equally preoccupied with moss, a substance that spelt romance and was an integral part of the hoary and picturesque world of antiquity with which everyone was in love. In particular, ladies adored moss. As a substance it fascinated them. So much so, that they began to incorporate it with so many of their parlour crafts either in its natural state or in imitation. For instance, this was the heyday of the Moss Mat, 'seen in every drawing-room and parlour with pretensions to gentility!' This mat was made in several shades of soft green and brown wools which, on completion was first sheared, then singed, to give it the genuine brown-tipped appearance of moss, proper! Moss mats were given pride of place by being placed underneath the lamp on the drawing-room rosewood table.

Another way ladies had of utilising moss was to glue fragments of it, as well as bark, onto the trees and rocks of an historic ruin they had painted to achieve a realistic effect.

By 1870, moss was no longer confined to the picture itself, but was transplanted as textural embellishment to the frame as well. For Victorians always aimed to frame a picture suitably. So a rural subject necessitated having a frame not adorned by shells as a seascape might be, but by moss or leaves or even spruce twigs freed of their needles! Dried, bleached and dyed moss was often formed into woolly wreaths to act as circular frames for some pictures and photographs. Even a wall-bracket did not escape this same treatment while a vase containing ivy was also decorated with moss.

Varieties of moss could be obtained from nursery gardens or at Covent Garden where it was sold in sacks.

One of the best-known authorities on moss-culture and moss-collecting was Margaret Plues, who published her *Rambles in Search of Flowerless Plants* in 1866. This book was very popular among ladies who had a taste for ferns, mosses and lichens.

CHINA MOSAIC WORK

Yet another extremely odd parlour pastime that made practical use of strange material was china mosaic work, evolved during the last decades of the nineteenth century. All a lady had to do to pursue this hobby was to hoard every small fragment of broken china. When she had amassed enough pieces she proceeded to glue them all over an urn-shaped vase or some other suitable object in patterns, if possible imitating the mosaic work done by Italian workers in coloured marbles.

It must have been a tricky and laborious task, but with perserverance and skill the result was quite handsome in appearance. In fact, the overall effect of a vase done in china mosaic work has a certain affinity to Limoges enamels especially, when fragments of sparkling lustre ware or gilt-decorated china had been inserted in the pattern.

In a copy of *The Girl's Companion* for 1876, detailed instructions are given on how to make a china mosaic pavement for the conservatory at little cost which would exactly resemble – says the writer – the tesselated marble floors found in

294 *China mosaic work. A pair of small plates and a flower vase, 1876*

Mediterranean villas. Incidentally, I have come across several stands for pot-plants and jardinières and even a little pedestal table done in china mosaic work for the conservatory.

POTICHOMANIE

It was Ethel May, the harum-scarum but wholly delightful heroine of *The Daisy Chain* (1856) who won 'two splendid vases of Etruscan pattern in potichomanie' at a Church fete. But who could say today what potichomanie is exactly?

The name *potichomanie* is derived from the French *potiche* (a glass vase) and *manie* (a craze or fad) and as an elegant hobby was pursued in Paris very much at the same time that 'drizzling' was fashionable. Potichomanie crossed the Channel to be taken up as a parlour pastime by the not-so-rich Victorians as a means of providing themselves with a passable copy of an ornamental Sèvres, Dresden or Oriental vase. This result was achieved by buying specially prepared sheets of paper motifs in the style of Sèvres and Dresden painted ornamentation. These motifs were first cut out, then glued, to the *inside* of the glass vase chosen; a task which demanded infinite patience and skilful, probing figers. On completing the decoration of a glass vase in this way, the potichomanist filled the interstices between his glued-on pictures with oil paint.

An interesting reference to potichomanie comes in a letter of Dante Gabriel Rossetti's, who was well-known as a picker-up of odd trifles used as background material for his pictures.

295 *A pair of bottle-shaped ornaments in potichomanie, c. 1880*

In 1874, while staying at Kelmscott Manor with William Morris, Rossetti dashed off a letter to Treffry Dunn, who had been left in charge of Tudor House, his home in Cheyne Walk, London.

'I remember there used to be somewhere at Chelsea a few classically shaped little white vases of the kind made for what is called potichomanie (i.e. covering white pots with patterns pasted on to imitate coloured china). Do you know whether these are still about or is there anything else white and of a suitable shape?'

In the 1880s, ladies took to pasting coloured motifs on the *outside* of common pottery jars known as 'Dolly Varden' jars. After doing this, they treated the surface with a coat of varnish and then set their jars up on the mantelpiece for everyone to admire. Later still, a more coarsened version of potichomanie was practised. This took the form of glueing gold and colour-embossed cigar-cards on to the under-surface of glass trays for display in the parlour.

Recently, I was shown a very charming and delicate example of potichomanie. It was a tiny glass flagon barely four inches long whose interior had been completely lined with tiny sprigs of coloured, paper flowers and then filled with salt to show off the decoration.

Before this curious craft ceased to interest Victorian ladies (c. 1880–90) *Enquire Within* describes it, together with its sister-craft, *Diaphanie*, which 'was capable of greater results than the mere imitation of porcelain vases by the introduction of glass panels papered with beautiful flowers on a white ground into drawing-room doors and on walls.'

DIAPHANIE

Again this is a craft derived from France, to which many Victorian ladies' magazines drew attention, declaring that though an Englishman spent what he could most conveniently afford on his home 'The elegancies and refinements of modern taste demand something more than mere comfort. How often are hall-windows, the library and staircase sadly neglected. Magnificent old historical glass can be envied by those who do not inhabit castles and palaces but all this can be remedied by the use of Diaphanie.'

Diaphanie, in fact, was 'a beautiful, useful and inexpensive art, easily acquired', the mastery of which produced imitations of the richest and rare examples of stained glass possible. Perhaps this was going a little far! But not too far, for parlour ladies residing in the new suburban villas where glass doors led into a small conservatory and glassed-in verandahs abounded. Diaphanie could be used on blinds, screens, skylights and Chinese lanterns besides hall windows and doors, we are told, in every variety of colour and design, all materials for this handicraft being obtainable at a fancy stationer's. Materials needed included specially prepared transparent sheets sold at 6s. per sheet. On each sheet, designs were printed in glass colours (*vitro de couleurs*) that remained unaffected by light. After these designs had been applied to a window-pane they were given a coat of clear white varnish. When this dried, another was added which produced the genuine appearance of rich old historic *stained* glass.

Diaphanie could also be applied with equally good results to silk, parchment, paper and linen after these materials had been treated to a generous dose of *liqueur diphanie*.

Vitremanie

This craft was evolved to improve on the methods used in diaphanie. It produced the same results but was simpler in operation and made success more certain. It was seen on glass doors and windows, etc. of the small halls and lobbies in Gothic-styled villas of outer Victorian London.

THE ALBUM

In the centre of the Victorian drawing-room or parlour, on a round rosewood table, there usually reposed a handsome book bound in dark morocco leather. This book was the Family Album, much handled and treasured and second only in importance to the household Bible. Whenever conversation languished or guests became restive during the evening, the Family Album was produced and talk then instantly revived as its pages were solemnly turned.

'It would be a difficult task to give the exact date of the first album', wrote Jane Loudon in 1849 when she was editing the *Ladies Companion*, adding that – 'the name ALBUM was given to a small register or little book which clever people carry about with them as a portable amusement, *un jeu innocent* of the pocket. Whenever they find themselves in a strange town or abroad, they knock at the door of a clever man and present their *album amicorum*, begging him to write something in it, so that they may carry away a scrap of his hand-writing as a souvenir of his talent. What is generally written is a riddle or a maxim, or a sentence of honey in favour of the owner of the Album which thus grows into a literary bonbon box of compliments.'

In point of fact, Mrs. Loudon's *album amicorum* is a direct descendant of the eighteenth-century commonplace book kept by aristocratic ladies, to preserve their favourite maxims and wise sayings, compliments paid, poetic verses and a valuable family recipe or two for the making of precious stillroom lotions and cordials.

Pages of an Early Victorian album, often tinted in a different pastel shade or left richly cream or white, have embossed borders in which to frame a water colour. Bindings differ from marbled boards, rich morocco leather or glistening black papier mâché adorned with a design of opalescent flowers and golden arabesques flowing all round! On their frontispiece, enclosed in a cartouche the word ALBUM is usually inscribed.

Sometimes serious, but more often gay and flippant, sentimental always and, on occasions not a little religious, early Victorian albums mirror the world in which their owners moved, and the higher placed that world was, the better, of course, their contents. But times were changing and money was passing into other hands than those well-bred. From about 1845 contributions to albums coarsened in character; in time they became facetious and nonsensical. In fact they suffered so much that books of 'Album' etiquette came to be published, reprimanding contributors who did not obey certain polite rules as to what might, or might not, be written in the album belonging to a young lady. 'Selections for the Album' were given in these books and used repeatedly, with the result that a dull uniformity prevailed everywhere. To counteract this, publishers weighed in by supplying new album-fodder for the ignorant. This took the form of steel engravings and later, gaudy lithographs, both of which were machine-produced. The once highly individual and aristocratic album was no more. Instead of charmingly decorated pages featuring embossed floral borders, delicately

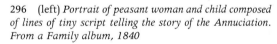

296 (left) *Portrait of peasant woman and child composed of lines of tiny script telling the story of the Annuciation. From a Family album, 1840*

297 *Sketch in water-coloured recording 'Souvenir of a Pleasant Excursion' at Sidmouth, 1836 signed* LEP. *From an Album*

298–9 (above) *Two pages from an album showing hand-drawn and painted borders surrounding two cartes-de visite of ladies, 1850s*

300 *Miniature screen drawn on an album page and stuck with early photographs of the members of a family, c. 1855*

301 *Sentimental poem written in old German script headed by a pen-and-ink drawing of a minstrel. Family Album*

302 (far right) *Coloured frontispiece to a young lady's floral album dated 1839*

drawn, that framed a poem or sketch, dozens and dozens of steel engravings celebrating national events were glued in on page after page.

Then, suddenly, about 1860, a new craze sponsored by German purveyors of fancy stationery struck England. Given the name of decalcomanie, this was the day when colourful and glossy 'scrap' pictures featuring robins, a rose, a pair of clasped hands were sold in sheets to be stuck in an album, cut to size and arranged prettily.

After decalcomanie there arrived, delightful and new, the first photographs referred to as 'cartes de visite' and which measured only $2\frac{1}{2}$ inches by 4. Eagerly collected as sentimental souvenirs of relations and friends, they were glued into albums. Heavy and ponderous to hold now, the leather-bound and brass-clasped photograph albums of the 1860s, '70s and '80s preserve the complete life of a whole generation of faded sepia-brown and grey figures. Ladies are pictured in ponderous skirts, beaded mantles and bonnets, while others, gayer and more trim, with pork-pie hats, play an antiquated game of croquet or tennis companioned by their swains in flannel blazer and straw boater.

Finally, about 1890, when the 'week-end' had been put on the social map with the full establishment of the railway and the first automobiles were on the road, there came the Confessional Album, forbear of the Truth Game and others of today. I still have my grandmother's, handsomely bound in red morocco with illustrations in delicate gouache by John Leech. On each page of fine, hand-made paper are posed such soul-searching questions as: 'What is your Pet Aversion'; 'Whom do you Admire most in Politics?' with answers, serious or facetious, written in and signed below.

PEDLAR DOLLS

Almost the last of Victorian parlour pastimes listed in ladies' magazines and journals where they were given certain prominence, was the 'Dressing', not of Amelias but of Pedlar Dolls. An interesting collection of them can be seen at the Bethnal Green Museum, London.

The Pedlar Woman was a familiar figure, well-known in Victorian England as she hawked her odd assortment of wares alongside the Glass-Blower, Image Man and Bible-and-Pamphlet Men. Because her clothes were peculiar to her as well as the goods she carried, she made an interesting subject for ladies who took infinite pains to reproduce her with all the needle-skill they pos-

303 *Pedlar dolls: man and woman with leather faces supposed to portray pair working in Portsmouth district, 1810*

304 *Essex pedlar doll. Ancient crone with wares, 1866*

sessed. In particular, they concentrated on making in miniature all the wares she sold, displayed on a tray suspended by a cord around her neck. Pins, buttons, reels of cotton, needles, button-hooks, a child's doll, chapbooks, boottees, a tin kettle, a knitted shawl – there was no knowing what the Pedlar Woman might not produce so as to tempt a cottage woman to part with her money. Pedlar Dolls were usually dressed to go on a stall at some local Fancy Bazaar or Summer Fête. Today, they are carefully preserved under a 'shade'. Dorothy Wordsworth, the poet's 'exquisite sister', knew one Pedlar Woman with whom she often talked when she passed her door at Grasmere in the Lake District. Dorothy wrote in her famous Journal:

'Friday, 10th October, 1800. A most heavenly morning. The Cockermouth traveller came with thread, hardware, mustard, etc. She is very

healthy; has travelled over the mountains these thirty years.'

A Pedlar Doll's outfit included a bonnet, shawl and apron worn over a dark stuff skirt or a printed, calico petticoat. Her boots were stout and made of leather. Faces shown are mostly old and wizened with small, dark eyes, greying hair and hooked features, for many women pedlars were of gypsy origin. Occasionally, though, a Pedlar Doll may be found of an attractive young woman such as Mrs. Jean Latham has in her collection. This doll is said to have come from Jersey and her date is *c*. 1830.

Today it would take all the skill of an expert needlewoman to reach the high standard of work achieved by Victorian ladies in 'assembling' a Pedlar Doll during the last decades of the nineteenth century, which saw the end of all those ornamental crafts once practised in the parlour.

10 **Cottage Art**

305   *Arrival of the itinerant artist into village. Centemporary engraving*
from a period album

As he entered the parlour, his eyes caught on two silhouettes, one of himself, one of Sylvia, done in the first month of their marriage by some wandering artist. They were hanging against the wall in little oval wooden frames; black profiles with the lights done in gold.

Mrs. Gaskell, *Sylvia's Lovers* (1863)

From the days of the eighteenth century, the journeyman artist trudged the muddy high-ways and by-ways of England, trying to pick up a meagre living with his pencil and brush. But he rarely had any academic training. More often than not, his artistic career began as a coach or inn-sign painter, from which work he acquired skill as a draughtsman and a love of precise detail. Later, he might turn to a more profitable form of naive portraiture based on old traditions, his sitters belonging to the same class from which he sprang.

As a case in point, the nineteenth-century painter, Walter Greaves, when put to work first in his father's boat-yard gained much experience there by having to draw exactly and simply the different boat-designs needed of him. An early picture of his, 'Hammersmith on Boat Race Day', belongs very much to the sampler-like world depicted by the journeyman artist. But how different is Greaves' later work, when he and his brother were taken up and patronised by Whistler whose disciple and ardent admirer he became. Once while gazing at some craft on the Thames, Greaves was heard to say: 'A boat is always a boat to me. But to Mr. Whistler it is a tone!'

When the itinerant painter was not first a coach or inn-sign painter, he might be an ordinary fellow possessed by the strong urge to draw and paint as nature dictated – like others before him. But whatever his personal background, he was the product of an age of austerity and isolation in rural England. With his portfolio strapped to his back and wearing a shabby velveteen jacket, he was a welcome figure always when he knocked on a cottage or farmhouse door to beg bread or a sip of water from its occupant.

During the nineteenth century strong links were forged between the hall, parsonage and doctor's house, and cottage homes, as domestic help came from them. From the age of 11, when rustic schooling for what it was worth ended, it was customary for little girls to enter domestic service at the local 'big house' or vicarage. For many years, pleasant informative years, these little girls knew a period of refinement in their lives when, under the eye of an efficient housekeeper or senior servant, they washed fine china, cleaned Georgian silver and, when dusting, gazed up admiringly, at family portraits by Hoppner, Romney or Gainsborough hung on the walls. Later, when they married and set up house either with someone met with in their working life or with the village lad who had long been their sweetheart, their homes were quite unlike those of their parents. For their furnishings and ornaments reflected in humbler form, of course, those left behind them in the hall or parsonage.

In her enthralling trilogy of autobiographical books, *Lark Rise to Candleford* (1945) Flora Thompson has described vividly the great changes that village domestic taste underwent during the 1860s, '70s and '80s. In every way, she says, cottage rooms became more comfortable and richer also in intimate possessions. There were 'dressers of crockery, cushioned chairs, pictures on the wall and brightly-coloured, handmade rugs on the floor' where there had hardly been any before.

But most preferred as a possession by a newly married couple was a portrait of themselves, done by the travelling artist, in their Sunday best. The groom, as it might be, in lavender trousers and tightly stretched kid gloves concealing his workworn hands; the bride in muslin gown with white lace fichu and a white poke bonnet trimmed with green paper leaves. Later, they might add to these twin portraits of themselves the picture of their child, or children, with the family pet; or a naïve rendering of a local view, the church maybe set round with trees or the village pub standing on the village green. Such pictures could be supplied at any time by the itinerant painter on his rounds.

Unfortunately, where the work of the itinerant painter during the nineteenth century has long been valued in America, in England it has been sadly neglected until recently. In consequence, many of our so-called Victorian primitive paintings have gone across the Atlantic to form part of America's folk art heritage and not ours. However, this fault is now being remedied and the work of our itinerant painters is diligently searched for and collected. As little of his picturesque life is known, it is interesting to come across one reference made to him by Charlotte M. Yonge in her novel, *The Three Brides* (1876). She draws attention to him through the mouth of an old cottage woman, Susan Reynolds, who remarks how 'She knew'd one who had draughted all the farmers' wives in gowd frames for five pounds a head; but satin gownds and gold chains was extry'.

306　*The Brontë sisters by Patrick Brontë, 1840s*

167

307   *Portraits of Sergeant and Mrs. Renham by David Lynch, 1854*   309   *Portrait of a young girl with book, unsigned, 1840s*

This is a valuable record of the prices charged by one travelling artist for his work. Mrs. Gaskell also knew of one who had made a silhouette of her heroine Sylvia Robson, on her marriage to her cousin, Philip Hepburn, in *Sylvia's Lovers*. When Charlotte Brontë showed her Branwell's portrait of Emily and Anne and herself Mrs. Gaskell described it as 'a rough common drawing like those done by inn-sign artists who tramp the country-side.' Actually, Charlotte's own rather charming picture of Anne with a black velvet ribbon tied round her neck, which is preserved at Haworth Parsonage Museum, might easily pass for the work of an intinerant painter of her flat technique is very much like his.

In *Victorian Miniature* Owen Chadwick tells the story of how one Victorian child, William Wayne Andrew, was painted by a travelling painter instead of his father who had refused to sit. Little William, who lived at Brixworth in Northamptonshire, was posed at his mother's wish in Findon church seated in a pew. But he was not given the traditional toy to hold or the pet to cuddle that most children painted by wandering artists were.

Though the pictures of the itinerant painter are seldom signed there are some which have a name and date. At an exhibition held in the summer of 1969 at the Rutland Gallery, in London, on *The Age of the Journeyman in English Painting and Pottery*, several pictures were on view which carried signatures. There was one, for instance, by Thomas Weaver (1774–1843) entitled: 'Prize sheep and cattle standing in the park of a manor house' (1803); Sydney Bown's 'A Gentleman with his Animals', inscribed on reverse 'Sydney Bown, Pinx, Leicester, July 1833; W. William's 'The Champion Bull and the Prize Cabbage', 1803; and 'The Berkeley Hounds', dated and signed D. Dalby, 1820.

The itinerant artist was never asked to set up his easel in a proper studio like his professional brother and draw, line for exact line, the replica of his sitter. For in his portfolio, he kept a

310   *The Housekeeper, unsigned,*   c. 1845

311   *Child with Apple, c. 1845*

312   *Little Boy with Drum, c. 1845*

number of appropriately dressed, and so readymade, bodies of men, women and children to whom he could attach the recognisable heads of those sitting to him. Thus his figures are never conceived in the round but are as flat as those limned in Tudor times. Moreover, traditional symbols were included that pinpointed the calling, or class status, of those whom he painted. Thus the wife of a well-to-do country solicitor, or a town alderman, wore a dark silk gown and clasped a book or lace-trimmed handkerchief; a young girl a rose; the coachman his whip;

313   *'Calved at one Birth' 4 September 1854*

314   *The Hunt: Landscape with hounds and house inset, unsigned, 1850*

315   *Farm Scene: unsigned, c. 1850*

and a child some favourite pet or toy. The children perpetuated by the travelling artist are legion but never pretty. They are too stylised for that. So, too, are the enormous number of Victorian servants whose portraits he drew. For it was at the back door of the hall, parsonage or doctor's house, reached generally by coming through the cobbled stableyard, that the travelling artist found his most profitable market. Here, at the sound of his merry voice, a crowd would gather of stable hands, footmen, maids in long print dresses, and pantry boys. Included was the sober and stately figure of the housekeeper in her dark stuff gown and mob cap; the butler too and the head coachman. Through the friendly office of this faithful clientele who all wanted their likenesses preserved for posterity like those of their masters and mistresses, the itinerant artist sometimes achieved his ambition. This was a meeting with the lady of the house from whom he might gain permission to draw her children or even herself wearing a plumed hat and carrying her pet spaniel.

Besides, though, the portraits of simple cottage folk, servants and members of the lesser gentry, the itinerant artist was inspired by sights and happenings met with on travel. For instance, many of his pictures deal with the simple but vivid presentation of the first clumsy traction engines he saw on the road; of a meet of the local hunt before a picturesque pub; fields with horsemen in pink streaming across it; a lonely castellated mansion standing in a derelict park or the London stage or mail coach arriving in the bustling square of a market town. All these subjects can be found faithfully depicted by the collector of itinerant paintings. Vigorously but simply rendered, they have a naïve charm all of their own. Such spontaneous original work presenting the rural life of Victorian England was not to be repeated till our own day and age with the welcome arrival of what is known as the Sunday School of Painters working in their own modern idiom.

THE BIBLE AND PAMPHLET MEN

Another source of procuring cheap pictures for cottage homes came through the Bible-and-Pamphlet Men who were travelling companions of the itinerant painter. But before disposing of any of the little holy pictures they carried, they made a sale of the large, brass-bound Bibles, sometimes illustrated, sometimes not, which were a necessity for cottage folk at this time. A Bible, after all, was often their only book; their sole treasury of poetic images; of words both familiar and strange over whose meaning brows were knotted and questions asked from those possessing more book knowledge than themselves.

Whenever a young couple was known to be setting up house, the Bible Men would call and for a few pence put down, the rest to follow, the couple became the proud possessors of a Bible of their own; a Bible destined to become a family heirloom. At the same time, they might buy a highly coloured little print, or two, in a black wood frame decorated at each corner with a brass rosette. These prints might show *The Flight to, and The Return from, Egypt; The Last Judgement; or Eleazer and Rebekah at the Well,* and were issued by P. & P. Gally, print-sellers of London. One of *The Last Judgement* springs to mind because each angel wore a hoop and periwig and had silly, expressionless faces, while those of the devils were wickedly full of character as they had been drawn with extreme care. As for Satan, he was quite an Adonis.

Besides these little religious prints, some glass pictures of crudely drawn flowers or simple, rustic subjects were also available. These were also

316 *'Lord Remember Me'. Religious cottage print, coloured, in original cruciform wooden frame 1860s*

317–8 (top) *'Return from Egypt', traditional example with frame, of an early Victorian print sold by P. and P. Gally;* (bottom) *'The Amiable Fruiterer', 1860*

hawked round from door to door or were sold in the market square of small country towns. Glass pictures were made to hang alone, or in pairs, and were originally framed with wide brass chains or if made of wood of cruciform shape.

The process of painting glass pictures (i.e. painting on the underside of glass with opaque colours) is better known in informed circles as *Verre eglomisé*, taking this name from its inventor, Jean Baptise Glomy, a Parisian artist, writer and antique dealer living at the end of the eighteenth century. In Europe, glass-painting was very much an early peasant art, some of the best glass pictures being found in the village of Sandler in Upper Austria.

The usual method of painting on glass was by coating the glass with turpentine and then soaking the paper print chosen in clean water. After being partially dried, it was placed on the glass with the print side down. Then it was thoroughly sponged all over with water and pressed gently with the fingers so that not a single bubble remained. When the back of the print began to peel off, the whole of the white paper was removed, leaving only the dark outline of the picture adhering to the glass. After the glass had dried naturally the colours were painted in by hand. The painting was always done in reverse, of course, which required skill on the part of the painter. A final layer of opaque white paint gave the whole picture a natural brilliance and glitter which was most effective. It has been recorded that one early Georgian glass portrait of Frederick the Great was advertised for 1/6 – this sum in the coinage of 1758. Sold to cottage people, Victorian examples of glass pictures framed in maplewood would not have cost more than a shilling or so.

THE TRAVELLING PENMEN

Elaborate penmanship or the art of fine calligraphy, as it was called, had long been an accomplishment of ladies and gentlemen. But it remained for the travelling Penmen in Victorian times to make known the different fascinating forms of lettering, and of illumination, to the illiterate poor living in remote villages. This they did by showing them their skill with pen and ink; by producing various examples of scripts; of inscribing their individual names with many a professional flourish in the family Bible or in their prayer and hymn books.

The strings of household texts suspended on rolls that were so loved, and prized, by cottagers could be embellished by a visiting penman for a few pence. His was the hand, too, that not only could write them a letter to send to an absent one but add decoration to memorial and anniversary cards. Elaborate funeral cards obtained at the undertaker were much valued by rich and poor Victorians and kept as precious family souvenirs long after the period for mourning had ended. Deeply bordered in black and inscribed with melancholy verses, these cards expressed feelings no longer felt today, when a brief crematorium service is preferred to one solemnly held in church. This couplet accompanying one memorial card is typical of many others:

Farewell, dear friends, remember me
When spring's young voice awake the flowers;
For I have wandered far and free,
In these bright hours, these violet-hours.

But the principal source of income for the travelling penmen came from farmers who commissioned them to ornament their waggons and carts and inscribe on them their names. This form of painted decoration by penmen has something in common with barge decoration. Traditional and highly specialised, it also has links with the gay paintings, lettering and figures, etc. found on costermongers' carts.

The decoration executed on farm waggons by travelling penmen is usually focussed on the front

319 *Memorial portrait of the Prince Consort showing the art of PENMANSHIP by J. Pichard, presented to Mr. and Mrs. Flood as a mark of respect on 25 December 1863*

and tailboard and consists of two panels with the owner's name and the name of his farm (also, sometimes, the painter's) in shaded lettering with many an additional scroll and curlicue.

In Thomas Hardy's *Far From the Madding Crowd* (1870) there is a reference to one itinerant penman of the day. For it was Gabriel Oak, Hardy's strong silent hero who 'could prent folks' names almost like copperplate with beautiful flourishes and long tails.'

When Oak arrived at proud Bathsheba Everdene's farm, he was told by one of her men, old Matthew Moon that 'Joseph Poorgrass used to prent Farmer Everdene's waggons but he could never mind which way to turn his Js and Es'.

By the end of the century, the travelling penmen had vanished along with the itinerant artist, and the Bible and Pamphlet Men. Village communities were no longer isolated and rustic taste changing. Besides, the education of the poor had become widespread owing to the establishments of the first National and Church schools and the rising generation could now write their own letters, whereas their parents and grand-parents had scarcely been able to 'prent' their names.

BAXTER PRINTS AND THE OLEOGRAPH

It was the Napoleonic wars that were said to have killed the fine era of colour printing from metal plates which, beginning about 1720, with James Christopher le Blon (the first printer of three-colour process) ended with the departure of Bartolozzi from England to Portugal in 1805.

The year before, 1804, had seen the birth of George Baxter who, at 23, went to London to be a wood-engraver and to print if possible in colour. Working very hard to achieve this object, Baxter produce a simple print of three butterflies in simple colours in 1827.

Though Baxter's first attempt at colour printing was treated as a great curiosity and rarity, nothing more happened till suddenly, in 1841, he produced two more colour prints; one 'The Coronation of Queen Victoria'; the other, 'The Opening by Queen Victoria of her first Parliament'. Both these prints were acclaimed and paid him handsome dividends. In fact, George Baxter and his 'oil prints' had arrived. To begin with he had printed his subjects in water-ink, but when turning to oil-ink his work was given its characteristic subtle and attractive quality. After issuing a whole and very successful series of Royal Portraits, he issued another called *Gems of the Great Exhibition* (1851).

Baxter had always aimed to take cheap but colourful, mechanically-produced pictures into the homes of the humble and poor and this he accomplished with enormous success during his lifetime. For his most decorative prints that feature flowers, children and genre subjects were sold for 1/6 each.

George Baxter died in 1861 and his prints today are eagerly collected. Possibly no other English colour printer – not even the great Bartolozzi in his prime – attained the popularity that Baxter did. His work will always appeal not only to collectors for the beauty of their colour effects but to the social historian, as so many of his subjects are of topical interest and picture ordinary family scenes.

Contemporary with Baxter prints ornamenting parlour and cottage room walls were daguerreotypes that took their name from Louis Jacques Mande Daguerre (1789–1851) their inventor. So successful was Daguerre's work that soon a considerable number of 'daguerreian artists' were selling their work not only in France but England too. So collectors can come across typical daguerreotypes that show 'Men in enormously wide duck trousers and women with many-flounced muslin dresses, black mantles, banded hair and straw bonnets' that make excellent companion portraits to George Baxter oil prints. After the daguerreotype came the day for cheap chromo-lithographs of Mont Blanc and the Lake of Lucerne with cheap reproductions of Sir Edwin Landseer's early and most popular, sentimental animal portraits and lithographs from Ary Scheffer. Then, in a big way, came the oleograph (i.e. printing in oil) which Mrs. Lang declared in her book *Men, Women and Minxes* was the *pièce de résistance*, the most favoured picture of all for country folk and was seen in the parlour of too many inns. According to Mrs. Lang the oleograph inspired four distinct types of subjects: Patriotism, Feudal Loyalty, the Domestic Affections and Religion; the last subject with a very big R, indeed.

Mrs. Lang describes with loving care and an eye to detail several large oleographs which she came across hanging in the parlour of a small North Country inn where she had put up. One in particular which took her fancy was supposed to represent *The Battle of Culloden*. But anyone with a little historical knowledge would have taken:

'The robust, red-faced elderly gentleman seated on a white horse with the Blue Ribbon of the Garter over his scarlet coat for George II, or the Duke of Cumberland, but *never* for Prince Charles at the age of twenty-five. A remarkable feature of this picture was the air of leisure about everybody, the wounded men included. No one would think they were retreating from a bloody battle while those on horse-back twisted themselves round in their saddles for all the world as if they were at the Waterloo Banquet.'

320–1   *Two contemporary coloured prints, showing the Royal children while out in the Home Park, Windsor Castle, late 1840s*

STEVENGRAPHS

The last contribution made to cottage art, to providing the poor of purse with pictures, cheap but gaily colourful, was by Thomas Stevens, an astute man of business, who being very much aware of the kind of goods Victorians bought if priced fairly, opened his Coventry factory in 1854 and launched what he called his first *Stevengraphs*. Actually, the association of the town of Coventry with silk-weaving goes even farther back than the evocation of the Edict of Nantes (1685) which saw the emigration of so many Huguenots to England followed by the successful establishment of many of their crafts, in particular silk-weaving. By the end of the eighteenth century, Coventry silk ribbons were being worn all over the world for ribbons were then the height of fashion. But owing to certain economic difficulties brought about by the Napoleonic Wars, the silk weaving industry of Coventry began to languish and, finally, almost packed up. Suddenly, though, new impetus was given and fresh blood pumped into the dying industry by the introduction of the Jacquard loom from France where it had been in wide use from about 1835.

It was through the invention, then, of the Jacquard loom that the automatic weaving of design in full colour was made possible in Coventry and enterprising manufacturers like Stevens began to produce attractive 'woven' pictures on plain and fancy ribbons which instantly captivated the public.

Thomas Stevens' first ribbon pictures – to which he gave his own name – consisted of a series of familiar but effective scenes concerned with the

175

hunting-field and with racing, rowing, football, tennis and cricket activities plus portraits of popular celebrities of the day and, of course, of the Royal Family. Success was immediate and another series appeared, inspired by religious, classical and legendary subjects including that famous local personality, the Lady Godiva and Peeping Tom.

Early Stevengraphs, well-drawn and coloured, were woven on the Jacquard loom with hair-fine, coloured silks on long silk ribbons and included nursery rhymes and bookmakers (Chapter V: The Library). Each picture along the ribbon was allocated enough space in between so that the buyer could cut it off, if he so wished, and mount it, separately, as a picture. Or he could buy one already mounted for him on grey cardboard (about 6 in. × 3 in.) for the sum of 'one shilling' each. This was a bargain, indeed. At the very beginning, Stevengraphs were actually sold on barrows in market-places as souvenirs and, in this way, were soon introduced in cottage homes.

After 1860, when a frame was asked for, it was supplied made of black wood with a gold inner line and black corner bosses. For the collector, the frame to a Stevengraph is of some importance as it carries generally the firm's trade label and date.

In 1875, Thomas Stevens had become so successful that he opened a new factory and called it The Stevengraph Works. Soon in full production, the factory poured out woven-silk pictures, fans, scent sachets, Christmas cards and book-markers. It is not easy to put an exact date on a Stevengraph but some of the woven hunting pictures carry the diamond-shaped mark with a large central 'Rd' indicating that the design was registered at the Patent Office to protect it for three years from being used by other firms. The marginal letters and figures point to registration on 2 August, 1879.

Unfortunately, Stevengraphs of a later date show the poverty of invention that was marring the whole field of artistic production towards the end of Queen Victoria's reign. The glowing colours that had once played such a strong part in their early appeal to rustic taste began to fade and finally assumed an over-all drabness. Even worse, many of Stevens 'woven' pictures came to be copied directly from engravings. This was not only plagiarism in its worst form but an artistic and technical set-back. For the technique of weaving silk pictures does not suit a reproduction of steel engravings. So the whole industry began to decline, steadily, from 1880.

As has been said earlier, almost the most popular woven silk 'ribbon' portraits were those of the Queen and Prince Albert. On the death of the Prince Consort, 14 December, 1861, he was mourned throughout England and a medallion portrait of him inscribed 'The Good Albert' was put out by J. & J. Cash and Dalton and other Coventry manufacturers of woven silk ribbons. Thomas Stevens made his own contribution with a Stevengraph of His Royal Highness surrounded by his bevy of daughters, the Princesses Beatrice, Helen, Louisa, Victoria and Alice which appeared in 1863. On a scroll shown below the Royal Arms are the words: 'The Earth is the Lord's and the Fulness Thereof.'

Before and after the Second World War, Stevengraphs were being collected only by the few. Today, however, whenever a sale of them is advertised to take place in a London auction room, buyers collect from near and far. Prices have soared. 'Leda and her Swan', the rarest of all Stevengraphs has been known to go for an extremely high price. A collector will have to dig deep, then, into his purse if he plans to buy a top quality Stevengraph unlike the cottage folk of a hundred years ago.

11 Cottage China

322 *Little Girl on Goat. Staffordshire chimney ornament, 1850s for cottage folk*

323 *Pair of coloured figures, Child with St Bernard Dog; Child reclining on period sofa. Biscuit china, unmarked, c. 1880*

The kitchen was a model of tidiness. The dresser was loaded with bright tins and blue-and-white crockery, with a neat cloth spread over the lower part, as white as the muslin window-blinds. The floor was perfectly clean as if the bricks were still in their yard, the round table shone like a looking-glass, the copper kettles were almost lilac with ruddy brightness. The curtains were white dimity, and so was the broad frill that was hung over the ample chimney beneath the mantelpiece covered with brass candlesticks, smart white china poodle dogs, holding each a black hat in his mouth (a perfect piece of reportage) and the like ornaments, and wherever there was room on the walls there hung or were pasted pictures in bright colours, a few small ladies and gentlemen, and several almanacs, with all sorts of shocking things going on in the picture at the top. . . . There were several Bible pictures, too.

This accurate and vivid description of a cottage interior in Hampshire was written by Charlotte M. Yonge. No one knew better than she what such interiors were like or what kind of things they contained for since childhood, she had been visiting village homes round her own at Otterbourne.

It was the itinerant painter and the Bible-and-Pamphlet Men who brought colourful pictures, cheap prints and chap-books to the notice of village folk. But it was to the Image Man they turned for their gaudy and gay chimney ornaments, flocking out to meet him as soon as his cry of:

*My casts are formed to get my Bread
And humble shelter for my head.*

was heard and he came into the village with his heavy pack already half-unfurled in readiness to display his wares. What he sold reached their rural market only by means of his own initiative and sturdy legs. Storms, rain, and high March winds or sudden biting flurries of snow in early spring, what did the weather matter to the Image Man. For he was sure of a warm

178

welcome at the end of his long tramp and appreciated the gossip that followed, besides tales of how his last china mug had been broken and another was needed!

In this way, did that vast range of Staffordshire chimney ornaments and their like reach their rural market; ornaments so zealously collected today and expensive. And not without reason either. For these one-time naïve and cheap earthenware 'toys', as they were first called, reflect like nothing else the simple tastes and enormously varied interests and habits of the people for whom they were produced and coloured. Above all, too, they speak for the love and pride that English people had for their country and national celebrities.

When cottage ornaments were not actually 'potted' by the Image Man, himself, he acted in the role of 'middle man' bringing to cottage doors the products being turned out in a steady stream from potteries operating at white heat in the Midlands. Materials used were chosen always for their cheapness or because they could be adapted to meet particular needs. Mass-produced in the end they lost their first charm and quality all except those splendid 'signed' pieces that were the work of individual potters, now famed. Like Enoch Wood (1757–1840), who modelled the first bust of John Wesley when he was his guest whilst touring the Midlands. Enoch Wood's work, together with that of Obadiah Sherrat, John Walton, Ralph Salt and others fetch astronomical prices today in the sale-room and historic collections have been made of them. Moreover as their pottery figures, etc. have long been recorded and given full and authorative treatment by notable writers on nineteenth-century ceramic, they will not be dealt with here. Instead attention will be drawn to some much later and less well-known earthenware ornaments. The following account of one small potbank working at full production in the 1840s to keep the travelling Image Man well-stocked with wares may be of interest to some collectors.

'The toy manufactory itself was a curiosity in structure and management. . . . The workshops were neither square nor round, nor oblong. They were a jumble of the oddest imaginable kind. . . . Only about a dozen people were employed at the bank.'

324 *Large white china Jubilee platter (1887) with black transfer printing of recent events*

325 *Prettily painted with floral border plate showing the Royal Family, c. 1845*

In such haphazard and makeshift surroundings repeated through the Potteries, the 'Image' maker worked for near-starvation wage assisted, sometimes, by his wife or weakling child labour. But in spite of such hard conditions he could, and did, turn out in marked contrast to his surroundings all those gaily-coloured rustic ornaments and figures which attract collectors today. According to one old 'figure' maker attached to a small toy manufactory:

'Napoleon was the leading article of our factory. He wore a dark-blue coat, tightly buttoned and white breeches. . . . We made cats, too, on box lids, representing cushions. We made dogs of all sizes from Dignity to Impudence. We made the gentlest of swains and sweetest of maids, nearly always standing under the shade of a tree.'

Historic busts of contemporary celebrities from The Grand Mogul to Merry Tom Thumbs; sentimental-looking Spaniels, gilt-collared and chained; Spotted Cows mildly chewing the cud; elegant, stream-lined rust-red Greyhounds; little Girls on Goats, little Boys on Plough-Horses – all these subjects were tackled and successfully 'potted' and sold by the Image Man. He knew his customers so his wares were produced only for the cottage chimney breast or farmhouse dresser, never for the display cabinets of the 'big' house or the whatnots in the pretentious parlours belonging to the rapidly rising trade class.

After the Great Exhibition of 1851, new earthenware heroes and heroines, new 'group' subjects made their appearance taking over from old, established favourites. Florence Nightingale with, or without, her lamp was more often seen that the Iron Duke; Burns and his Mary instead of Grace Darling and her Boat. In 1845, after the purchase of Balmoral and the Queen's obvious delight in her well-publicised Highland life, an attractive series of Scotch lassies and lads wearing the bonnet and kilt flooded the market. They were followed by characteristic Welsh figures, by old women in scarlet cloaks and tall black hats when the railroad opened up romantic Wales to tourist traffic.

That fascinating observer of the Victorian rural scene, John Ashby of Tysoe, describes two typical cottage rooms at this time when new ornaments were taking over from the old ones, the one belonging to his dear grandmother Harriet; the other to his Aunt Rouvray. His grandmother, who was of the old school, wore a linen apron and goffered cap. A small, red cross-over shawl covered her black bodice.

'Her cottage was bright with polished furniture and with red and blue damask table covers and woollen antimacassars. There was a bookcase full of volumes of the *Girl's Own Paper* and *Good Words*. On the mantelpiece were china figures of old-fashioned policemen, pale blue-and-white, and small yellow lions with crinkled manes. On the wall above hung long hollow glass 'walking-sticks' twisted like barley sugar. One of them was filled with tiny coloured balls like confectioner's "hundreds and thousands".'

Aunt Rouvray, with more money to spend, had in place of her sister-in-law's common blue-and-white policemen:

'Wedgwood jugs with swelling stomachs, rope handles and narrow necks. Rough brown jugs with metal rims and bodies encrusted with trees, dogs and a deer. A patchwork cloth covered an octagonal table, the centre made of tiny octagons of broadcloth, scarlet and black and green. Around were squares, also tiny patches of the same cloth and then again octagons filled with more mosaic and every patch braided with gold. There was a picture of 'The Bay of Naples' and a piece of painted velvet with passion-flowers of ivory and red, large cornflower-like blossoms of deep blue and brown roses whose pink had fled.'

Not only was Aunt Rouvray a skilled needlewoman, it seems, but a dab at Oriental Tinting or Poonah Work, for that was what her piece of velvet painted with passion-flowers amounted to!

So much for the general décor and ornamentation of cottage rooms by way of china and pottery figures; what of the farm house? Well, here very much the same kind of patchwork cushions and rag rugs, of gleaming brass and gaily-coloured earthenware figures bought from the Image Man prevailed, though on a slightly larger scale and with some differences. According to Miss Gertrude Jekyll in her *Old English Household Life* published in 1939, the enormous dresser found in every farm kitchen always featured 'a garnish of pewter'. These silvery-looking objects, mugs, plates, sugar castors and jugs, etc. were handed down carefully from one generation to another, while the large chimney piece with its broad, accommodating shelf displayed Staffordshire ornaments that included 'Shepherds and shepherdesses, rustic groups, dogs and cow jugs supported by an earthenware money-box, spill-holders and a tobacco jar.'

Both in farmhouse and cottage kitchens, Chesterfield domestic ware (i.e. dishes, plates, bowls and stewpots) were in constant use. The jugs that appealed most to a yokel's sense of humour were those known as 'Puzzle' jugs, of which there is an enormous variety. Butter and cucumber dishes made in amusing shapes also had their appeal; so did squat bottles of greenish-tinged glass with long necks and short bodies, besides horn mugs to take out to the fields. The heavy pestles and mortars used by country wives were often made of stoneware or marble by Wedgwood at this time. Before they were of brass. A pottery hen seated on her nest, whose plump form could be lifted up by her scarlet comb to reveal a clutch of smooth, brown, newly laid eggs below was much prized. All these objects and more like brightly painted tin canisters, stoneware spirit flasks, wooden snuff boxes in the shape of shoes and mocha ware, are now collected and growing harder to find every year.

181

327–8 *Chesterfield brown ware: jampot with bramble-berry and leaf ornamentation;* (centre) *Stoneware cottage pitcher, Doulton, c. 1855;* (right) *Richly ornamented in relief grocer's canister with metal stopper, 1860s*

CHESTERFIELD BROWN WARE

Throughout the nineteenth century, Chesterfield Brown Ware was used extensively for domestic purposes in kitchens everywhere and sold by London retailers under the trade name of 'Nottingham' ware, for reasons unknown! This hard and opaque, salt-glazed stoneware made by Derbyshire potters has enduring qualities, besides an attractive rich brown sheen, engendered by the introduction of salt into the kiln when being baked.

Much of this ware has been wrongly catalogued as 'antique' on account of patterns based on eighteenth-century ones being used in Victorian times. By and large, domestic articles such as stewpots and oven dishes though made by different potters differ little from one another and carry no mark. Traditional shapes are still being reproduced today. There are, too, some very attractive little ginger-brown canisters with metal lids, also jam and pickle pots, to be found that used to be supplied to small village grocery shops once

to keep snuff in or dry goods like lentils and peas, etc. They carry raised designs of leaves and berries which are very pretty. Brown ware tobacco jars have similar decoration, only theirs usually show sporting scenes in relief and their lids are dome-shaped. This line of ware dates from about 1850 to 1890.

In *Victorian Pottery and Porcelain* (1959) Mr. Bernard Hughes lists the following names which can be found impressed on Chesterfield Brown ware. KNOWLES, the Welshpool and Payne Potteries, Brampton: OLDFIELD, John Oldfield and Co., Brampton; BRIDDON, William Briddon, Brampton; BOURNE, in several styles, such as Bourne & Son, Denby; WILLIAM BURTON (Codnor Park) until 1833.

Recently, I was shown a small kitchen entirely equipped with genuine old Chesterfield Brown Ware collected over the years. One object calculated to catch the eye of any collector was a most endearing little brown colander perfect in its modelling and having two tiny ear-handles like an Owl Jug.

PUZZLE AND HUNTING JUGS

Puzzle jugs appealed strongly to rustic humour and were found in pubs as well as in cottage and farm-

house homes. In Chesterfield Brown Ware, they were sold in shapes unaltered from the preceding century. For identification these have a baluster or bulbous body with a long wide neck; or they may be spherical with a narrow neck and be either plain or decorated with incised patterns. Or, again, they may carry figures and other designs in relief. Perforations round the neck are carried out in heart and diamond patterns or in semi-circles and circles formalised in group patterns. Spouts on them can number up to three, four or five. The joke derived from drinking out of a 'Puzzle' jug when merry-making was at its height in a bar was to hold the jug up in one hand closing, with a spare finger, a hole under the handle. With the other hand, the drinker in question tried to close two of the spouts and then proceed to quaff the contents without spilling a drop. This was a difficult feat.

Elsmore and Forster, Clay Hill Pottery, at Turnstall in Staffordshire specialised in some ironstone 'Teasing' jugs from about 1860 to the mid-1870s. In capacity, their jugs ranged from 1 to 4 pints and beer was generally served in them. After mine host had placed a full jug on the table, anyone picking up the jug was horrified to see the liquid pouring out from the bottom. This was brought about by using a hollow handle which ran from the rim and entered the side of the jug continuing down the inside to a half inch hole situated in the centre of the base. A small hole was then bored into the underside of the handle. So, whenever the jug was lifted, fingers had to cover this hole to prevent the liquid from spilling. When an unsuspecting customer picked up the jug, naturally without stopping the hole, out poured the liquid to his consternation and amazement.

Elsmore and Forster 'Teasing' jugs sometimes carry pictures of clowns on their sides with a cock fight in progress on their fronts. They can be marked with a coat of arms on the base with the words 'Warranted Ironstone China' and below the name *Elsmore and Forster*. But when this partnership broke up in the mid 1870s their teasing jugs ceased to be made.

Hunting jugs were the trade name for the Chesterfield Brown Ware jugs that were decorated by hunting scenes or pictures of dead game in high relief, such as Aunt Rouvray displayed in her parlour when John Ashby of Tysoe visited her as a boy. Other characteristic designs on these jugs show trees, windmills and village cronies smoking, drinking or walking about in groups. Handles are often modelled in the form of a greyhound. The name 'hunting' jug derives from the custom of serving hot punch or toddy in them, as this type of ware retains the heat better than any other stoneware. Loving cups and two-handled posset pots incised with names and a date were also marketed in Chesterfield ware as late as the 1880s. Jugs in the form of a bear hugging a poor dog to his chest were reproduced from traditional eighteenth-century moulds till 1880. The bear's head was detachable and could be used as a separate little drinking-cup.

Some unusual cylindrical jugs listed as *canettes* with greyhound handles belong to this group of 'hunting' jugs.

MOCHA WARE

Mocha Ware, once taken into little account, has recently been brought to the notice of collectors largely because of its unusual colours, designs and character. Its origin is humble and stems from a rustic background. Large quantities of ½ pint and 1 pint mugs, besides quart and pint jugs, were produced for use in public houses and taverns, together with spill vases and mustard pots and other containers.

The name 'mocha' derives from the semi-precious stone, the 'moss agate' which was sold by Georgian jewellers as *mocha* stone. This milky-looking gemstone with its delicate moss-coloured threads running all over it, sometimes in green,

329   *Half pint size tavern beer mug, Mocha ware*

sometimes in rust-red hues, gave its eighteenth-century name, *mocha*, to a creamware when it was produced with similar coloured patterns and veinings. This was about 1780. The invention of mocha ware has been traditionally attributed to a well-known potter of that day called William Adams.

From the late eighteenth century and through the nineteenth, mocha pottery, basically made of creamware, pearlware or caneware was produced in enormous quantities for all kinds of domestic utensils such as tumblers, mustard pots, pepper and salt cellars, cups and butter dishes as well as tavern serving jugs and mugs. These when found may be inscribed below the glaze with the name and address of the house they belonged to, together with the landlord's name and occasionally a date. For village shops and shellfish stalls one pint and half-pint containers were made in which to measure out dried peas or nuts or shrimps or winkles. For a more expensive market some finely potted ornaments like flower vases and spill jars were issued with success, including a quart-sized coffee pot and teapot.

The delicate markings and patterns on Mocha Ware that suggested to the countryman the shapes of windblown trees, ferns, mosses, or a bird's feathers known from childhood, were achieved, of course, by the skill of the potter. In *The Art and History of the Potting Business* (1846) William Evans has described the process of banding with mocha dip. This, he says, was applied by skilled operators on the ware as it rotated in a lathe. While the dip was wet on the unfired ware, moss agate effects were produced by a diffusing agent known as *mocha tea*. This was composed of a strange witch-like brew made of tobacco juice, stale urine and turpentine. Later, in a more

hygenic climate of opinion, hops and tansy were used instead of urine. It was said that a spot of 'mocha tea' dropped on wet mocha dip immediately spread into the shadowy images of those moss, ferns and feather motifs which so endeared this ware to country people.

Although nearly every earthenware potter could supply Mocha Ware on demand, little of this pottery is marked.

The fascinating Teulon-Porter collection of Mocha pottery bequeathed by Mr. Teulon Porter to the Stoke-on-Trent Museum has few marked examples, for instance. One is a quart mug marked 'Edge Malkin & Co., Burslem (1870–1903); the other, is a quart mug carrying a pink rose which was the mark used by John Rose & Co., Coalport (1820–1840). But Mr. Bernard Hughes gives some other known makers of Mocha Ware. These he lists in his book *Victorian Pottery and Porcelain*, as Pinder and Bourne, Burslem; John Tams, Longton (1874–1912); Maling and Son, Newcastle-on-Tyne; and the Kirkcaldy Pottery, Fife, which produced thistle-head like patterns by means of a blow-pipe used on a caneware body.

A cheaper form of Mocha Ware called 'Moko' pottery is sometimes mistaken for it. Moko pottery goods come in plain buff or red earthenware covered with white slip which is mottled by splashing different coloured slips on it with a flexible brush made from the long hairs in a donkey's tail – hence, its name.

Owing to the popularity today of Mocha Ware, many mugs and jugs are being reproduced from old moulds. Collectors drawn to this ware should procure a small book written by Mr. Teulon-Porter which is published by the Stoke-on-Trent City Museum.

OWL JUGS AND HARVEST BOTTLES

To quench his thirst, the farm labourer used to carry a jug, or bottle, out with him to the fields. It contained either beer, milk or water according to his preference. At first, a field jug or bottle was made of stout leather which blackened with time and usage. Then came those in earthenware or stoneware that were left plain or decorated. Like a countryman's smock or a fisherman's

jersey or guernsey, the knowledgable countryman could identify from which county, or district, these bottles and jugs came. For instance, in Dorset, farm hands carried a small, squat, pot-bellied jug with two, tiny ear-handles made in a darkish-red unglazed clay which was known by the name of an 'Owl Jug'.

In Essex, where I lived for many years, our harvest bottles were made of a greyish-brown stoneware, semi-glazed. They held a gallon of

330 *Example of a pot-bellied 'Owl Jug' (Dorset) in unglazed clay*

slip, scratched away and cut to show the darker ground. Inscriptions on jugs run on very much the same lines and are often repeated like this one:

He that by the plough must thrive,
Himself must either hold or drive.

Other centres for local pottery wares to interest collectors might be named as Tickenhall in Derbyshire, credited with a special kind of ware featuring designs cut out from pads of white clay applied on a dark ground, and near Salisbury, Wiltshire, a red-bodied type of earthenware was produced with a purplish-brown glaze decorated by incised or applied inscriptions. One of these read:

When I was in my native place
I was a lump of clay
And digged was from out the earth
And brought from thence away.

But now I am a jug become
By potters' art and skill
And now your servant am become
And carry ale I will.

At Gestingthorpe in Essex, a ware of eighteenth-century origin, with a yellow glaze marked with dark-brown flecks, has long been known and appreciated by Essex people. Sometimes this ware is decorated roughly with floral sprays; sometimes, with incised inscriptions. At one time, Gestingthorpe pottery works appear to have been operated from Pot Kiln Chase, the last potter working there being recorded by the name of George Finch. This was in the year 1912, but recently I heard this kiln had been reopened. Another Essex potter who achieved considerable fame in his lifetime and whose wares are well-known to collectors was Edward Bingham. His products ranged from ordinary dairy pitchers to puzzle jugs; from plain utility ware for the rustic many to ornate vases, etc. for the county's select few. Edward Bingham's pottery is characterised by a beautiful glaze; his decoration by an odd and completely individual combination of classical and folk subjects subtly mixed. He is still remembered by people as a remarkable personality who was never seen at work without wearing his bowler hat and who always carried an umbrella. Today he is recognised as a first class artist-potter.

home-brewed cider or ale and are more of a tall shape than squat. They had only one handle. On special occasions, as it might be for a local wedding or harvest home, farm jugs and mugs and harvest bottles might be given preferential treatment by being initialled or inscribed with the date of the ceremony and then kept to decorate the dresser. Sometimes, too, they were ordered from the local pottery and given away as presents. A small but interesting collection of local Essex pottery including harvest bottles is on view at Great Bardfield's little museum.

Today, many oldtime, county potteries once operating to supply the demand for their goods from near-by farming and village communities have vanished forever. In North Devon, for instance, several small potteries flourished once between Barnstaple and Bideford and produced decorated slipware in traditional local styles that collectors drawn to preserve rustic bygones like to possess. Another pottery centre dealing with characteristic wares was Donyat in Somerset, one of whose pieces, now in the Taunton Museum, commemorates the birth of local Siamese twins joined together, dated 1680. The prevalent form of decoration for Donyat harvest jugs is a coating of

ORNAMENTS FROM THE DAIRY

'On the right of the hall-door a broad gravel path led in a serpentine sweep towards the stables, a long low building spread over a considerable area hiden by shrubberies. The dairy was a little way further off. It had been originally a barn but was now a model dairy with outside gallery and staircase of solid wood work and with a Swiss roof. . . . The dairy itself had a solemn and shadowy air, like a shrine, and was as pretty as the dairy at Frogmore. The walls were lined with Minton tiles, the shallow milk pans were of Doulton pottery and quaintly-shaped pitchers of bright colours were ranged on china brackets along the walls. The windows were latticed, and a pane of ruby, rose or amethyst appeared here and there among the old bottle-green glass and cast a patch of coloured light upon the cool marble slab below.'

Miss Braddon, *The Fatal Three*

This description of a Victorian dairy house belonging to Mrs. George Greswold of Enderby Manor I find quite enchanting, besides being an accurate one. From the eighteenth century, the great lady as well as the squire's and farmer's wife could be found working with her maids in the dairy attached to the house in the same way that Marie Antoinette made milking a cow or churning butter fashionable at the Court of Versailles. Eighteenth-century dairies, such as the Chinese Dairyhouse at Woburn Abbey, besides Queen Victoria's later one at Frogmore had much time, thought and money lavished on them, especially when Josiah Wedgwood, the great potter produced the pans and implements needed for them.

Whether belonging to the 'big' house or to a mere farm the dairy was always a pleasant place to work in, with its white, plastered walls and stone-flagged floor. Everything in it had to be kept scrupulously clean. Brass milk churns of every size with brass ladles to match gleamed bright with polish. Other equipment was usually made of sycamore wood, while shallow pans with long handles, or none, of pewter, china or earthenware for cream and cheese-making were daily scrubbed and dried; otherwise the milk turned sour and the butter rancid.

One Essex dairy room I knew was attached to the back of the farm house, where it lay sheltered from the mid-day sun by green elderberry bushes. The two windows that ventilated it had gauze shutters to keep flies out. The roof was of slate with two feet of thatch over it, and a large churn was turned by a wheel outside rotated by a donkey. Every dairy utensil made of sycamore wood was washed in boiling water after the day's work. Friday's milk was made into cheese. A change from the old days, I heard, when it was 'turned' always into butter ready for sale at Saturday's market near by.

At the receiving-end of dairies like this one, well-run by the farmer's wife, was the Dairy shop proper, which sold its produce like butter and home-made cheeses and milk, etc. This might be cited in the nearest market town or even farther away – in London. Here, again, everything was kept cool and clean and until about 1914 followed a traditional pattern of furnishings. For instance, a town Dairy nearly always had soft-green, majolica tiles lining the walls, half way up, while a long marble slab did duty for a counter. On this marble slab, a pottery hen might sit, concealing under her smooth brown eggs or white. Near her might stand some miniature wooden churns, bound with gleaming brass with doll-sized brass-handled gill and half-a-gill measures hooked on to their sides. With these measure the thick cream was ladled out. Today these little churns have completely vanished and have been replaced by plastic cartons. A large white swan with golden bill often

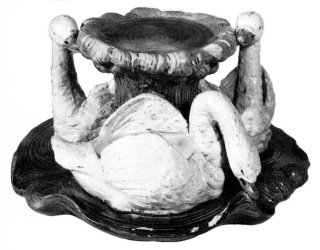

331   One of two similar dairy window 'Swan' majolica ware ornaments, marked Bretby Art Pottery, Woodville, 1870

sat in the Dairy Shop window, flanked on either side by more pottery hens or two long-legged storks or cranes in majolica ware.

Some years ago I bought a large set-piece in majolica ware that was composed of three white swans posed on a flat green platter imitating lily pads. It had come out of a recently demolished,

old-fashioned dairy shop. It was a marked piece coming from the Bretby Art Pottery, Woodville, Burton-on-Trent which later moved, under the direction of Henry Tooth, to Linthorpe near Middlesborough in 1879. This firm specialised in majolica dairy ware besides umbrella stands made in the form of storks and cranes.

Pottery Hens

Pottery hens with or without their chicks in earthenware, or in coloured opaque or clear glass, are legion and in great demand today. At one time, they were produced purely for a rural market but today they are being reproduced from old traditional moulds in their hundreds for London stores. Mr. Geoffrey Godden has garnered some fascinating material about pottery hens. In particular, he tells the story of how a widow with the name of Jane Beech took over the Old Bell Pottery Works at Burslem on the death of her husband and became quite noted for her pottery hens, besides other fanciful wares. So much so that she had a poem written about her activities by a Canadian traveller, James Lidstone when he toured the Potteries in 1866.

332   *Pottery hen (unmarked) with buff, speckled plumage seated on a yellow nest, c. 1860s*

JANE BEECH
Manufacturer of China, Parian and Earthenware Fancy Goods

Here ev'ry form of life in Heaven above,
Or in the Earth beneath
All that of inanimate we love,
Or like of things that breathe.
All you can mention of Bird or Animal,
Jane Beech as b' Fairy Wand doth readily up-call:
I've seen of the Legendary Red Riding Hood
Many representations, but never one so good;
While the Fowls for egg Dishes charm each
    wond'ring land,
As if straight from some mighty Sculptor's hand.

It would have been nice to know industrious Mistress Jane Beech, who carried on with her Fowl Dishes and Birds and Little Red Riding Hoods till 1873. But her factory, the Old Bell Works, did not long survive her for it was demolished about 1876.

Butter and Cucumber Dishes

Butter dishes were a highly profitable line and taken out of a travelling potter's pack with a flourish if they happened to be ones in a new shape. But whatever the shape was, dishes were made in two sizes; one to hold half a pound of butter; the

other, a pound. Usually cottage butterdishes come in pressed glass or a palish-brown earthenware; a small cow sits on the lid for use as a handle.

At one time, cucumber was considered to be a high-class relish, but somehow or other it descended in the social scale along with cockles and shrimps until it was only seen in a cottage parlour

333 *Green glazed with yellow lip cucumber dish (un-marked)*

334 *Farmhouse half-pound size butter dish in pale-brown ware, quilted pattern, cow on lid*

for 'high tea'. The most attractive cucumber dishes are made in the long slender shape of a cucumber itself, in a shiny green ware. Another attractive farmhouse or cottage item, until quite recently a drug on the market, was a dome-shaped cheese holder in prettily patterned china or in mottled lustre Sunderland ware. For some reason or other, they went completely out of fashion for a time, but now they are 'in' again, and fetching quite a price.

PAINTED TINWARE

Another medium that supplied colour and ornamentation to a cottage interior, in particular to the dresser, was painted tinware. This ware included painted tin tea caddies, canisters, tobacco jars, biscuit boxes, trays, etc. produced by the travelling Tinman on his rounds, besides the essential tin kettle or pots and pans.

This type of painted tinware was known in earlier days as *japanned ware,* for *japanning* was one of the many skills learnt by Europe from the East and when the English made an attempt to imitate Oriental lacquer in the seventeenth century it was called *japan.* But on tinware, craftsmen first used varnishes without trying to achieve relief decoration, as they did on furniture by the use of a composition called gesso, and followed up their varnishings by a baking process to fix the glossy finish.

While originally suggesting a hard shiny finish, *japanned* ware finally came to mean any kind of metalware with painted decoration; for pewter as well as tin was treated in an identical way.

The first centre for the production of decorated tinware was Pontypool in Monmouthshire. Ponty-pool had primarily been an iron-manufacturing town, but experiments with the craft of *japanning* took place about 1700 and industry spread its tentacles eventually to Birmingham, Bilston and Wolverhampton. Painted tin domestic utensils both for well-off and humble buyers were produced from about 1760 to 1820. Typically the background for this ware is black, brown, crimson or a mottled hue like tortoiseshell; decoration features flowers, exotic birds, scenes and festoons, delicately painted, on goods like tea trays and caddies which had a great vogue in Victorian homes for almost a century. Japanned goods from Pontypool, Bilston and other Midland centres have been fully documented and made known to collectors. But humbler versions made for the rural market like tea caddies, biscuit boxes and grocery canisters in painted tinware are not so well-known. Famous biscuit firms have long supplied their customers, for instance, with decorated tin boxes of every amusing shape and size which are now claimed by collectors anxious to preserve this kind of bygone. A similar appeal is attached to metal tea canisters and tin cigar and tobacco jars.

Another manifestation of painted tinware of a highly decorative character has been brought to notice by the opening up of England's fascinating network of Midland canals to holiday traffic by 'narrow boat', motor launch or steam barge. This is the painted 'barge-ware' belonging to the colour-loving and picturesque canal folk some of whom come from gypsy origin though they do not like to admit to this background.

The attraction of painted barge ware lies in its flat style of painting similar to the itinerant painter's art. When lettering gives the owner's name on his 'narrow boat', it is full of the same little twists and curls used by the travelling pen-men on farm carts and waggons.

Many of the old-time homes of the true 'barge folk' of England are still found, happily, afloat. In them, the Long Buckby can and other canal gear is still in daily use. The Long Buckby can features the traditional pattern of gaudy, full-blown roses and multi-coloured, flat-petalled daisies on a background with vermilion bands, while its base is done in what is called the 'Scotch plaid' design. The can took its name from the little canal shop near Buckby Wharf, Norton Junction, on the Grand Union Canal, where it was once produced.

Traditional paintings of romantic castles and hills, winding rivers and humped bridges, cottage roses and daisies are still being painted today on reproductions of 'barge ware' (i.e. on stools and trays, watering-cans and dippers) by canal-ware painters, some of whom survive in their work-shops along the Grand Union Canal. All their work is done in free-hand with no guiding lines and is bought by enthusiasts using the canal for their holidays as well as by collectors with an eye to their value rising in the future.

Another 'collecting line' which stems from this same source, are some very distinctive lattice-rimmed china plates decorated with floral patterns and some big, shiny, brown Measham teapots used by canal folk. Teapots are festooned with floral garlands and often carry an inscription like: 'Remember Me' or 'Love at Home'. Sometimes a name is printed on a scroll, such as 'Mrs. Ashbee, 1880' or just simply 'Thomas Wright, Builder.'

Many stories of a legendary quality have gathered about the age-old designs found on the painted tinware, the crockery and even on the sides of the 'narrow boats' themselves belonging to the canal folk. It is said that they were first seen about the time the first canal was built by James Grindley for the Duke of Bridgewater. One story goes that the castles which compose an ever-

335   *A white tinware coffee jug with painted roses, 1860s*

336   *Canal 'Bargeware' coal bucket with traditional hand-painted flowers etc*

recurring theme of boat-decoration represent the domed pottery kilns along the Trent and Mersey Canal and that the pennants flying from their towers, the plumes of smoke when these same kilns were being fired. The small rounded hilltops which rise in the flat landscape are the waste heaps which surround the old pottery towns and so on . . . All this is as may be. But the gaudily painted great tin cans and dippers, the coal scuttles and latticed-rimmed white china plates, the brown Measham teapots together with the decorative braces and wide 'spider-web' belts worn once by every boatman, will never cease to attract both tourists and collectors to acquire them whenever possible.

LATE VICTORIAN COTTAGE FIGURES

Towards the 1870s and '80s, a whole new range of little pottery figures, including some in biscuit china, came to be produced, many to do duty as love-tokens or as fairground prizes and cheap 'fairings' for villagers out on a shopping spree. Another market for these figures were the garish stalls strung along the piers of South Coast towns like Southend, Margate and Brighton; or, up North, Blackpool and Scarborough. Vulgar in taste as many are and florid, lacking the simple but appealing artistry of the Image Man's chimney 'Toys', nevertheless an interesting collection can be made of some of these figures, which have quality and interest through displaying the fashions and habits of their day as their prototypes did of an earlier epoch.

For instance, the sudden rise to popularity of the Christy Minstrels, together with the London appearance of individual 'Coon' artists like 'Jim Crow' Rice at the old Surrey Theatre, gave rise to many small china figures being modelled to impersonate them, including one of Billy Waters, a celebrated 'blacked-up' street musician whose picture by a contemporary artist was actually seen in the Royal Academy.

Later came the small china model of Piper Findlater, V.C., who during the India-Tirah campaign was wounded during the storming of the Dargai Heights by the Gordon Highlanders on 20 October, 1897. Propping himself up against a rock and under heavy fire, Piper Findlater continued playing the regimental march, *The Cock of the North*, to encourage his comrades to fight even harder round him.

For his gallant act, Piper Findlater was awarded the Victoria Cross, receiving it from Queen

337–8   Striking Victorian figures 'Jim Crow Rice a famous music-hall artiste and 'Billy Waters', a well-known London street musician

339   Biscuit china. 'Edinburgh fishwife' from the Rathbone Pottery, Portobello

Victoria herself at Netley Hospital on 20 May, 1898. Soon after this event, in spats, kilt and solar topee his figure could be bought in biscuit china to be placed on the mantelpiece.

Another figure in this same genre shows the well-known Edinburgh Fishwife in traditional dress, and with her big creel strapped on to her bowed back. She wears a bottle-green dress hitched up for work so that her pretty pale yellow-and-brown striped petticoat shows below. Her face is exceptionally well-modelled and painted and she is among the few marked pieces of this time, being produced by the Rathbone Pottery, Portobello, Edinburgh.

In the 1880s, the drawings of Kate Greenaway (1846–1901) began to have a phenomenal success, the quaint dresses of her children creating a new romantic type of clothes for children. For a time all smart little girls wore high-waisted muslin gowns with sashes and beaver bonnets; little boys frilly low-necked shirts and pantaloon trousers. Lithographers grew rich by selling hundreds of coloured prints that reproduced the sentimental world created by Kate Greenaway's romantic vision. Little pottery figures invaded the china market that were the exact replicas of her children in their

343–4 *Telegraph boy in terra-cotta, product of the Watcombe and Clay Co., Torquay;* (right) *Piper Findlater, V.C. hero of the India-Tirah campaign, 1897*

340   *Young Girl with Billy goat*

341   *The Squire*

342   *The Lovers*

345–7   *Another version in biscuit china of 'The Bathers' by E. B. Stephens (1815–82), same pose but mother in different garment; (centre) Portrait china figure of the well known prison reformer Elizabeth Fry (1780–1845) as a candle-snuffer; (right) China 'Kate Greenaway' child (coloured) as a candle snuffer*

pseudo-Regency clothes. There were special Trade Cards, too, bearing Kate Greenaway figures, while white linen cloths, etc. were embroidered with illustrations taken from her books.

After the death of Queen Victoria, pottery figures became more and more debased. Folk art, as expressed through the medium of earthenware and cheap china, was dead and the Image Man with his tray of pretty rustic ornaments vanished forever.

12 **Cottage Glass**

348 *Charming one-time fairground vase in spangle-ware when mica flakes in the glass gave glittering effect. Handles and trim in plain clear glass, mottled pink and green c. 1860*

The glass-blowers made a goodly array and gave away tokens as they went. The men wore hats and caps brittle and brilliant with wavy plumes of spun glass whilst birds, ships, goblets and decanters on their poles glistened in the beams of the hot sun. (Coronation Day, 19 July 1821)

Mrs. Linnaeus Banks, *The Manchester Man*

349 *'An elegant and beautiful ship' in Bristol glass, c. 1820*

Round the important glass centres of Sunderland and Newcastle in Northern England and at Stourbridge, Bristol, Nailsea and Wrockwardine in Shropshire, the glass men lived in small cottages whose front gardens often showed a glittering coloured glass ball (later known as witch-balls) which were stuck up on a pole so as to avert the evil eye cast by someone passing by. For they were a superstitious lot, these glass-blowers, many of whom took to the road at intervals, hawking their fancy glass wares from village to village like the Image Man his china. From time to time, too, one of these glass-blowers might be seen seated working 'at his lamp' in the small square of a market town watched by a fascinated group of gaping yokels. One such man was seen by a little girl called Emily Shore one day in October, 1831, when she visited Potton in Bedfordshire. She recorded this sight in her journal.

'He made glass baskets, candle-sticks, birds and horses. And the way he did them is as follows. He sat at a little table and before him was a little furnace which contained a flame of intense heat though it was only kept by tallow.

'He had a great many glass sticks of various sizes and of every colour; when he wished to make anything – a basket for instance – he took a small one which he used merely as a prop; he held one end of another in the flame till the end of it melted into a sort of paste which could be drawn out into any fineness. By this way, he made a vast number of things. One was

Charles II under the Oak; another was the Lord Mayor's Coach; and George IV lying in state. Some of these things were handsome and expensive. We bought a few of the minor things. One was a glass pen and an elegant and beautiful ship.'

The Journal of a Young Naturalist (1891)

Within the limits of his craft, the Glass-blower was far more inventive than his opposite number the Image Man, though his wares on account of their fragility did not endure so long as his companion's earthenware 'toys'. As a race of artisans, glass-blowers were the merriest of men; here today, gone tomorrow. But their most attractive trait, possibly, was their communal love for, and participation in, processional ceremonies and out-of-door gatherings. One of the former took place on the Coronation Day of George IV in Manchester and many years later Mrs. Linnaeus Banks, born Isabella Varley (1821–1877) being told about it, described it in her well-known regional novel, *The Manchester Man* (1876). Another ceremony known as 'The Glassmakers' Picnic' took place further south, round Stourbridge in Worcestershire. On this day, the men taking part tricked themselves out in glass feathers and stars, and promenaded the streets, each one carrying an example of his skill like a cage of glass birds or a long, striped, glass walking-stick. They sang as they marched along 'A Glass Maker's Song' whose opening verse went like this:

> *Bonny's backed the winner,*
> *We're on the booze today,*
> *We'll have a goose for dinner,*
> *And drink whisky in our 'tay'!*
> *We'll line our coats with five pound notes*
> *And drink our noses blue.*
> *For Bonny's backed the winner*
> *And we don't care what we do!*

Nailsea House was founded in 1788 by John Robert Lucas, a cider maker, to produce a new-shaped bottle of brownish-green glass which he had designed himself, and which came to be known as pot-glass. This glass was free of the heavy tax levelled on flint-glass. John Robert Lucas was so successful that four years later, in 1792, he was approached by Edward Homer, an enamel painter, who proposed to him that his pot glass might be decorated with a view to selling it for cheap domestic ware. When Lucas agreed the two men joined forces and in this way variegated Nailsea glass appeared on the market. It was an instantaneous success. By 1830, John Robert Lucas's onetime humble glass-house for bottling cider was in full production with fancy glass wares, so much so that more buildings were added till they covered five acres of the surrounding scrubby heathland.

All over England, glass from Nailsea was having a phenomenal success and being copied, too, by other glass houses. Among the most popular goods from Nailsea were jugs and fancy flasks, rolling-pins and bells. These wares were produced about 1800. The glassmen sold their garden witch-balls, now as novelties with painted or transfer-printed scenes on them; with flowers, too, and mottoes. Then from about 1845 came those exquisite hand-bells and gimmel flasks. Hand-bells, which stand about 9 to 18 inches tall are found in many colours or they can be stripped. They are usually of flint glass. Their clappers should also be made of clear flint glass and a loop is often found at their top for a thong to pass through. Once upon a time these bells were hung in chapels and meeting houses where they were struck with a padded hammer to mark, with their soft clear ring, a period of silence for prayer.

Gimmel flasks are really two bottles blown separately then fused together and mounted on a crimped or petal foot. Some gimmel flasks were used for oil and vinegar; others sold to contain sweet-scented toilet waters.

Another rewarding novelty was glass coaching-horns over a yard long (*c.* 1850) in amber glass to represent brass. Shepherds' crooks, walking-sticks and long slim pipes for measuring ale in pubs – all these wares can form individual 'collecting-lines' for lovers of Nailsea and other types of nineteenth-century coloured glass.

FAIRGROUND LUSTRE GLASS

At one time, many churches in the slum quarters of a city or in country parishes off the beaten track used altar vessels of silvered glass in imitation of genuine silver. It was not long, then, before silvered glass vases, candle-sticks and other ornaments came to be gaily painted on the outside with bands of bright colour or a coarse spray of flowers, for a secular market. The best market happened to be the world of the fairground, where the glitter and gaudy decoration of this silvered glass was quickly snapped up or came to be used as prizes in side-shows like 'Aunt Sally'. Many a cottage chimney shelf boasted at least one pair of silvered glass candlesticks or a vase brought home by a victorious coconut shier.

350 *A small 'Fairing' vase of shocking-pink biscuit china with applied forget-me-nots. Silvered glass candlestick decorated with coarsely painted flowers, c. 1890*

SLAGWARE AND MARBLE GLASS

Slagware, which was in production from about 1842 to the 1870s, has been called sometimes 'poor man's porcelain', because it looked so much like glazed china. In fact, it was first made as a substitute for expensive china table ware which only the rich could afford. At one time, it has been

recorded, slagware was produced in novelty forms so that it could be put into packaged groceries, as give-away presents to customers'.

The name slagware derived from the way it was made. This was by glass-makers buying silicates from a nearby steel works in the form of 'slag' drawn off molten steel which was mixed with clear glass. The result – slag glass! Though most of it is purple and white, it can come, too, in green, brown and blue. Objects found in slagware number small, squat vases and tumblers, spill-holders, cream jugs and a kind of 'pinched' or 'poacher's' type of bag or basket. There are also attractive flat-sided flasks impressed with pictures taken from nursery tales. Registry marks come in a diamond-shaped mark which gives the year, month and parcel number of the design.

Marble Glass is twin-brother to slag glass the only difference is that it has a slightly wider range of colour which includes mulberry and cream, jet black, blue and orange (rare) and tortoiseshell (very rare). Covered dishes, cake-stands, match-holders, and jam pots may be found but lidded sugar bowls and celery vases have all but vanished.

FRIGGERS

The name 'frigger' comes from the verb 'to friggle' or 'fuss' and it describes the habit indulged in by some glass-blowers of 'frigging abaht' with odds and ends of unused glass towards the finish of a day's work. This was the time when in jovial mood they decided to make something practical for the wife, or fanciful for the children to take home with them. From this haphazard occupation of whimsical glassmen — to produce an object entirely for their own pleasure and to show off their skill — good business resulted, for it was not long before they realised that their 'friggers' might be appreciated as much in the open market as at home.

So, whenever the glass blower went tramping along the roads with his ordinary wares, he took a number of multi-coloured glass whips and pens, top hats and eggs, household 'dumps' and rolling pins as well.

Always a good selling-line and attractive to the cottage wife was a set of glass balls varying in size but similar to the glass floats used by anglers; these she could put in a tumbler or on a jam pot to act as a seal, allowing no fly or wasp to creep in. Another useful but pretty object the glass-blower produced was a door-stop or 'dump', as they came to be known in West Country parlance. These kept a cottage door open during hot weather while baking was in progress and could be custom-ordered. Made of pale-greenish glass, 'dumps' contain bubbles often in their rounded, transparent hearts or a pot of flowers.

Yet another attractive glass gadget for the cottage home was a glass rolling pin, with one open end that could be filled with water and so keep the pastry cool and short when used. Early in the nineteenth century, it has been recorded that Chance Bros., Birmingham, made 'glass rolling pins and milk pans'. As glass was subjected to penalising excise duty between 1745–1845, the first glass rolling pins were made of untaxed green and amber bottle glass. Decoration was kept to a minimum and an owner's name or initials merely

351–2 Two cottage glass door stoppers; a heavily leaded flint glass with smokey look, Birmingham & Stourbridge, 1840s; (right) a green glass 'Dump' enclosed airy bubbles, Nailsea, 1828–60

scratched on with the point of a nail. In the 1840s, bottle glass rolling pins were flecked with white coloured ornamentation; later, they were given beauty treatment by way of decoration known as *latticinio* introduced by Italian glass workers coming to England on a new 'exchange' system. Latticinio featured delicate loops and whorls of coloured glass threads, known as 'quilling', being embodied in the clear glass form. From now on, the glass rolling pin lost its functional use and became purely ornamental, often being given away as a love-token or souvenir present. Sometimes filled with salt (a precious commodity still), or expensive tea or rum, stories have gathered about them and queer superstitions. One is that given by a sailor to his sweetheart it should be hung up carefully to ensure his safe return. Should his rolling pin suffer damage then news might be heard of his death at sea or the loss of his ship.

Because of their romantic appeal, glass rolling pins are still being reproduced of heat-resisting glass at Sunderland. When first reproduced in 1930, they were hand-blown, but now they are churned out at the rate of some 100,000 per year by semi-automatic processes.

The 'friggers' made by the glass-blower to please and amuse his own children have been delightfully described by Mr. S. Taylor-Seago in an article that appeared in *The Lady* called 'Friggers Afloat'. Mr. Seago tells of some charming little cottage glass paperweights known as 'Man-in-the-Moon'. They were made by the glass-man dropping a small 'gathering' of molten glass onto a smooth stone slab which ran out to form a circle. Before it set and became solid, he drew, roughly, on it a pair of eyes, nose and mouth-a-grin with the end of an iron tube. Another glass whimsy of his were some long-necked little flasks called 'Flip-flops' by children, on account of the curious sound they made, a kind of metallic 'flip-flop' when held up to the mouth and blown upon.

'Crackers' or 'Prince Rupert's Drops' were small glass tadpoles that could be hit and hit again without ever breaking! But one astute blow on their tails and the little creature broke into a thousand pieces with a shattering report that seemed a piece of pure magic to juvenile beholders.

Glass swans, pigs and piglets, glass eggs, a bellows-shaped bottle and a glass pistol filled with liquorice 'all sorts' or just water, all these delicious and airy fancies could be 'dreamed up' by the itinerant glass-blower crouched over his incandescent lamp placed within the protective shelter of a cottage porch or set up in the bustling market square of a country town like Potton to fascinate wide-eyed and silent audiences.

GLASS SHIPS AND WALKING STICKS

Besides Emily Shore's 'elegant and beautiful little glass ship' bought from a glass-blower, there were other ships much bigger and grander in conception to be obtained by order. In fact, glass ships exquisitely rigged and manned, too, by tiny glass figures were a favourite subject of skilled glassmen and preserved by their owners under a shade in the parlour. The City Art Gallery, Bristol, has an interesting advertisement printed by a Mr. Davis to announce the recent arrival from South America of his Swedish partner, Mr. Johnson, and:

'To assure the public that they are the only glass ship-builders travelling the Kingdom and that they will blow any article wanted while the company are present. Glass Blowing, Spinning, Linking and Modelling. Mr. Davis makes a variety of ornaments for sale such as feathers, pens, plain and ornamental necklaces, ships, flowers and pipes, tobacco stoppers, cigar tubes, microscopes, spirit levels, trees, birds and birds' nests, seals with a variety of other articles too numerous to insert. Mr. Davis is capable of spinning one thousand yards of common window glass in the space of one minute so fine that ten grains will extend to 18,000 in length.'

Mr. Davis must have been a master glass-blower, indeed; almost a magician. What must it have been like to see him spinning his yards of common window glass into those shimmering threads of silvery nothingness. Did his skill measure up to walking sticks as well or did he leave such everyday objects to Mr. Johnson? Today, glass walking sticks placed in decorative patterns on a wall or illuminated by concealed lighting in an alcove, have come very much into fashion and there are several well-known collectors of them. Lord Boyd of Merton has over 70 examples, all different, in regard to their colours, patterns, heads and handles. In plain or opaque glass, spirally threaded,

353 *Superb confection
of the glass blower's
skill and artistry. Glass
birds with spun glass
tails perched on glass
fountain, ship below.
Bristol, c. 1820*

354 *Three different ship models in glass white and coloured glass, c. 1840*

twisted, knobbed and ribboned; with latticino ornament, pink or white on a green glass; striped or flecked – walking sticks with their companion shepherds' crooks express a world of pure fantasy created by glass-blowers. Stories are attached to them, too, as they are to rolling pins. For instance, in East Anglia, a glass walking stick was given to a bride and her groom on their wedding day to ensure that he, the husband, never took a stick to beat his wife. A shepherd's crook might smooth the bridal sheets for luck as a rolling pin smoothed a sailor's collar. But if a walking stick twisted like barley sugar hung on a cottage wall as the one did in Grandmother Harriet's room then it might be filled; 'with tiny coloured balls like a confectioner's hundreds and thousands'. For a trade-sign, they were put up outside a sweet shop in the same way that a long coloured tobacco glass pipe hung above a tobacconist's door.

TOP-HATS AND SHOES

In her book on *Victorian Glass* Ruth Webb devotes a whole chapter to glass hats which were sold for a few pence to cottage people who loved them. For they did duty as inkwells and mustard pots; salt and celery containers; candle-snuffers and tooth-pick holders besides little vases to stick a few primroses or wild violets in. Another use for these endearing objects was as 'gift' souvenirs and Christmas presents. By and large, they were pro-duced by glass-men in a wide variety of shapes reproduced from the mould selected by their maker. One glass hat known as a 'tumbler's' hat; another with a curly brim as a 'Parsons's'. Both derive from an inkwell mould.

'Blown-moulded hats', as they were called, were produced over a long period of years in clear glass, characteristic colours being amber, pale ruby and an olive-green. Many of these hats were blown from moulds other than the inkwell, such as bottles and whisky tasters. There is one brand of glass hat which goes by the name of 'caster place hat' after the 'caster place men' who 'blew' them scorning the use of a mould. A clown's hat, tall steeple hats, a policeman's helmet, a jockey's cap were produced by the glassmen, who were always inventive.

For the Christmas and 'souvenir' market, some little glass hats have 'Compliments of the Season' or an individual name printed in gilt letters on their brims. Between 1850 to 1860, hats in a milky-white opaque glass, known as 'Derbies', appeared which were very popular. They were 'blown-moulded'

335   *Blown moulded hats: curly-brimmed hat in amber glass and diamond-patterned hat with hat-band in ruby glass, c. 1850*

356   *Opaque white bowler hat or 'Derbie', c. 1865*

from old pharmacy bottles and often decorated with a little garland of painted flowers or have printed on their brims 'To a Good Boy'. As small ornaments, glass hats in a wide range of amusing shapes and colours can be most rewarding to collect.

The same thing may be said of boots and shoes in glass, clear or opaque. It is extraordinary really what an odd fixation Victorians, rich or poor, had for boots and shoes. Whenever they could, they bought them in different mediums to display in their rooms, and this went for a cottage kitchen as well as for a rich lady's boudoir.

A long association between footwear, luck and marriage dates far back in time, in fact, to the Bible when the plucking off of a shoe signified the confirmation of a contract for redemption or change of ownership which could include marriage. As faithful Bible readers, most Victorians knew of the symbolic importance of shoes as good-luck emblems and so liked to possess them. From amber glass shoes with buckles or without to tiny glass slippers as transparent as Cinderella's, glass footwear is eminently collectable. While on this topic I should

like to mention some shoes in quite another medium which appealled to cottage housewives. These were large carved wooden boots which acted as tea-caddies and which are sometimes found quite complete with simulated eyelets and laces. They are most attractive. Village men, on the other hand, favoured another type of small wooden boot or shoe hollowed out as snuff boxes. These date round about the 1870s and 1880s when they were made in large quantities. Usually they have sliding lids or, sometimes, tight-fitting rebated ones made to lift out. They vary in size, too, from 1″ to 2″ long, if they were for the pocket or up to 5″ if not.

Occasionally a wooden shoe snuff box is found with a carved date but more often than not the year appears on the sole in small brass pins. These little shoe boxes are miniature works of art when they carry elaborate brass-pin decoration that is reminiscent of piqué work usually the little brass pins are let in flush to look like fine stitching on the soles and uppers. Again, there are some shoes, parts of whose 'uppers' have been stained black in imitation of black glacé kid. This brings me to one very

357   *Clear Glass Hats: 'Tumbler' moulded hat; (right) Tophat blown possibly from an inkwell mould, c. 1840*

odd but ornamental boot seen recently. It was carved out of coal, ordinary shining black coal. Was it some fantasy conceived by a miner in his free time when, overcome by the urge to do something entirely different with his hands than he hew

out coal, all day and every day, in semi-darkness, he turned to carving this boot for a lucky emblem? One will never know. But it survives to this day, one complete and very dramatic-looking coal boot and, as yet, I have come across no other.

CUP PLATES AND COMMEMORATIVE PIECES IN PRESSED GLASS

As I have already stated (Chapter II: The Dining Room) pressed glass was first produced in America, appearing in England later, about 1830. However, it was not until the 1870s and '80s that pressed glass scored a phenomenal success when it came to be recognised everywhere as a modest substitute for English sparkling cut-crystal long used by the upper-class. Quite rightly, pressed glass was first known as 'poor man's glass'. But who cared? Certainly not the public for whom it was being mass-produced. So many domestic utensils, in particular table items that poor people had never been able to afford before in glass, were now available. Custard cups, pretty glass bowls for jellies and trifles, cream jugs, butter dishes, cup

plates – they were on sale in towns and village shops, on market stalls or given away as popular fairground prizes. How pleased must Flora Thompson's mother (and others who had been in service with the gentry) have been to handle glass plates and jugs, once more, even though they lacked the superior quality and weight of cut-crystal long-known to them!

One of the prettiest and most unusual objects to be found in pressed glass are Cup-plates which are extremely collectable. These charming little platters, slightly smaller than the average-sized tea plate, have a flat instead of the recessed base belonging to a saucer, with which and its saucer it was sold as a threesome. This trio was produced for those who did not consider it vulgar to sip direct from the saucer into which their tea had been poured out to cool. Because this way of drinking tea necessitated putting the cup down on the table cloth, where it sometimes made a slight stain, the cup-plate was invented to hold it. Cup-plates are stippled all over to give a 'lacey' effect and feature, as their decoration, stars, flower and fern patterns, sunburst and rosettes.

Because pressed glass was cheap and lent itself so well to mass production, manufacturers found it the perfect ware in which to reproduce their endless 'Commemorative' or 'Royal Occasions' souvenir pieces by way of large and handsome Jubilee chargers, (these include both the Golden and Diamond Jubilee) jugs of every type, candlesticks, bowls, mugs and plates, etc. No Victorian, especially those with middle-class taste, could resist buying, so royalty-conscious were they and Establishment-loving, some pressed glass ornament marking a Royal Wedding or Death – the more so if it was in amber glass to display on a whatnot shelf or mantel-piece. Many interesting examples of pressed glass 'Commemorative' pieces are still available to tempt admirers to start a worthwhile collection whose value will steadily rise with the years.

358 *Small candlestick in amber 'pressed' glass commemorating the Royal Jubilee, 1867*

13 **Souvenirs of Travel**

359   *Souvenir china plate with painted decoration from Cromer, 1890s*

360 *Coloured frontispiece by Benjamin Fawcett (1808–90) for the Rev. Houghton's* Seaside Walks of a Naturalist, *1870*

The Victorians, rich and poor alike, loved the sea and spent a holiday on the beach whenever they could. Their choice was wide, having been opened through the means of cheap travel on the newly established railroad. From the garish delights of Southend, then, with its many 'Cockles and Winkles' stalls, its chain pier and loud hubbub of Cockney voices to the better class amenities afforded by Brighton, Bognor and Bournemouth, or even the primitive joys known to the gentry frequenting Devon fishing ports and Cornish coves – Victorian families could sample them all!

It was not until the reign of Queen Victoria that the sea-side was mass-enjoyed. From this period date many new holiday ploys; many new fashions in clothes, food and social habits. Above all, an enormous stimulus was given to sea-side trade, to the manufacture of local goods to supply an ever-increasing demand for 'Souvenir Gifts' of every kind that would remind sentimental Victorian tourists of their visits to the sea.

In 1844, the young Queen Victoria herself set the royal seal of approval on sea-side excursions by buying Osborne House on the Isle of Wight, which became one of her dearest possessions. Eight years later, two typical middle-class families set out, the one to Torquay, the other to Paignton, the heads of which were to wield great influence over the holiday life of their compatriots for several generations to come.

To begin with, Philip Henry Gosse who, suffering from overwork and physical strain, rented a cottage near Torquay in 1852 to which he took his wife and 'a dear little naturalist in

204

petticoats'. This was his son, Edmund, destined to become the leading literary critic of the 1890s and the author of *Father and Son* (1907).

Very much aware of the flora and fauna awaiting discovery on England's still virgin shores, Gosse began to take notes for his first book on marine biology while staying near Torquay. A year later, in 1853, *A Naturalist's Ramble on the Devonshire Coast* came out and scored an immediate success, with its fine chromolithographs done by Gosse himself. In 1854 *The Aquarium* followed, for which work Gosse had formed a summer party of students to assist him in his research and to whom he had given out-of-door classes on marine life. So a completely new pastime for cultured Victorians (or those who wished to be thought cultured) was inspired by Gosse.

In the meantime, Charles Kingsley (1819–1875), Rector of Eversley in Hampshire, who greatly admired Gosse, followed his lead by taking his own family to Paignton in Devon. Here, accompanied by a young friend, Miss Grenfell, he studied the marvels of shore life and produced in 1855 his own charming *Glaucus: or, the Wonders of the Shore* which he dedicated to his youthful partner.

The Victorian taste for Aquaria began about 1854 and became widespread when Philip Gosse's *A Handbook to the Marine Aquarium* appeared in 1855. The frontispiece of this book carried such a magnificent illustration of an octagonal indoor tank standing on an ornamental pedestal of wrought-iron leaves that ladies craved to possess one just like it for their drawing rooms.

Eventually, the honour of having the first sea-water aquarium in her London home was won by a Mrs. Anne Thynne when, in 1856, she brought back to London living madrepores from Torquay. When interviewed by a reporter from *The Girl's Home Companion* she explained how to save herself 'the trouble of agitating the water for further supplies in her tank she had

361–3 *Outside cover of* Seaside Walks of a Naturalist*;* (centre) *Coloured plate by William Dickes (1818–92) from* Glaucus: or, the Wonders of the Shore *by Charles Kingsley, 1855;* (right) *Plate from* Beautiful Shells *by H. G. Adams, 1871*

  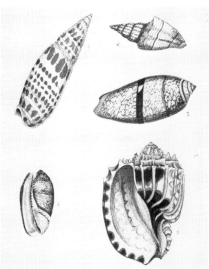

sent all the way to Torquay for living seaweeds to purify the water for her flagging corals!'

To have an anemone pan in which to house the pretty anemone *Daisy tyriensis* found in delightful Lyme Regis harbour in such abundance, together with the Gem anemone (*Bunodes gemmaces*) was the aim of every lady with *avant garde* tastes. Especially when dear Mr. Shirley Hibberd high-lighted 'Marine and Fresh-Water Aquariums', anemone pans and their like as embellishments of much interest and beauty in his book *Rustic Adornments for Homes of Taste*.

Suddenly, though, the fashion for aquaria – like all fashionable crazes – changed course and instead of corals, madrepores and sea-anemones being the rage, pebbles began to be collected instead with fossils and semi-precious beach stones like cornelian and amber. Little books appeared now on *Beach Rambles in Search of Seaside Pebbles and Crystals* (1859) which sparked off the vogue for pebble jewellery, particularly in Scotland. Where fossils and agate (cat's eye), quartz and amethyst could be found, shops opened to attract buyers. One of these was established at Lyme Regis by Richard Anning, a carpenter and seller of geological specimens for which the little sea-port was famed. For it was his daughter Mary Anning (1799–1847) who by discovering the historic remains of the Ichthyosaurus in a cliff between Lyme Regis and Charmouth had brought celebrity not only on herself but to her home-town. Charmouth close by soon cashed in on Miss Anning's much publicised find and opened its own shops for fossils, etc. to cater for the tastes of budding holiday geologists.

Gradually, though, as the century advanced, the typical Victorian sea-side holiday, with its simple pleasures like rambling on the sea shore looking for shells and pebbles, competing in donkey races and making a seaweed album underwent many changes. Instead of marine biology, the full-time study of photography was taken up and mild attempts made at rock climbing in Devon were exchanged for the real thing in Switzerland. The Royal and Ancient game of golf arrived and yacht-racing took the place of quiet hours spent boating and fishing in the company of an old retired salt. By the time that the Queen, aging rapidly, was living in semi-retirement at her beloved Osborne, the whole pattern of holiday life had altered for her subjects at the sea-side.

SAND PICTURES OF THE ISLE OF WIGHT

Among the most attractive of sea-wide souvenirs in demand today are sand pictures; in particular, those which owe their origin to the existence of the variegated sands found at Alum Bay in the Isle of Wight.

It was from about 1840 that an important centre for the production of sand pictures was established at Newport, chief town on the island. Here, pursuing their odd craft lived a group of sand painters chief among whom was Edwin Dore, who nearly always inscribes his name and date in a minute hand on his pictures.

Alum Bay lies about six miles from Newport where Dore and his fellow artists obtained the materials for their work. For here the cliffside,

composed hitherto of glaring white chalk, suddenly alters its geological character and in the words of George Brannon, Artist and Author of *Vectnis Scenery*, a period guide book:

'. . . . there is a sudden transition to a very extraordinary exhibition of various COLORED sands, clays and ochreous earths disposed in alternate vertical strata – white, black, red, blue and yellow, blending into every variety of tint; and so vivid are the colors that they have not frequently been compared to "stripes on the leaves of a tulip" and to "stripes on silk".'

It was from these fascinating coloured sands, instead of from fat tubes of paint, that Edwin Dore, J. Neat and others created their pictures. During his lifetime Edwin Dore declared himself to be the creator of sand-painting, but this is incorrect,

364 *'Shanklin Chine'*
by Edwin Dore, in
maplewood frame, 1844

though he was, I think, the leading exponent of this minor art while he lived. It was Benjamin Zobel, born in 1762, who came to England shortly before 1791, married an Englishwoman and was later made 'Table Decker in Coloured Sands to His Majesty King George III', who was the first creator of the sand pictures by inventing a foolproof glue by which coloured sands and marbles, crushed to dust, could be stuck to a sheet of millboard, the usual support for painting with sand. Incidentally, it has been recorded that Zobel did pay a visit, some time, to the Isle of Wight where he probably viewed the cliffs of Alum Bay with awe. But this was long before Edwin Dore had realised the commercial potential in producing sand pictures that featured local views and picturesque subjects for a booming souvenir market. For to take mementoes of their holiday home was of paramount importance to most Victorians.

The subjects chosen by Newport's sand painters vary little and many of the same beauty spots,

historic homes and ancient churches appear, again and again, rendered by different artists.

A charming and detailed conception in sand of Shanklin Chine (1844) a famous beauty spot, frequented by tourists, is one of Dore's best pictures and interesting to compare with George Brannon's engraving of the same place which appears in his guide book. Both pictures of the same place vary little in composition except that Brannon's engraving entitled 'Sketched off on the Water at the time of High Tide' was done at a much later date than Dore's. For his sandy track leading up from the shore has become Brannon's proper levelled path up which people stroll to admire the view from the top of the chine.

Another pretty picture by Dore, also signed, shows the 'Entrance to Carisbrooke Castle', a favourite subject often tackled. It is dated 1849. In my possession is another rendering of The Keep of this same castle by W.F., (initials only); Norris Castle by James Symonds, 1846; and West Cowes

365 *'Norris Castle' Isle of Wight by J. Symonds, dated 1846*

366 *'Entrance to Carisbrooke Castle' by Edwin Dore, 1849*

Castle (artist unknown) which was first built in the reign of Henry VIII, to protect the Wight from pirate raids.

But by far the most interesting and intriguing of sand pictures with a curious history is the one of Edwin Dore's entitled:

'This was the Residence of the "Young Cottager", Brading, I. of W.', signed and dated 1844.

To fix the identity of the 'Young Cottager' one must read a long-forgotten volume of three extremely pious and sentimental, semi-religious tales, or tracts, published in 1814 under the title of *Annals of the Poor* by the Reverend Legh Richmond, 1772–1827. Legh Richmond was Vicar of Brading, then an obscure and small village in the Isle of Wight during the years 1797 to 1805, when he left to become Rector of Turvey in Bedfordshire, where he died.

For all their excessive piety and heavy sentimentalism, Richmond's short and simple annals of the poor', as he himself described them, have an underlying touching quality. They reveal not only the charm and gentle kindness of their author but his tender concern for his parishioners living in the direst poverty at that time.

Soon after the arrival of the Reverend Legh Richmond at Brading, with its long straggly street and ancient church, dating back to the 7th century and in much need of repair, he managed to collect a small group of village children every Saturday evening in his garden. He taught these children to read and repeat the catechism, psalms and hymns besides part of the scriptures. Among them was little Jane S——, aged 12. She was a quiet, mild, undistinguished child but one keen to improve her mind.

However, after attending the Vicar's classes for 15 months, Jane suddenly vanished and it was not until Legh Richmond met an old woman, one day, in the village that he discovered what had happened. Poor little Jane had 'fallen into a decline' and was dying.

'. . . the next morning I went to see the child. Her dwelling was of the humblest kind. It stood against a high bank of earth which formed a sort of garden behind it. . . . The front aspect was chiefly rendered pleasing by a honeysuckle which climbed the wall, enclosing the door, windows and even the chimney with its twining branches. As I entered the house-door, the flowers put forth a sweet and refreshing smell!'

The Vicar found Jane upstairs, in a bare, comfortless room whose floor was broken and whose sloping roof sagged pitifully. There was no furniture to speak of; only two tottering beds, a three-legged stool and an old oak chest.

The rest of the story concerns itself with what the Victorian reading-public most enjoyed and shed copious tears over – the prolonged death-bed scene of a saintly child who converted her erring, non-church-going parents to seek God in her name before she died, clasping their hands in her own.

So widely read and loved became Legh Richmond's tale of 'The Young Cottager' that all visitors to the Isle of Wight immediately hurried off, as a matter of course, to see her home and to hear something more, if they could, of her.

Little Jane's cottage still stands today but it is now in private occupation. Edwin Dore's memorial to her in sand also survives but it is in America, owned by Mrs. Kenneth W. Heyt of Hanington, West Virginia. It was about 1871 or 1872, she told me, that this picture was given as a wedding present to her grand-parents Thomas Rowson Morris and Isabella, his wife, by the Reverend Thomas Rowson, a Congregational minister in the Isle of Wight. Thomas R. Morris emigrated to the United States where he was joined later by his wife, their three children, and Dore's sand picture. This picture was inherited by their eldest daughter, Mrs. Thomasson, on whose death it came into the possession of her daughter, Mrs. Kenneth Heyt, the present owner.

Another favourite subject dealt with by the sand painters of Newport was Arreton Church about $5\frac{1}{2}$ miles from Sandown. A very old Saxon building carefully restored about 1886, the porch is sixteenth century and there are several interesting tombstones. One of these, like little Jane's home at Brading, was a tourist attraction for Victorians as it contained the remains of Elizabeth Walker, *The Dairyman's Daughter* whose pathetic tale, second only to Jane's, was published separately as a pious tract. Two million copies were sold.

One more local industry that made use of Alum Bay coloured sands was centred round the production of some little glass bells which were much loved by visitors to the Island. Inside each bell that could be used as a paperweight, a local view was shown in variegated sands. In *Glimpses of Nature During a Visit to the Isle of Wight*, 1843, a commissioned guide book, Jane Loudon describes the tour she made with her husband and daughter, Agnes, in a hired pony carriage to obtain her material. Before the Loudons returned home, they visited a newly built Gothic-styled cottage near Brixton village that overlooked Black Gang Chine. Here, Jane Loudon bought Agnes 'a curiously-shaped bell filled with coloured Alum Bay sands arranged so as to represent the Needle Rocks washed by the tide'. One can imagine the child's delight. Little glass swans have also been filled with the same sands in striped patterns and sold as holiday souvenirs.

They are still inexpensive as antiques. Glass bells from the Isle of Wight in good condition once obtainable for a shilling are becoming scarce and dear.

367–8 *Two glass swans filled with coloured Alum Bay sands and traditional bell-shaped paperweight;* (right) *lighthouse with shell stamp-holder*

SEAWEED ALBUMS AND PICTURES

In the summer of 1833, the Duchess of Kent took her lively 14-year-old daughter, the Princess Victoria to the Isle of Wight, having rented Norris Castle, West Cowes, for some weeks. In between official engagements and boring social functions, Victoria went rambling along the lovely sandy shores of the island with her governess, Lehzen. Together they indulged in the innocent pastime of collecting pretty shells and seaweeds. In fact, seaweeds with their multi-coloured, feathery fronds found in a rocky pool fascinated Victoria.

Gathering them in her basket she returned to the Castle, where a long, enjoyable evening was spent sorting, washing and drying choice specimens to fix with gum in graceful patterns between the pages

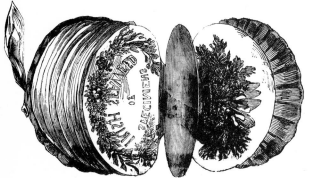

369–70 (top) *Example of a 'Shell-Book of Seaweeds' illustrated with instructions in* The Lady's Newspaper, *10 March 1852, and* (bottom) *actual Seaweed Album, itself, with Biblical quotations added in tiny script on each leaf, 1850s*

of an album. Later, in the summer, when Victoria met the little Queen of Portugal, Maria da Gloria, on a State Visit to England, she generously presented Her Majesty with her Seaweed Album. In turn, Her Majesty gave Her Royal Highness a herbarium of Brazilian plants which she had collected and dried herself. So honour on both sides was satisfied.

This was how Royal patronage was given to the hobby, of making a seaweed album, which was destined to become so fashionable. From now on, young girls and matrons in cloak and bonnet could be seen bending over seaweed-strewn rocks on the beaches of elegant South Coast towns like Weymouth, Sidmouth, Torquay and Dawlish while seagulls screamed, unnoticed, overhead.

From the 1840s, a number of charming little books on algology, with hand-coloured plates, were published. In fact, they quite replaced the flower books of an earlier date.

Isabella Gifford (1823–1891), born at Swansea, who lived for over 40 years at Minehead in Somerset, was a pioneer in the study of algae for ladies. Her *The Marine Botanist: An Introduction to the Study of Algology* has delicately drawn illustrations and is a very pretty example of Victorian book-production in this genre. Miss Gifford described many seaweeds common to our shores and how to preserve

Each attractive plant, that sucks and swells
The Juicy tide, a twining mass of tubes.

When young ladies and their mothers were too lazy to collect their own material for a seaweed album but wished to take one home all the same, they visited the shop where they were on sale almost completed but for a few last personal touches. Alternatively, they might purchase what was known then as a 'Seaweed Group', now much sought after. These groups were arranged on cardboard in garland or nosegay patterns which could be cut out and rearranged individually by the buyer. Charming little bas-reliefs of dried sea mosses were also available.

One of the best-known of these shops was kept by Mary Wyatt in Torwood Street, Torquay. One time maid to Mrs. Amelia Griffiths, a pioneer lady marine biologist, Mary had opened her shop to earn a living by selling madrepores, dried sea-woods and mosses and other seaside souvenirs as her husband, Henry was a permanent invalid.

371 *Fine example of a seaweed picture in its original gilt frame showing a view of Langland Bay, Glamorganshire and signed 'From a Grateful Patient', 1855*

Mary Wyatt had often accompanied her mistress, Mrs. Griffiths, on her exploring expeditions and learnt from her much about seaweeds. Otherwise she was quite illiterate, having had no education. In 1833, the well-known algologist, Doctor William Harvey, asked Mary to prepare him some named collections of seaweeds under the supervision of Mrs. Amelia Griffiths. This she did. Later, Mary produced her own four volumes of *Algae Danmoniensis* and a Supplement which were well received. Botanically these books were not only a valuable contribution to the study of seaweeds but sold well to visitors. Coming from a very humble background, Mary Wyatt's is a success story, indeed, only to be equalled by pretty Polly Perkins of Poole in Dorset whose stock-in-trade was shells

and who taught shellwork (Chapter IX: Parlour Pastimes).

In 1852, *The Lady's Newspaper* came out with a new way of preserving, and presenting, too, dried seaweeds in:

'A fanciful and very elegant Book, the binding of which is composed of large shells, fan-formed, enclosing leaves of fine paper where on patterns of SEAWEEDS are stuck in their many varieties.'

At last the Seaweed Album had arrived! Moreover full instructions to make 'a beautiful Seaweed Landscape' was obtainable according to *The Lady's Newspaper* on application at Messrs. Ackermann, The Strand, London. I have come across one example only of a 'Seaweed Landscape'. It shows a river-scene with banks fringed by delicate, waving

211

greenish and brown fronds. This example was found in a lady's album of the period and is now on view at The House of Shells, Buckfast, Devon.

The Seaweed Picture is the natural companion of the Seaweed Album and good examples can still be found in their maplewood frames, although they are becoming scarce. They are by no means cheap. Like the Seaweed Album, these pictures follow a strictly traditional pattern showing carefully dried specimens of seaweeds and mosses arranged usually in a small wicker basket. The engraving of a local view is sometimes included. Below the basket, written in a sloping elegant hand, the following lines are always quoted. They are possibly by the Reverend David Landsborough who wrote a book on British Seaweeds that went into three editions. Here they are:

Call us not weeds, we are flowers of the sea,
And lovely and bright and gay-tinted are we,
And quite independent of sunshine or showers;
Then call us not weeds; we are Ocean's gay flowers.

Not nursed like the plants of a summer parterre,
Where gales are but sighs of an evening air,
Our exquisite, fragile and delicate forms
Are nursed by the Ocean and rocked by the Storms.

In his book, the Reverend David inscribes these lines with a footnote:

'Motto on the title-page of a pretty album, called "Treasures of the Deep" containing about fifty specimens of Scottish algae, prepared by the author's daughters and sold for charitable purposes.' The sum asked for this album was 'Fifteen shillings'.

SAILORS' VALENTINES

There has been no greater stronghold for the preservation of Victoriana than the parlour of a seaside lodging house. In *Men, Women and Minxes* Mrs Andrew Lang gives evidence to the truth of this, for she writes:

'The mantelpiece of the lodging house parlour is a museum in miniature. Above it hang memorial verses and funeral cards, deeply edged in black, all in perforated board. A large black-and-white china cat guards one end of it and is matched at the other by a red-and-white spaniel. Next to the cat and dog if the cottage is anywhere by the sea and the son a sailor are probably some large shells which, in their beauty and mysterious colouring, must always lend grace to the commonest surroundings. But, alas! shells are only considered naturally ornamental when they are of a sufficiently large size. At other times, they are mounted on velvet and tortured into frightful little watchstands, pincushions, paper cases and similar horrors.'

I wonder what Mrs. Lang would have to say if she knew what high prices are being asked today for the same frightful little shell horrors she names? As for Sailors' Valentines, they head the list for anyone after such items.

According to tradition, this name was given to those wooden octagonal-shaped boxes, sometimes found singly, sometimes hinged together as a pair,

under whose glass covering specie shells were arranged in patterns like mosaic work but with a five-pointed star, an anchor or some other nautical emblem put in the centre. Underneath this nautical emblem picked out in shells might be the words: TRULY THINE; or, FORGET-ME-NOT. Hence the name, VALENTINE.

However, the tradition that these valentines were made by individual sailors in their leisure hours on long sea voyages had been entirely exploded by Mrs. Judith Coolidge Hughes writing on Sailors' Valentines in *Antiques* (February 21, 1970). After closely studying a wide range of sailors' valentines, she has been able to identify and list some 35 different shells used in them which are native only to the West Indies. So are the tiny red seeds known as 'crab's eyes' (*abries precatorins*) which also appear. Yet another important piece of evidence is that these sailors' valentines always follow the same rigid pattern so that they cannot be the work of one particular shell-artist but are far more likely to have been mass-produced for commercial purposes. Produced, then, in the West Indies, they were sold *en masse* to sailors of all nationalities calling at Barbados, almost an international port. In this way, these shell valentines have been distributed among such countries as France, Holland and England where, turning up, they all reveal the same pattern. Even the octagonal wooden boxes in which they are produced fall into two distinct classes: the one made of inexpensive wood like Cedrela (or Spanish cedar); the other, as if for officers, of a much finer wood, smoothly polished and well-finished.

SHELL ROUNDELS

A shell roundel, sometimes called a 'Bull's eye', usually encloses a local seaside view or the cheap colour-print of a sailing-ship or steamer (usually a *bona fide* one with a registered name). In shape, these little seaside pictures can be round, rectangular or heart-shaped. They are always shell-encrusted, and sometimes have dried moss decor-ation under the glass. Mass-produced, they were sold well within living memory in South Coast towns as cheap souvenirs of a seaside holiday. In a humdrum way they might almost be called early 'shell collages', but little skill – or taste – has gone into their making. All the same, these small Victorian Shell Roundels appear to have a market as collecting items.

SAILORS' PINCUSHIONS

In the category of genuine sailors' handiwork carried out for seaside souvenirs come large, plump and very ornamental pincushions first made for their mothers, wives or sweethearts but later sold to tourists for threepence each. Elaborately tas-selled and heart-shaped for sentiment, utilising gaudy scraps of scarlet, golden and blue material, cloth or silk, they were sewn all over with pearl shell buttons or gilt beads, pinheads and sequins. These pincushions have a lusty appeal all their own. Some spell out in glittering pin-heads a loving message like 'Kiss Me Quick' or 'Think of Me'; or just simply 'Merry Christmas'. Although an enormous number of these pincushions have perished long ago some remain preserved almost in their old pristine glory, with pinheads and beads still a-glitter while their ornate tassels looped round them swing, still, intact.

372 *A Sailor's decorated pincushion on a black velvet ground with beadwork motifs, 1860s*

SAILORS' GLASS ROLLING PINS

By the time that Queen Victoria was well estab-lished on her throne, glass rolling pins (Chapter XI: Cottage Glass) had evolved into their most picturesque form, and among the many inscrip-tions found on them, the majority apply to the ways of sailors and fishermen. One of the earliest pins on record, for instance, is made of brown bottle glass with these letters on it: 'W.T., 1843, ARUN. G' which has been deciphered as 'W.T.' initials of the sailor who owned it, plus the date and the name of his ship, *Arun*, built and registered at Sunderland. The 'G' stands for the name of his sweetheart it is thought. This same rolling pin carries a crude representation of Sunderland Bridge, a steamer, a two-masted vessel, railway carriage, the sun, two birds and a masonic emb-lem. By far the most popular and ever-recurring motif on a sailor's rolling pin was the transfer picture of the cast-iron Sunderland Bridge with its huge span of 236, first opened in 1796. It appears over and over again, on mugs, jugs and bowls of Sunderland lustre wares from 1807 to 1865 as well as on rolling pins.

From the busy north-east coastal ports of Sunderland and Newcastle, Hull and Great Yarmouth, coal ships and barges were always in transit, making their way down south to Dover and Portsmouth and beyond. As part of their cargo, rolling pins were taken and sold by sailors for beer money, etc. These rolling pins often bore the name of the ship and its image, with other applied decoration like the words 'Kiss Me Quick' or a national slogan like 'Peace and Plenty'. Beyond Southsea, though, and Poole, Sunderland glass rolling pins were joined by others of a different type made of white opaque glass, more often than not, and with the painted decoration on them of a sailing-ship or paddle-steamer, according to fancy, which grew faint over the years and sometimes even rubbed off. This kind of glass rolling pin,

with its preponderance of West Country, even Welsh, surnames and place names, suggests that they were made for sailors plying their trade on South Coast ships rather than those belonging to the North.

Because they are larger, longer and more finely blown than others, Sunderland glass rolling pins can always be identified. They can measure as much as 30 in. in length, but the average length is 15 in. Predominating colours are a deep blue or opaque white (milk glass), followed by amethyst. Green is apt to be rare and turquoise (opaque) even more so. Open at one end, a glass rolling pin could be filled with tea, rum or sugar and then sealed with a cork. Salt was used, too, to give them weight when used in the kitchen for ironing a collar or ribbon; water when pastry was being rolled. But on the whole, decorated glass rolling pins were treated with care and hung up as pretty wall ornaments.

PICTURES OF SHIPS IN WOOL

Pictures of needleworked 'Ships in Wool' attributed to sailors have never been held suspect like their Shell Valentines. This is due to their air of complete authenticity and because every detail in regard to their sails, masts and rigging is correctly carried out. They are nearly all different, too, in design and were never produced *en bloc* for commercial uses like shell valentines.

Generally the wooden frames for these pictures were produced by the ship's carpenter and they remained un-glassed. They are worked for the most part in coloured wools with touches of silk on a canvas, light sail-cloth or duck background whose surface was sized to prevent puckering. Rarely dated or signed, their age can be roughly gauged by studying the kind of wool used or the type of ship shown. Genuine specimens of 'ships in wools' appear at the beginning of the nineteenth century and remained in production till the period 1920–1925 saw their demise owing to the end of the old-time seamen. For those that followed on took no part in producing any form of handicraft, woolworked pictures or otherwise.

An imaginary ship rarely appears in a picture. Nearly, always, it is one that actually sailed the high seas; from a Royal Naval frigate to a Five-

373 A 10-gun brig worked in coloured wools on canvas by an A.B. (RN) seaman, c. 1800, from Glynde Place, Sussex

374 *H.M.S.* Pique *worked in fine stitches in natural colours. Rigging detailed and accurate. Flies her red paying-off* *pennant*

Masted Barque, flying before the wind with all her sails unfurled. A ship's rigging was usually done in white silk and some sailors produced quite realistic effects of cloud-shapes and foam-tipped waves by additional touches of cotton wool!

One splendid picture, The Hakon Castle, an iron barque built at Liverpool in 1862, done in silks on parchment hangs today in the National Maritime Museum at Greenwich. The *Hakon Castle* was lost with all hands during a fatal voyage made in 1881 between New York and Queenstown. The picture of her only survives because it was not finished at the time she went down and so was not on board.

In *Country Life Annual* for 1962, Miss N. M. Woodall, an authority on this subject, has contri-

buted a very interesting article on what she terms pictures done by 'Artists of the Watch Below'. For it was during the hours they were off duty that sailors took up their needles and wools to compose the picture of a ship they both knew and loved. Miss Woodall has affirmed that Poole in Dorset is still a happy hunting-ground for collectors of 'Ships in Wool'. Moreover as this old port had long associations with Newfoundland and Naples, pictures found here often show the Bay of Naples in the foreground. Two embroiders of ship pictures were a father and son of Italian extraction called Masarilli. Mr. Masarilli, senior, worked during the last half of Queen Victoria's reign; his son continued till as late as 1920. Another sailor who pursued this craft was William Gibb, a tailor's

215

375   *Three warships in frame of red curtains with yellow braid and tassels, worked on canvas, waves of cotton wool. From Glynde Place, Sussex*

son who went to sea at 16 and served for 52 years on every kind of ship from luxury yachts to grimy coasters.

I have found some small East Anglian tidal ports like Maldon in Essex and Woodbridge in Suffolk profitable not only for picking up a handsome 'Ship in Wool' but the pictures too of homely village pubs worked in cross-stitch, as so many of these used to be run once by an old, retired salt and his wife. This genre of rustic picture worked in wool is quite as decorative as those showing a schooner under full sail ploughing her way through high seas and foam-tipped waves.

SOUVENIRS IN SERPENTINE

One very hot July day in 1870, like many another romantic-minded Victorian tourist visiting Cornwall, the Reverend Francis Kilvert drove with friends from Truro in 'a nice roomy wagonette large enough to carry ten people' and drawn by a pair of handsome greys to Mullion to explore the Serpentine district. After a picnic meal taken at the Old Inn, they drove on to Kynance Cove, where the wagonette was left on the moors and a descent made into the dramatically bouldered cove below. In his now well-known, enchanting diary, Francis Kilvert records how with the tide ebbing fast:

'We wandered about among the huge Serpentine Cliffs and the vast detached rocks which stand like giants guarding the Cove. I never saw anything like the wonderful colour of the serpentine rocks, rich, deep, warm, variegated, mottled and streaked and veined with red, green and white, huge blocks and masses of precious stone marble on every side, an enchanted cove, the palace of the Nereids.' (July 22nd, 1870).

Afterwards Kilvert paid a visit to the shops that stood round the green of Lizard Town watching the serpentine craftsmen at work. The floors of the little wooden shanties in which they worked were deep in marble dust and the sound of whirring lathes filled the air. He was much impressed. But not so an equally distinguished visitor who came with her parents to Lizard Town from Falmouth some 22 years later. Her name was Beatrix Potter. She wrote in her Journal:

'There are nine to ten little booths for the sale of Serpentine goods, all very moderate in price, honest in workmanship and bad in pattern. They have one design, the old Cornish water jar which they repeat over and over again but unluckily

216

without any true comprehension of its really elegant shape.'

Beatrix Potter thought the best piece of work she saw 'an inlaid table slat but I consider stone mosaic a hideous perversion and chopping up of a naturally harmonious and beautiful substance'. She made no mention of the two most sought-after souvenirs in serpentine (at this time and now) which sell in thousands. These are a copy of Cleopatra's Needle and the Eddystone Lighthouse. They were once made in a striped crimson, dark-green serpentine which is difficult to come by today so other serpentines in particular a lightish grey-and-green one, are used instead.

Other popular items fashioned by Cornish workers in serpentine were vases, buttons, beads, paperweights, inkstands, candlesticks, spill vases and little bowls, etc., besides small pillars and fonts commissioned from churches near and far. Truro Cathedral (begun in 1879) has pillars of deep crimson and dark green serpentine, highly polished.

In Victorian times, handsome but massive mantelpieces in serpentine were in great demand and so were pillars for the porticoes of London houses. These pillars still abound in many squares and crescents of the Royal Borough of Kensington. It has been said that it was the Prince Consort who first realised the potential commercial possibilities in serpentine; this multi-hued and extremely hard volcanic marble which so nobly resisted fire but could succumb to the vagaries of the British climate when placed, unprotected, out in the open.

Serpentine-turning is still one of the least publicised of the dwindling number of local industries that survive in different parts of England. Incidentally, serpentine is found at Portsoy in Banffshire, Scotland, where it is called Portsoy marble. Skill in working serpentine appears to be hereditary and well-tried techniques are handed down from father to son. At the Lizard, work has been carried on for several generations by the same families. Serpentine is quarried about half a mile from Kynance and is prospected for with a crowbar. It can take as long as six weeks to localise a new site for quarrying. Serpentine is cut, shaped and finally polished; this polish, that never loses its high gloss, is carried out on a treadle lathe.

Recently some interesting details of the early beginnings of serpentine-turning in Penzance

376–8 *Souvenirs in Serpentine: small bowl and spill vase; paperweight enclosing painted view of St. Michael's Mount, train in foreground; traditional form of serpentine Eddystone Lighthouse*

were given to me by Mrs. Diane Cotterell of The Curiosity Shop, Copperhouse, Hayle, whose great grandfather, called Stevens, led a party of turners sent about the 1860s from the Blue John mines in the Castleton area of Derbyshire to Penzance by their employer when his mines were no longer fully active. These highly skilled turners settled down in a row of houses on the sea front which had fallen vacant owing to a disaster at sea in the 1850s. Very soon above the door of one house was seen this sign: 'Patronised by Royalty: Stevens & Sons. Serpentine Workers.'

Later a trade-notice was circulated locally which read:

CORNISH STONE WORKERS:

STEVENS & SONS

WESTERN ESPLANADE

& MORRAT ROAD

PENZANCE.

ESTABD. 1870.

PRIZED MEDALLISTS

WORSHIPFUL CO. OF TURNERS,

LONDON.

Two distinct types of serpentine are found: one is pale and translucent; the other, dull and opaque. The former kind is known as *Noble* serpentine; the latter, *Common*. There is also a rare black variety found at Carlin Cove which contains glittering crystals of bastite. Mrs. Cotterell spoke of a darkish-green serpentine with silvery flecks known as 'silver spray serpentine'. Dark red serpentine is considered to be the most lovely by workers and much prized by reason of its rarity. Yet another type of serpentine called 'verdite' was found at one time to be injurious to the health of those who 'worked' it, while other kinds did them good as it contained a certain amount of calcium.

Today Eddystone lighthouses (with or without metal gulls round their bases) in greyish-green serpentine are being churned out as they are in demand still by tourists. Stone eggs are popular, too, and are produced by several local firms. I have seen some lovely specimens made by an old craftsman now dead. One larger than a duck's egg was made of *steatite*, off-white, scrawled and splashed all over with russet and dark brown; another of an orange so brilliant that it hurt one's eyes almost to look at it! Quite large sums are asked for these eggs as they are much collected and those who produce them belong to a race of dying craftsmen.

SOUVENIRS IN JET

What serpentine was once to workers in Cornwall so was jet to the carvers of this semi-precious, black gemstone who lived in Whitby, that ancient seaport on the Yorkshire coast. Along the narrow streets and alleys of this fishing town, notorious once for its smuggling trade, the whirr of lathes

379 *Pretty hand-brooch in jet, holding flowers, c. 1860*

was once heard as it was in Lizard Town. But today only a few skilled men remain cutting, carving and polishing raw black gleaming jet with high speed precision machinery to meet a demand that has suddenly risen for ornaments in jet.

It was Queen Victoria who first started the fashion for jet by appearing at a banquet on 27 August 1850, in a black silk dress with a parure of jet. The Duke of Cambridge, her cousin, had died and she had gone into mourning. From that evening, jet was 'in' and by 1870 some 1,400 men and boys in a total population of 11,000 inhabitants were employed at Whitby turning out not only a stream of jet necklaces, earings, chains and brooches but a whole host of other attractive items like paper-knives, egg cups, etc. for a thriving souvenir traffic. Everyone coming to Whitby, then heralded as 'The Gem of the North-East Coast', wished to take away 'something in jet' with them.

Like amber, jet is supposed to possess strong magnetic qualities and many old customs and superstitions have gathered about this odd, coal-

380   *A ship's wheel, Caedmon's Cross and model of a boat. All in Whitby jet*

like substance. For instance, when a piece of jet is carried in the purse, the bearer will never lack for money, it is said; it has been alleged, too, that jet will cure dropsy, loose teeth, and epilepsy. When mourners could not afford to wear real jet ornaments they bought, instead, those made in *obsidian*, a stone similar to jet and which is obtained from a black vitreous type of volcanic rock that can take on a high polish.

Yet another variant of jet is a fine, smooth, ebon-black basalt (i.e. *basantite*) imported to England in Victorian times from Mount Tonolous in Lydia, Greece, where it is known as *lapis lydia*. This pebble or stone, hard as flint but with a smooth velvety surface, was used to test gold and silver alloys from the colouring the streak obtained when rubbed with it. Hence the name, touchstone, used in the working language of gold and silversmiths.

It was not long before jewellers were producing the lockets of touchstone set in silver which were worn by Victorian ladies as emblems of luck and to attract good fortune.

Jet jewellery has come into fashion once more and shop-keepers in Whitby are trying to lay their hands on every remaining piece of antique jet jewellery that turns up as they can sell it rapidly. Anyone fortunate enough to find an exquisite lace-like jet ornament or a delicately-cut chain and locket may possibly have acquired something produced by William Roe, who was one of Whitby's leading jet workers in the 1860s. His grand-daughter, Miss Roe, still lives in a seventeenth-century house overlooking the harbour where she sells *bric-à-brac* in much the same way that Mrs. Cotterell sells antiques and serpentine souvenirs at Copperhouse in Cornwall.

TARTAN WARE

'All the tourists in the world rose up like one man and flocked to the scenery Scott described so vividly. . . . In remote places like Lake Katrine and the Trossachs, great inns and hostelries sprang up and tourists became a multitude.'

So wrote William B. Scott in his preface to the 1883 edition of Sir Walter Scott's poetry at a time when the whole Victorian world appeared to be flocking *en masse* to Scotland to assume for a time the kilt and plaid and to buy either little wooden

knick-knacks decorated with clan-tartan designs, or a piece of Wemyss china, or to take home large, plaid-painted tin boxes of butterscotch and Edinburgh rock.

From that day to this, tartan materials have never been out of fashion, especially in France, a country which has always adored them. It was at William IV's coronation in 1831 that small snuff boxes decorated with clan-tartan designs and having gold and silver name-plates fixed on to them were carried by titled Scotchmen. These snuff boxes originated from Laurencekirk, a

381 *Two small 'souvenir' gifts in tartanware, flat heart-shaped pincushion and stamp box. Small plump pincushion covered in tartan silk, embroidered, 1890s*

village in Kincardine where Charles Stiven first started to produce them in white wood ornamented with sketches in Indian ink preserved under clear varnish. At the beginning, Stiven's pictures showed only rural scenes and views; later, there came a display of interlacing lines on them known as 'worming'; later still, designs in checks which soon developed into the presentation of Scotland's most celebrated and loved clan tartans in full colours. When I was a child living abroad, I used to be taken on a round of visits to my Scotch relatives about every two years. Then, I remember, I was showered with presents of small pen-holders and pencil trays, little round wooden boxes for stamps in tartan ware and plump pincushions and needle-cases bound in tartan silks besides a small book, *Songs of Robert Burns* bound in clan-tartan boards – my mother's clan colours, of course – which I still have. Subsequently, years later, my old Scotch housekeeper always gave me at Christmas wooden knick-knacks, again, of her tartan and mine.

It was at the Great Exhibition of 1851 that a special showing was made of Tartanware and the Jury's Report quoted the following items to have been on view and their wholesale prices: 'Cigar cases, 42s. per doz; Paper knives, 10s. to 17s. doz; Snuff boxes 22s. to 168s. per doz; Netting cases from 5s. a doz.'

Sycamore wood was used exclusively for this ware as it was found that its close texture and light weight was more suitable than others. A length of raw sycamore wood that cost about 25s. could produce snuff boxes to the value of £3,000.

Throughout the 1850s and '60s, then, ladies touring Scotland eagerly bought any amount of fancy articles in tartan-decorated wood not only to keep as sentimental souvenirs of their holiday but to keep handy for putting on a stall at a local Fancy Fete or Charity Bazaar. Many of these little wooden objects like a pair of candlesticks, a spectacle case or pen tray had a label on them giving the names of William and Andrew Smith of Mauchline. For in November, 1853, this firm had taken out a patent for a mechanised method of drawing tartans in full colours. This was achieved by fitting a single drawing-pen into a simple, hand-worked machine and using water-colour, when it was possible to draw straight lines with ease and precision. However, this method was superseded three years later in 1856, by a second patent granted to William and Andrew Smith by which small wheels, or rollers, were used instead of a pen. For the first time it was possible to employ oil and to varnish colours. This greatly improved machine, operating several rollers at the same time, drew all parallel lines of one colour, too, at once. Although this method remained in use for some time, less costly tartan patterns were printed by lithography.

By now the market for souvenir articles in Tartanware was such a wide one that many new examples were added. The following items produced by Messrs. Clark & Davidson of Mauchline were listed by them in their Great Exhibition Catalogue: 'Portfolios with wooden boards in imitation of tartan and views, Holyrood Palace and Balmoral Castle in ornamental shields . . . note-books, flower vases, crochet boxes and egg cup stands, thread and reel boxes, needle books, match boxes, razor cases, pomatum and scent boxes, scissor cases, etc.'

It was not surprising that when Queen Victoria had a special tartan designed for Prince Albert, besides ordering all kinds of tartan furnishings by ways of carpets, curtains, etc. for Balmoral, tartan materials were the rage during the nineteenth century.

Clan-tartan brooches, rings and card cases, tooth pick-cases, work boxes, reticules, etc. can all be found by the collector and a recently published book *Tunbridge Ware and Scottish Souvenir Woodware* by Edward and Eva Pinto (George Bell) should most certainly be studied as *the* authorative work.

SCOTTISH PEBBLE AND PEARL JEWELLERY

'I counted seven brooches myself on Miss Pole's dress. Two were fixed negligently in her cap. One was a butterfly made of Scottish pebbles which a vivid imagination might believe to be the real insect.'

Mrs. Gaskell, *Cranford* (1853)
But Miss Pole was not the only lady who might have been seen at this time, the 1850s, wearing a brooch made of Scottish pebbles. For some time now they had been the rage as holiday souvenirs, owing to the latest holiday pastime which was to collect stones like moss-agate, cornelian and topaz while on a sea-shore ramble. After acquiring some of these stones, they were taken along to a small working jeweller who, after cutting and polishing them made them into a large handsome brooch mounted in silver. At one time, in the 1930s, such brooches and bracelets were almost a drug on the market. Now that they are in demand they are as expensive as others.

In Scotland, regular itinerant craftsmen known by their Gallic name of 'Ceard' used to roam the countryside hawking their pebble jewellery. In Shetland, indigenous *antigonite* and *scapolite* was fashioned into pendants for local beauties to wear besides other small ornaments. When a heavy purchase tax came to be levied after the 1939–45 War on all forms of modern jewellery, not only did Victorian jewellery become highly fashionable but Scottish Pebble Jewellery as well.

Genuine old brooches featuring moss-agates, cornelian, bloodstones, sard and amethyst have a very handsome appearance when set in heavy silver or thin gold, circular mounts with an open centre. Such brooches can measure anything up to 4 and 5 inches, as they derive remotely from the great Brooch of Tara, itself, besides other heavy Celtic shoulder brooches which were necessary to secure the folds of a plaid. Another type of brooch can be found that has its stones cut flat; these are set with a solid back.

Another branch of Scottish jewellery which belongs, distinctly, to the souvenir class may still be found on Tayside. It was a little over a century ago that an inconspicuous advertisement in a Perthshire paper announced the opening of a small watch-maker's shop in Perth by two brothers called Cairncross. Their business flourished and by the 1890s, a second generation of two Cairncross brothers were in charge. The elder, James Charles, became deeply interested in the delicate beauty of the small freshwater pearls being taken, locally, from the Tay by a William Abernethy. Buying the best pearls he could from Abernethy, Cairncross began to design, and make, some small pearl Tay brooches which were quickly snapped up by the local gentry or by visitors holiday-making in Perth. The Tayside pearl has a characteristic range of colours, from cream to pale mauve which is due, it is said, to certain acids and calciums found in Tay water. It has a unique lustre, too, all its own, nor does it need to be cut or polished.

Iron jewellery was first produced at the time of the Peninsular War and was resuscitated when the Franco-Prussian War began. At both these times, patriotic ladies surrendered their gold ornaments (as English ladies did their wedding rings during World War II) to be melted down. In exchange they were given (as we never were) certain items of iron jewellery, often stamped or marked, which they could show to others with natural pride. Many examples of iron jewellery were on show in the Great Exhibition of 1851 and were cited as being well-designed and wrought. As the iron with which these ornaments were made was enamelled black, much of this jewellery resembles jet. A book has just been published on this little-known branch of a jeweller's craft never before covered. It is by Anne Clifford and is called *Cut-Steel and Berlin Iron Jewellery* (Adams & Black).

'A PRESENT FROM . . .'

This class of Victorian souvenir, crystallised for collectors today in the words 'A Present from . . .', is the largest of all, embracing almost every kind of object in nearly every medium, from a miniature ivory umbrella, to hold needles inscribed 'Present from Brighton', to a 'shocking pink' china mug whose gilt lettering spells out the same message, only this time it is *'From Yarmouth, 1867'*.

Before the middle-class Victorian world set out in ever-increasing numbers on their travels, at home or abroad, it was the aristocracy who alone had visited the Continent in their great rumbling family coaches to do the Grand Tour and to pick up, by fair means or foul, what can only be called loot, by way of sculpture, bronzes, antique pottery and paintings by old masters which they brought back to adorn their homes. In contrast to their cultured plunder, the middle-class Victorian travel-ler spread his net much wider in one sense but narrower because less esoteric in another, to gather in the treasure that caught his eye and by which he could remember his travels.

By and large, it was the middle-class travellers who brought into being the nineteenth-century local shops supplying picturesque but cheap 'souvenirs of travel' wherever English tourists appeared. One of the first places recorded to supply these 'Presents from' was the Field of Waterloo. Here, from about the 1820s, the excursion-minded British were met with the welcome sight of stall owners, ready to sell them on the spot a variety of elegant little ivory toys which, in turn, gave rise to a thriving industry based at Dieppe that pro-duced miniature ivory umbrellas in whose carved handles were set tiny glass lens. Engraved or painted on these lens were seven minute pictures of French seaside places that could be studied by holding the lens to one's eye and looking towards the light!

It would be impossible to dwell on all the kinds of ingenious 'souvenir' toys and china ornaments that eventually came to pack the whatnot shelves or mantel-pieces of prosperous Victorian homes till the end of the nineteenth century, when so many of the small individual manufactories that had produced them ceased to function and the glass-blowers and itinerant potters who had also contributed to their sale from John o' Groats to Land's End had passed away.

However, there was one class of superior 'souvenir china' which was unrivalled in popu-larity in Victorian times and which after long years

382 *'Present from . . .' coffee cup and two saucers, transfer-printing of Southend views, black on pink china, c. 1850*

383 *Large china platter showing local views of Hastings, 1860*
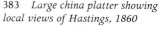

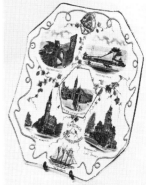

384 *Three china mugs: 'A Present from the Crystal Palace, 1851; (centre) from Southend; (right) hand-painted: 'A Gift for a Friend', London 1881*

of neglect, is attracting attention from collectors, again. This is Heraldic Goss China largely created by Adolphus W. Goss, the son of William Henry Goss, founder of the famous Goss pottery works established at Stoke-on-Trent in 1858. William Henry Goss specialised first in terra-cotta ware, parian statuary and ivory porcelain. A man of many interests and wide views, Goss aimed to produce as many different types of decorated china as he could. So, in 1872, he took out a patent for further improvements 'in manufacturing articles of jewellery, dress ornaments, dress fastenings, smoke shades for lamps and gas-burners, etc. . . .' In fact, there was nothing really that the Goss pottery works did not cover by way of fine china ornaments, including some be-jewelled ware even, and floral brooches, whose flowers and leaves modelled in the round were paper-thin and left either pure-white or tinted in natural colours.

Towards the 1890s, Adolphus W. Goss, a keen

student of heraldry, then a fashionable pastime, had the brilliant idea of issuing an ornamental ivory porcelain ware that could be decorated with civic coats-of-arms in full colours. For this means, he invented a series of brilliant enamels suitable for application – with staggering commercial success. Victorians went mad to secure some piece of china showing the armorial bearings either of the town where they had been born, or married in, or were just visiting for pleasure. For many years a range of china models of antiquities from all over the country, each piece bearing the heraldic arms of the town where it was sold, were produced to catch the acquisitive eye of a Victorian traveller while on holiday. But almost the most attractive and unusual of Goss china models are those that illustrate about 40 different styles in domestic architecture. In natural colourings, these little china houses range from medieval, plaster-and-timber thatched cottages to elegant Gothic villas or

385–7 *White china swan bearing civic arms of Weston-super-Mare, imitating Goss, unmarked; (centre) Fish vase in natural colours; (right) Blue-and-white fish reposing in a wreath of applied forget-me-nots, sentimental seaside souvenir, wall plaque. 1890s*

a baronial Scottish castle with pepper-pot towers. Norman keeps, lighthouses, romantic gateways besides authentic homes as it might be John Bunyan's celebrated Elstow cottage in Bedfordshire or Charles Dickens' Gad's Hill mansion at Rochester, Kent, can be found by the collector. Well-known inns, too, have been commemorated such as 'The Cat & Fiddle' at Buxton and 'The Feathers' Hotel' at Ledbury. Miscellaneous items such as copies of 'The Old Bar' at Gretna Green or 'The First and Last House' at Land's End should not be overlooked as possible finds round which to form a collection.

Mr. J. R. Goffin, who owns a superb collection of Goss China in all its different manifestations besides much interesting data concerning the workings (and correspondence) of this pottery works, told me that a rare model representing an actual potter's oven of the kind in which Goss china was first fired is still in existence but seldom come by. This model, which looks very much like a cottage in design, has a central front door and one window on either side of it. The huge, coal-fired beehive-shaped oven, topped by a fat chimney, so characteristic of the bottle-shaped potteries of the Midlands, has been faithfully reproduced in this little china ornament.

Early examples of Goss china has the name 'W. H. Goss' impressed on them. Adolphus Goss's 'Heraldic' china is similarly marked. Later examples have the rising goshawk, ducally gorged, added or else the latter appears on its own. This elegant bird figures in the armorial bearings of the Goss family.

Goss's 'Heraldic China' may be said to be the last manifestation of the sentimental craving commonly felt by most Victorians, irrespective of their class, to possess something in their lives, representative of their travels when they stepped out of the ordinary norm of their daily lives.

In our own day and age of space-travel, as we fly from one corner of the world to another there is little time or opportunity for that matter to indulge in the extraneous joys of souvenir-hunting after the manner of our forebears, the Victorians. Moreover souvenirs of the calibre found in the past no longer exist except in a debased form, mass-produced, to satisfy the taste of those who go only on package tours.

388   *Sunderland lustre wall plaque – 'The Mariner's Compass'*

Further reading

Author's Note: It would be just as difficult to give a complete Bibliography which has gone into the making of this book over so many years as it would be to compile another today to assist would-be collectors of Victoriana. Once books on this subject were few and far between; now they abound. Every aspect, indeed, and every side-line has been covered. On Victorian Sentimental Jewellery, on Paperweights, Postcards, Buttons, Stevengraphs, the specialist collector has only to look at the crowded shelves labelled ANTIQUES in a good bookshop and make his own choice of book and writer.

There are a few books, though, which I have found invaluable to have to hand and these are:

The Antique Buyer's Dictionary of Names by A. W. Coysh (David and Charles).
Victorian Antiques by Thelma Shull. Charles E. Tuttle Co., Rutland, Vermont, U.S.A.
Antiques International, (Collectors' Guide to Current Trends) Michael Joseph.
Decorative Art of Victoria's Era by Frances Lichten, Charles Scribner, Ltd. N.Y. U.S.A.
The Connoisseur's Complete Period Guides, The Connoisseur, London.
Victoriana: A Collector's Guide by Violet Wood, G. Bell & Sons.
Victorian Taste by John Gloag, David and Charles.
Life in Victorian England by W. J. Reader, B. T. Batsford Ltd.
The Victorian Home by Ralph Dutton, B. T. Batsford Ltd.
The Price Guide To Antique Furniture, The Antique Collectors' Club, Woodbridge, Suffolk.

Index